A CAPITAL CURRENTS BOOK
Insiders look at topics of concern today

OTHER CAPITAL CURRENTS BOOKS

TORN BETWEEN TWO CULTURES
An Afghan-American Woman Speaks Out
MARYAM QUDRAT ASEEL

THE $100,000 TEACHER
A Teacher's Solution to America's Declining Public School System
BRIAN CROSBY

THE OTHER SIDE OF WELFARE
Real Stories from a Single Mother
PAMELA L. CAVE

DAVID, GOLIATH
and the
BEACH-CLEANING
MACHINE

DAVID, GOLIATH
and the
BEACH-CLEANING
MACHINE

How a Small California Town Fought an Oil Giant—and Won!

BARBARA WOLCOTT

CAPITAL
BOOKS, INC.
Sterling, Virginia

Capital Books, Inc.
P.O. Box 605
Herndon, Virginia 20172-0605

ISBN 1-931868-31-X (alk. paper)

Library of Congress Cataloging-in-Publication Data

Wolcott, Barbara.
  David, Goliath and the beach-cleaning machine : how a small California town fought an oil giant and won! / Barbara Wolcott.
    p. cm.
  Includes bibliographical references and index.
  ISBN 1-931868-31-X
  1. Unocal Corporation—Trials, litigation, etc. 2. Liability for oil pollution damage—California—Avila Beach. 3. Rizzo, Saro. 4. Environmental lawyers—California—Biography. I. Title.
  KF1866.U56W65   2003
  344.73'046332'0269—dc21   2002154037

Printed in the United States of America on acid-free paper that meets the American National Standards Institute Z39-48 Standard.

First Edition

10   9   8   7   6   5   4   3   2   1

To my families

Contents

Acknowledgments   ix

Introduction   1

Stakeholders   4

Timeline   6

Avila Beach Pollution Plume Areas (Map)   7

1 Rizzo's Date with Destiny   9

2 The Beginning of the Partnership Juggernaut   17

3 The Little Dig—The Peril Below   27

4 Conflicts in Technology   37

5 Partnerships Draw a Line in the Sand   45

6 The Battle for the Plan—The EIR   59

7 Rizzo Loads His Sling with Small Rocks   67

8 Small Town Fight in the Big Leagues   79

9 Corporate Coming of Age   93

10 Padlocks on the Pipelines   103

11 Shootout Stalls—Sheriff Comes to Take Over   111

12 Strangers Muddy Paradise   123

13 High Noon at Avila Beach   135

14 The Cost of a Company Town   145

15 Truce and Consequences—Settlement   153

16 The Way We Were   161

17 Dawn on the Battlefield   171

18 Dust, Destruction, and Dismemberment   179

19 The Last Good-Bye   185

20 Holding Hands with Heritage   197

21 Rizzo's Dolphin Calling   205

22 A Pebble in the Water—Ever-Widening Rings   219

Epilogue: People   231

Glossary   233

Bibliography   237

Index   241

Acknowledgments

MANY people were involved in the completion of this book, even though writing is often seen as a solitary undertaking. I'm a product of my original family, which includes five sisters and one brother, a host of in-laws, nieces, nephews, aunts, uncles, and cousins, all of whom have taught me that family is first and foremost. The generation my husband and I produced—three sons and three daughters—proved they were right. These children have brought immeasurable joy and a number of wives, grandchildren, and more in-laws to the mix.

More specific to *David, Goliath, and the Beach-Cleaning Machine,* my professional family includes a remarkable literary agency, D4EO Allen O'Shea Literary Partners; a daring publishing house, Capital Books, Inc; a workshop of writers in San Luis Obispo; plus many newspaper and magazine editors I know, but have never met in person.

Now I have another close connection: my Avila Beach family. No one likes to have old wounds reopened, and for these people to talk with me at length about this calamitous event in their lives was nothing less than valiant. The bibliography lists those who were willing to beard the lion and a few I got to know only through media coverage. I am eternally grateful not only for the opportunity to tell their story, but also for the kindness and consideration they offered me as a stranger in their midst.

As a group, all these people taught and inspired me. There is no way I can list them in order of importance, because they all have a unique place in my heart. Instead, I will revert to the library system and do it alphabetically. You all know who you are!

Allison, Ann, Annabelle, Art, Audrey Mc., Audrey Y., Barbara B., Betty, Bob, Carol H., Carol Mc., Catherine, Cheri, Christopher, Christy, Cindy, Coleen, Cricket, Deb, Diane, Don, Dorothy, Dot, Earl, Elaine, Elise, Eric, Erica, Fern, Flo, Floyd, Franny, George, Grace, Gus, Harold, Harry H., Harry R., Herb, Howard, Jack, Jackie, Jane, Janet, Jason, Jeane, Jeff, Jennifer, Jerry, Jim, J.J., Joan, Joe, John M., John O., Judy C., Judy K., Judy R., Judy S., Judy W., Karen, Kathleen, Kathy, Ken, Kent, Kimberly, Kyle, Laura, Lori F., Lori W., Lynne, Margaret, Marguerite, Maria, Marilyn A., Marilyn M., Mark, Marti, Mary H., Mary L., Mary Beth, Maxine, May, Michael, Morgan B., Morgan M., Myrt, Nancy, Nathan, Norm, Oliver, Pauline, Peggie, Polly, Rocky, Rosemary, Sally, Sandy, Shirley, Skeeter, Skip, Steve, Willma, Zachary.

Introduction

AS a specialist writing about technology, nothing prepared me for the precedent-setting Avila Beach environmental cleanup. Avila Beach is a small California town located about halfway between Santa Barbara and Monterey. Isolated by a ring of mountain ranges and ocean from the rest of the world, this tiny beach community retained its unique character for a hundred years as a company town with a close connection to the oil giant originally called the Union Oil Company, now known as Unocal. Secluded though it was, this little town was thrust upon the international stage in the mid-1990s because of an environmental disaster of epic proportion.

The story unfolded as a young attorney, Saro Rizzo, stumbled over some picnic debris during a morning run on the beach and decided to ask Unocal to donate a beach-cleaning machine to the community.

Avila Beach has been described by national media as "frozen in the 1960s," which residents consider a compliment. It has an eclectic resident population of fewer than four hundred souls whose identities and lifestyles range from original hippies to active octogenarians living in the same homes their grandfathers built, with a sprinkling of professionals who work in surrounding cities. Fiercely independent, this ragtag band stood up to a multinational company that had allowed nearly a half million gallons of petroleum products to pool under the main street business district. The leader of the charge was a fresh-faced lawyer with the ink hardly dry on his diploma.

It doesn't seem like a fair match to pit a young man two years out of the Jesuit Santa Clara law school against Unocal and a host of Harvard and Princeton lawyers, but this is one of those hard-to-believe stories. Rizzo and his environmental partners won big time, to the tune of $18 million in damages as well as an estimated (Unocal isn't telling how much) $100–200 million to clean up the town.

From the moment Unocal was embarrassed to discover a pool of stinking petroleum products in a dig they predicted would reveal dry, degraded crude, to the final blow in a Los Angeles meeting of top U.S. attorneys, things kept going Rizzo's way. Rizzo's suit was the first of nearly sixty by others to follow, including some by Ed Masry of *Erin Brockovich* fame.

Longtime Avila Beach residents were not surprised to learn there was a massive pool under the town, but the discovery appeared to have brought Unocal up short. The oil company went into court so confident that Rizzo's suit would be dismissed they never consulted with the plaintiffs. After being rebuffed by the judge, Unocal retrenched in a corporate legal stall with both Rizzo and San Luis Obispo County. That tactic cost the company dearly, because during the delay, the information about the pollution damage only increased.

Even as county test results painted a bleak picture of the extent of the contamination, Rizzo realized the state agencies involved were legally stymied in their negotiations with Unocal; neither were his own negotiations for settlement of the suit progressing. With few financial resources to push the suit forward, Rizzo announced at a press conference that he would file the suit in federal court as well.

That news made headlines and woke up the state capitol in Sacramento. Now every California agency stopped playing possum about the pollution as they realized this court action would take all authority from them and place it in the hands of the federal government. The state attorney general came to town, and Rizzo enlisted the help of an 800-pound gorilla—Milberg Weiss, a premier law firm known for their successful prosecution of the Exxon Valdez spill and Holocaust victim restitution. The oil giant at last sent in their top corporate attorney, a practical man who saw the writing on the wall and negotiated the settlement quickly and amicably.

The cleanup followed in short order, but it required that the little town's homes and businesses that sat directly above the massive leak be completely torn down or removed, then moved back again. Only two of twenty-seven buildings were deemed both historically significant and able to withstand the destruction. Thousands of truckloads of contaminated sand and the residue of destroyed homes and buildings were hauled out, and clean materials were trucked back in.

Unocal has sold that part of their business that encompasses Avila Beach and has cleaned up the majority of the huge spill. The remaining underground plume, which is asphalted under the beach, will be monitored for movement—both sides agree that removing it would be more hazardous than leaving it, because of the action of tides and winter storms. The town is slowly rebuilding, but it has paid a terrible price. Residents used to love to be called funky, but no one could clearly define what that meant when it came to the task of replicating it. Restoration is under way. While Unocal only had to shell out the money to do it, the people of Avila Beach had to surrender part of their spirit.

The beach-cleaning machine arrived at Avila Beach in the spring of 2001.

STAKEHOLDERS

The Town

Mike Rudd—owner The Sea Barn
|
Lucy Lepley/Dolores Lepley
|
| Cotchett, Petrie
| James Duenow
| Alan Bond
|
Perry Martin
|
Bill Price—owner of Beachcomber Bill's
|
Archie McLaren
| | Cal Poly State University
| Daniel Levi
|
Betty Woody
|
Betty Terra
|
Gladys Misakian
|
Evelyn Phelan
|
Sharon Morrison—owner of motel
|
Bob and Elaine Gorman Jr.
|
Marvin Dee—owner Avila Grocery
|
Saro Rizzo and the Avila Alliance
| |
| Matt Farmer |
| Avila Beach Foundation
| Environmental Law Foundation
    James Wheaton
| Communities for a Better Environment
| Milberg Weiss
    Steve Crandall
    Al Meyerhoff
| California State Attorney General's Office
    Deputy Attorney General Ken Alex

The Agencies

U.S. Army Corps of Engineers
U.S. Coast Guard
U.S. Fish & Wildlife Service
U.S. Occupational Safety & Health Administration
U.S. Environmental Protection Agency

California State Water Resources Control Board
  Regional Water Quality Control Board
       Gerhardt Hubner
California Coastal Commission
California Department of Justice
California Air Pollution Control
California Environmental Health Hazard Assessment
California Department of Toxic Substances Control
California State Bar Association
California Department of Fish & Game

San Luis Obispo County Board of Supervisors
      Evelyn Delany
      Peg Pinard
San Luis Obispo County Planning Department
      David Church
San Luis Obispo Department of Environmental Health
      Curtis Batson
San Luis Obispo County Counsel
San Luis Obispo County District Attorney
San Luis Obispo County Public Works Department

Avila Beach Community Services District
Avila Beach Fire Department
Port San Luis Harbor District

Unocal

Roger C. Beach
William Sharrer
James Bray
Denny Lamb
Paul West
First Bank of San Luis Obispo
California Polytechnic State University
      Dr. Nirupam Pal
      Dr. Raul Cano
MidState Bank
Environmental Impact Review
      A. D. Little Company
      Steve Radis
      Chris Clark
      Sara Kocher
Jacobs Engineering
      Rich Walloch
      Arrie Bachrach
      Leilynn Olivas Odom
      Robert Gibson
      James Allen

Independent

Ed Masry
      Erin Brockovich

Timeline: <u>Avila Beach from Discovery to Restitution</u>

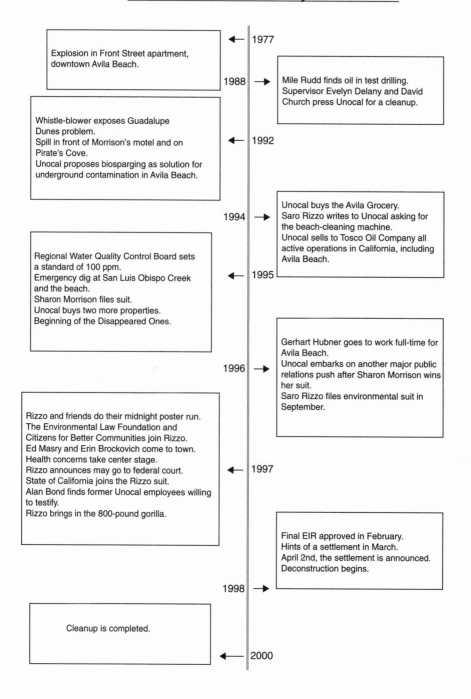

Explosion in Front Street apartment, downtown Avila Beach.

← 1977

1988 →

Mile Rudd finds oil in test drilling. Supervisor Evelyn Delany and David Church press Unocal for a cleanup.

Whistle-blower exposes Guadalupe Dunes problem.
Spill in front of Morrison's motel and on Pirate's Cove.
Unocal proposes biosparging as solution for underground contamination in Avila Beach.

← 1992

1994 →

Unocal buys the Avila Grocery.
Saro Rizzo writes to Unocal asking for the beach-cleaning machine.
Unocal sells to Tosco Oil Company all active operations in California, including Avila Beach.

Regional Water Quality Control Board sets a standard of 100 ppm.
Emergency dig at San Luis Obispo Creek and the beach.
Sharon Morrison files suit.
Unocal buys two more properties.
Beginning of the Disappeared Ones.

← 1995

1996 →

Gerhart Hubner goes to work full-time for Avila Beach.
Unocal embarks on another major public relations push after Sharon Morrison wins her suit.
Saro Rizzo files environmental suit in September.

Rizzo and friends do their midnight poster run.
The Environmental Law Foundation and Citizens for Better Communities join Rizzo.
Ed Masry and Erin Brockovich come to town.
Health concerns take center stage.
Rizzo announces may go to federal court.
State of California joins the Rizzo suit.
Alan Bond finds former Unocal employees willing to testify.
Rizzo brings in the 800-pound gorilla.

← 1997

1998 →

Final EIR approved in February.
Hints of a settlement in March.
April 2nd, the settlement is announced.
Deconstruction begins.

Cleanup is completed.

← 2000

Avila Beach Pollution/Plume Areas
(Reprinted from the Draft Environmental Impact Report,
a public document)

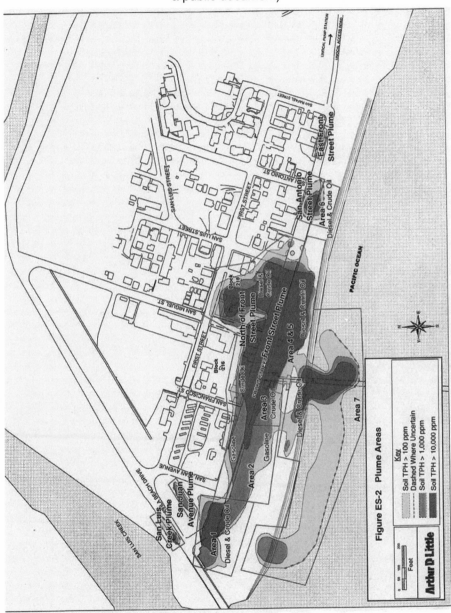

RIZZO'S DATE WITH DESTINY

THE sky above Avila Beach was cloudless, but thick fog shrouded the mountains surrounding the town. On his morning run, Saro Rizzo turned off the road and headed toward the water's edge, where a flock of terns dotted the high-water mark. The birds scattered as he approached, and Rizzo watched them fly out toward the sea. He turned his attention back toward the direction he was headed, in time to spot a large piece of broken glass sticking out of the wet sand directly in his path. Unable to break stride to miss it, he twisted in mid-step and fell awkwardly into the receding surf.

The birds seemed to laugh at his predicament, but Rizzo was not amused. From ground level he could see that the glass he had tried to avoid was not the only hazard on the beach. The sand was littered with the remains of bonfires and meals. A gull pecked at a hamburger wrapper, and the sea breeze rolled two empty beer cans along the firm sand like wayward bowling balls. The beach looked like it typically did on a Monday before the cleanup crew arrived, but the broken glass and the rusty nails that had been left after the lumber had been burned in the bonfires stirred Rizzo to action.

He picked himself up and trotted home, dumping his clothes and shoes into the washer on the way to the bathroom. He showered quickly, and with hair still dripping onto his thick terry robe, he headed resolutely toward the computer. For the next hour Rizzo searched the Internet for beach-cleaning machines, finally printing out information about one that cost $70,000, which he considered a reasonable price. He had no idea that he was launching a series of events that would involve him for the next year and a half. In the coming seventeen months, Rizzo set off an unprecedented chain of events, together with others traveling separate routes toward the same legal confrontation. They would bring a global oil corporation face-to-face with its responsibilities.

"I was living in Avila in a condo with one of my brothers," he remembers. Although his father was American-born, his mother came from Italy, and the family spent part of his growing years in that country, including his early school years. When the family moved back to the United States, they settled in San Luis Obispo, California, to open Café Roma. The restaurant was an instant success and remains one of the region's favorite dinner houses. Two of his brothers followed the family into the restaurant business, but Saro chose to study law.

A 1994 graduate of Jesuit Santa Clara Law School in northern California, Rizzo feels he absorbed an extraordinary sense of justice from his father, who believed strongly in the importance of being straightforward in all things. This philosophy helped form Rizzo's own personal convictions. "I believe in karma," he says, "what goes around comes around." He doesn't hide his passion and is not afraid to speak his mind, even when his is an unpopular view, sometimes prompting people to ask why he is so incensed about the world's injustices. His father passed away during Rizzo's first year in law school, and he remembers the older Rizzo as a kind of sage, whom he tries to emulate.

After he passed the California State Bar, Rizzo searched for a way to put his education to work. Although clients for an inexperienced lawyer were few and far between in San Luis Obispo County, his new practice, which was based out of his condo, did get a few criminal defense cases. As a result of this lack of work, he spent a lot of time at the beach, becoming increasingly concerned about the trash that littered the strand.

On that fateful day when he decided that something should be done and he was the one to do it, the solution appeared to be simple—get a beach-cleaning machine. When Rizzo approached the Harbor District to ask about getting the machine, although they thought it was a good idea, they told him there was no money in their budget to buy it, and encouraged him to ask Unocal Corporation for the money.

The suggestion was not unreasonable, because Unocal had actively supported many community projects in the past. With a large number of storage tanks sitting high on the bluff above the town, Unocal's tank farm, as it is popularly known, had been part of the community for a century. Employees of the oil giant considered work at Avila Beach to be a plum assignment, and they became part of the fabric that held the tiny town together. The idea of theirs being a company town was not unpalatable to Avila Beach residents; they all felt like part of a big family.

Unsatisfied with the Harbor District's answer about budget constraints, Rizzo looked into their finance records to see why a beach cleaner couldn't have a higher priority for purchase. His research revealed that a Unocal pipeline had broken in the Avila Beach area in 1987, and as a result of that spill, the oil company had paid the Harbor District thousands of dollars in penalties. Noting that the money had been earmarked in the settlement for "beach activities," Rizzo returned to the Harbor District to find out exactly what kind of beach activities the money supported. Again, the answer he got was less than satisfactory, so Rizzo took the information he had to the *New Times,* a local weekly with a reputation for gutsy reporting. The newspaper published a feature story about nails at the beach and Rizzo's proposal to buy a beach-cleaning machine. That article apparently got the attention of the port authorities, because, after it appeared, they came to Rizzo, saying they liked the idea of the machine and agreeing to pay half if he could come up with the other half of the money.

Rizzo went to San Luis Obispo County Supervisor Evelyn Delany, who was responsible to the Avila Beach constituency, and asked if the county could pay for half of the machine. Delany suggested that instead he write to Unocal and ask them for funding.

Having heard the same source suggested twice, Rizzo wrote to Unocal identifying the need for the machine and including a videotape of the one he wanted to buy. "I told them it would be a good thing for the community, but never got a response from them. I guess to them I was just some crazy guy asking for a beach-cleaning machine." Not only did Unocal not respond to his letter, the company never returned any of his follow-up phone calls. "I was insulted," he recalls.

Over the months, Rizzo's quest for a clean beach took on new meaning, as reports of a serious Unocal spill beneath the town's beach began to make front-page news. Rizzo knew that in 1988, businessman Michael Rudd had discovered oil a few feet below his Front Street property, during a soils test that was required for him to get a building permit. At that time, San Luis Obispo County and the Regional Water Quality Control Board met with Unocal staff to discuss how to deal with the leak, and in 1992, a vapor extraction system was installed to take care of the problem. No further testing was done to determine the extent of the underground plume until the mid-1990s, when additional petroleum products were found under the beach.

Even after the Regional Water Quality Control Board issued an emergency order in October 1995 to clean up one section of the underground western plume, there was still no agreement on how to proceed with additional cleanup, because Unocal objected to the standard the board had set of a residual of no more than 100 parts petroleum products per million of water. The company demanded that the board set a new standard more to their liking, without benefit of an Environmental Impact Report, and refused to submit a cleanup proposal until they got a more favorable ruling.

Without a cleanup proposal from Unocal the whole process was at a standstill. An EIR appraises a proposed method of cleanup and its resulting consequences to the town, the people, and the beach, and, in many cases, no work can proceed without such a document first being approved. Rizzo could see that it would be years before anything would be accomplished, and he feared that over time Unocal would wear down its opposition and eventually walk away from the entire mess. While regulatory agencies met with Unocal lawyers, rumor fed additional uneasiness that Avila Beach was floating on a petroleum pool that could make everyone sick or cause an explosion that would dwarf the one that had occurred seventeen years earlier.

Rizzo's proposed beach-cleaning machine fast became a small symbol of a huge environmental problem that threatened the existence of the town itself. Unocal testing revealed a large deposit of petroleum at one end of the beach and more under the downtown business district. It was clear that the sands and soil were dirty above and below, even though air monitoring in the town showed no vapors or emissions from the plume.

Spills are a part of everyday business for oil companies, and with the volume of traffic that had moved in and out of Avila Beach, residual pollution was expected. A Unocal pipeline spill in 1992 caused a drastic drop in business for motel owner Sharon Morrison. In the suit she brought against the company, she was awarded a million dollars in damages.

As summer days shortened toward autumn, Rizzo sat on the beach with his brother Marco and complained bitterly that Unocal appeared to understand the language of law only when it was pressed on them. If he couldn't even get the company to buy half of a beach-cleaning machine, he knew they would also resist cleaning up the underground spill.

Marco challenged him to do something about it, and, seeing no alternative, Rizzo began to look into the spill, beginning with old records. The Unocal pier at Avila Beach was private access for the company to load ocean tankers from storage at the tank farm on the bluff above the town. Pipelines from the tanks on the hill led directly to the end of the pier by way of the downtown area and continuing across the beach, so a leaking pipe was likely the source of the contamination.

In the process of doing his research, Rizzo learned that since the early 1990s, California regulatory agencies had been investigating an underground oil spill close to the beach near the farming town of Guadalupe, fifteen miles south of Avila Beach. That predicament grossly overshadowed the one in Avila Beach because of the volume and location of the spill, and, as a result, it was a much higher priority for Unocal than Avila Beach, a town that was no more than a half-mile across at its widest.

The Guadalupe Dunes area contains the last remaining intact wind-sculpted dunes in the entire state of California, outside of Death Valley. The long, undeveloped beach is home to a number of endangered and threatened plant and animal species, and has an underground spill of monumental proportions. Unocal was directing its attention toward the contamination from the Guadalupe spill, which was estimated to be a minimum of 8 million gallons of diluent, an agent used to thin thick western crude so that it can move through pipelines. The extent of the spill—still not determined—is likely to exceed that of the Exxon Valdez disaster in Alaska. The spill endangers the vast Santa Maria Valley aquifer, the underground water source for thousands of square miles of central California. If the diluent were to reach the drinking and agricultural water for northern Santa Barbara County, the result would be an economic disaster of incalculable consequence. In the view of one regulator, there would not be enough money in all the oil companies in the world to repair the damage.

When Rizzo read about the Guadalupe problem, he realized that, by comparison, the situation in Avila Beach appeared minor. But he also believed that didn't justify Unocal ignoring his attempts at communication. His father might have pointed out that there are no small cases, only small people, and the oil company should have had the courtesy to answer his letter and phone calls.

His continued research in 1995 led him to contact the Regional Water Quality Control Board, as the agency responsible for working with the county on the Avila Beach underground pollution. That spill was described in official documents as a threat to groundwater and was termed dangerous. Rizzo sifted through files and other paperwork at the water board and found that there were many more pipelines under the town than he had realized, some carrying crude oil, others used to transport gasoline, benzene, and diesel to the end of the pier for loading onto the ships.

He also discovered information indicating that the plume of toxic petroleum products under Avila Beach was growing.

The trash he'd been concerned about on top of the sand was nothing compared to what lurked below. The danger it posed to the small town was formidable.

Rizzo had never handled an environmental case, nor, for that matter, had he filed *any* court case, but he considered the beach a public treasure. He decided to file suit against Unocal, asking the court to direct the oil company to clean up the beach *and* to buy the town a beach-cleaning machine. In preparation for filing, he again turned to the Internet, this time schooling himself in environmental law, especially a little-known one—California's Proposition 65.

Considered a somewhat minor law in the state, Proposition 65 has a provision for forcing commercial enterprises to publicly list any toxic materials under their care that are in proximity to the public. Grocery stores, gasoline stations, hardware stores, and any other enterprise having an inventory of substances deemed toxic by reliable science must post a sign at their front door warning people entering the premises about the presence of the toxic substance. Aside from the environmental groups that had lobbied for its passage, the law was considered to be a nuisance by the buying public.

However, Proposition 65 has a second provision, dealing specifically with water contamination and giving power to the people to act as state attorney general for suits brought on behalf of all state residents. Rizzo was the first to use the ten-year-old law as a basis for filing his Avila Beach suit.

In San Francisco at the state archives, Rizzo copied files of similar consumer protection complaints and other relevant court documents for use as legal precedents. When he was confident that he had enough material to file the suit, he and a friend combined the information into a comprehensive, forty-page complaint, asking only that Unocal clean up the mess they had made, and requesting no punitive damages. Once the document was complete, all Rizzo needed was plaintiff status, as required by law.

Unlike a classic class action suit, which requires a group of about thirty people to support a complaint, a Proposition 65 suit needs far fewer people to establish plaintiff status. After all his complaining to friends about the beach-cleaning machine, it didn't take Rizzo long to find enough who were willing to form the Avila Alliance, an unincorporated association with legal standing as a nonprofit group. The membership reflected the population of the town, with surfers, blue-collar workers, and a few professionals. "We put the name on it, I typed it at home, and for $186 bucks, you file! That was it," remembers Rizzo. With that, the wheels began to turn in earnest for what was to become an epic battle between the little people of a tiny beach town and the oil giant.

On September 6, 1996, the day after filing the suit, Rizzo was wakened by an early call from a local reporter. The story of the lawsuit was on the front page of the *Telegram-Tribune*, San Luis Obispo County's daily paper, and people wanted to know what was going on. The reality of the potential impact of the suit began to sink in, and Rizzo's euphoria about tackling such a large company was replaced by a sober appraisal of his chances of succeeding. It had felt like an impossible dream to the young attorney as he prepared the paperwork, but, bent on meeting the challenge, he had paid scant attention to the fight he would have to face in order to win.

Rizzo had gone from school and two years of minor casework to the world litigation stage in one step and faced a phalanx of top attorneys with many years of experience. David dared Goliath, and the battle was on. The young attorney was not the first to file suit by a private party against Unocal over the contamination at Avila Beach, nor was he the last to attempt to solve the problem. He was, however, the first to file for the people on environmental grounds, and his action would prove to be pivotal in meeting a challenge that had begun more than a hundred years before, when Unocal first began operations in Avila Beach.

THE BEGINNING OF
THE PARTNERSHIP
JUGGERNAUT

O VER the years that Unocal was the major economic player in Avila Beach, there had been a number of known aboveground spills and one underground leak with a spectacular announcement of its presence. Restaurateur Pete Kelley remembered that one particularly well.

A big man with a gentle manner, Kelley had a dream of opening a restaurant, and when he got the chance to launch his first enterprise, he did it in Avila Beach, in the downtown area on Front Street, where the beach is a stone's throw from the front door. The area was described in an issue of the long-gone *Avila Community News* as the place "Where the Bikini Meets the See."

It was an exciting time for Kelley to open an eatery and have it be successful from day one. Offering Caribbean cuisine and signature black beans, Pete's Seaside Café quickly became an area favorite as well as a return tourist destination. Kelley recalled that when the town went off septic tanks, oil appeared in the trenches that were dug for sewer lines. People were aware of contamination underground, and they also knew there were many pipelines running under Front Street. According to Kelley, by the time he opened his café, anyone who dug in the downtown area always hit oil. However, there was a more volatile spill waiting to be ignited—gasoline.

Kelley had been open only a week in July 1977 when the explosion happened. A basement apartment adjacent to the restaurant became ground zero, when the pilot light of a water heater set off the vapors. Kelley said, "It was almost humorous, because Everett and Linda, the students involved, were painting their apartment, and they were thrown through the window. They ended up outside, upright with their hair kind of singed, still holding on to their paintbrushes."

Kelley said Unocal was very aware of the problem, and they were ready with what he called "an invisible shield solution"—polyurethane injected into the sand to keep the spill from migrating. Electronic monitoring devices were used to measure the vapors, and monitoring wells were drilled to measure the volume of gas underground and were connected to air pumps used to disburse the gasoline vapors.

"Every twelve hours the wells would register gas, then it would disappear," said Kelley, "and the company figured the problem was cleared. It's obvious to me that it has to do with the ocean and high tide, but most people who have to deal with Avila don't know the ocean from their elbow." In spite of the shortcomings of Unocal's solution to the gasoline leak, there were no more explosions, but the gasoline underground remained like a silent plague threatening the little town.

The owner of the damaged apartment and his shaken tenants settled with Unocal for an undisclosed amount. Large fans that were brought in to clear vapors in the building used so much power that the wiring in Kelley's restaurant was destroyed. Still not willing to cause a stir, he had a friend rewire the place, and the cost was underwritten by Unocal's insurance company. When it was all over, Kelley realized that the spill had not been cleaned up, and he predicted at that time that it would take about a million dump truck loads to do so.

"My landlady, old Miss Barbara, had fumes in her apartment,

and I think she suffered some health problems because she lived closest to the leak," he said.

Kelley was also uneasy about the "invisible shield" between the leak and the apartment. He believed that if the contamination were prevented from moving toward Front Street properties, it would just migrate somewhere else. He was right. Not only did the gasoline remain, it was joined by benzene, crude oil, diesel, and other petroleum products to form a series of pools—later designated as "plumes"—beneath the town. Avila Beach was a time bomb waiting to explode again, and four hundred residents and thousands of tourists lived, breathed, and played atop the toxic soup. Years later, an internal Unocal memo would reveal that the company had typed and analyzed the soil and found the cause of much of the contamination to be their own 76 Premium gasoline.

The townspeople were caught between wanting the economic stability Unocal brought and worrying about the effects of long-term exposure to the noxious brew that was a part of their everyday life. As the 1980s drew to a close, more and more information came out about the silent threat that lurked under Avila Beach, but the news came to light slowly, in bits and pieces.

The underground leak became the "elephant in the parlor" in 1988, when Michael Rudd, one of the businessmen along Front Street, wanted to build a larger store. He had outgrown his original location, having done well selling souvenirs and Hawaiian shirts and renting boogie boards and surfboards. As part of the permit process for new construction, he contracted for a soil test, which immediately indicated that fumes were coming from underground. The fumes were so strong that engineers were afraid that if one of them lit a cigarette they would all be blown away. Rudd worked with the San Luis Obispo County Planning Department, where he had begun the process of securing a building permit, to solve the problem, but he would find, to his dismay, that there was no quick fix available. His discovery was just the tip of the iceberg.

For four years, without ever knowing the extent of the leak under the Rudd property, County Planning Department staff met informally with Unocal representatives, trying to get the company to commit to some kind of testing and cleanup. County Supervisor Evelyn Delany read reports from planners and stewed about the lack of initiative toward solving the problem. "Everybody noticed the fumes," said Delany. "It was a part of the package, like how Avila smells, and some days were worse than others. It was blamed on traffic. It was because of the tank farm. It was the fishing boats."

Then, in 1992, a Unocal pipeline broke, spilling five hundred barrels of crude oil at the edge of the ocean. Pirates Cove and Fossil Point on the eastern edge of Avila Beach were blackened, and the shore was strewn with dead birds and a small number of otters. Ten thousand salmon fingerlings that were being tended by the Central Coast Salmon Enhancement Program were also lost in the bay, and their holding pens were damaged.

Delany said that, although Unocal did a good job quickly cleaning up the water, they dragged their feet on doing the same for the fouled shoreline. She tried for months without success to get the company to finish the job. It was at an information exchange meeting in Santa Barbara with Unocal and their academic associates that Delany was able to raise the matter in public.

At that meeting, company and university experts who dealt with environmental problems claimed, with the support of scientific material and illustrations, that oil drilling and transport were harmless. During the public comment period that followed the presentations, Delany asked why the company had left the mess on the beach at Pirates Cove, and before she got back home an hour later, Unocal had contacted San Luis Obispo County to arrange the cleanup. "They did not like being embarrassed in front of their colleagues," observed Delany.

Negotiations about the Rudd property problem had been the responsibility of County Planner David Church, who was dismayed that the matter had dragged on for so many months. Delany, in her capacity as supervisor, finally set up an official meeting, where she learned that Unocal had proposed to the Regional Water Board, a state agency that also had jurisdiction in the matter, remedying the situation through use of a soil vapor extraction system.

"They told us how great their air-sucking wells were going to be," Delany said, "what they looked like and where they were going to be. Then they showed us the tank farm where the gas would be accumulated and burned off. That was their solution."

Unocal did not deny that the spill was their responsibility, and, it appeared to Delany, the company was proud of their proposed remedy. After having long discussions with the County Planning Department and the Regional Water Board, without much action, Delany was not in the mood to suffer further delays. "They were so sure it was going to work and it was the best thing since sliced bread. I said in effect 'sure, stick it in your ear.'"

Prior to Delany's first meeting with Unocal, the extent of the toxic plume had only been guessed at. "It was, 'maybe it's here, maybe it's there, maybe it's deep, maybe it goes under the beach, maybe not,'" she said, "and after all the guessing about it without benefit of testing, Unocal simply said, 'we'll just put in the air-sucking wells and solve the problem.'"

Toward the end of the meeting, Unocal agreed that something had to be done, but, to Delany's surprise, said they were not sure that they were responsible for the contamination. "We said, 'who else?' And they said they didn't know, but they still weren't sure," said Delany. Clearly the communication between Unocal and the county was guarded at best, and it was not destined to improve in the near future.

It made sense to determine the extent and location of the underground plume before the company could realistically develop a plan to clean it up, but it appeared to Delany that Unocal was in no hurry to get it done. At the same time that problems with the contamination in Avila Beach were unfolding, a discovery a few miles to the south promised to muddy the already roiling waters. Although that problem was in neighboring Santa Barbara County, the source was the same oil company.

Unocal employee Dan Tucker reported to Santa Barbara County regulators that the company had been concealing diluent leaks at the Guadalupe Dunes facility since the 1980s. According to county documents, Tucker claimed that readings on constantly checked individual meters never matched those on master meters, and he said he believed that at least one hundred barrels of diluent were being lost each day. Tucker added that when he had reported the discrepancies to his supervisors, he was told the meters were not registering accurately. Tucker was unconvinced and unable to accept the continued losses. He finally reported his concerns to a Santa Barbara County environmental health investigator.

Shortly after the information came to light, armed California Fish & Game officials raided Unocal offices in Guadalupe and, using a warrant, confiscated scores of records that clearly supported Tucker's fears. From the records themselves, regulators learned that the Guadalupe Dunes' underground spill dwarfed that of Avila Beach. Delany was dismayed to find that Unocal attorneys dealing with Avila Beach were also assigned to Guadalupe, and they had adopted the same strategy of stall and talk with no action. The problem at Guadalupe served to increase the turmoil and began a new era in negotiation, because of the additional jurisdictions.

Responsibility for the cleanup in Guadalupe, just as in Avila Beach, involved a mind-boggling number of county, state, and federal agencies. Complicated by the fact that there were two counties and two sites involved, coordination became a nightmare for everyone except Unocal, which was able to play the waiting game to its own benefit. Little by little it became clear that company attorneys were adding to the confusion by pitting one agency against another, claiming a request from one agency conflicted with that of another, or that one allowed more latitude in the negotiations than yet another.

Although testing had not been done to confirm it, the leak of diluent at Guadalupe was monumental and estimated to be in the millions of gallons, judging from Unocal records alone. "It was the same company," Delany said, "and we knew some of the same players in the suits. We knew the drill." In an attempt to inject a little levity into the sea of accumulating gloom, lawyers for Unocal in both problem areas became known to the regulatory agencies as the "Santa Maria Group." This was a reference to their formidable presence that spoke as one, despite their numbers. By contrast, the agencies each had a specific frame of reference.

None of the negotiations helped Mike Rudd in the least. He was left without financing for a new store, because, despite his own excellent credit history, the contamination put his property in the lenders' high-risk category. Avila Beach residents sat up and took notice, realizing that if Rudd couldn't build on his lot, none of them could even consider building an addition onto their homes. Even more ominously, they couldn't buy or sell any property, nor could they refinance the existing loans they had on their properties.

The timing of the economic disaster could not have been worse for Rudd and the entire town. Except for the abalone industry, there had been no economic growth for Avila Beach immediately following World War II. While the rest of the country enjoyed an unprecedented upswinging economy after the war, Avila Beach continued to be an oil company town with limited growth.

That all began to change in the mid-1960s, when Pacific Gas and Electric announced plans to build the Diablo Canyon nuclear power plant on another bluff a few miles west of town. The entire San Luis Obispo region was rocked by a long-lasting protest against the construction of the plant by antinuclear factions from around the United States and the world. Protestors tried to shut down the project, and while they succeeded in getting some additional safeguards, the construction was allowed to commence.

Once the issue was settled and construction actually begun, the influx of workers made Avila Beach a boomtown for several years. Every available room, apartment, and closet was rented, and businesses along Front Street thrived year-round instead of closing at the end of the summer tourist season, as had been their practice. Interest in building began in earnest, making the town a destination location for tourists instead of a stopover on the way to places of greater attraction like Big Sur, Yosemite, or Lake Tahoe. Plans for extensive construction were abruptly aborted in 1977 because of a lack of sufficient water to sustain increased development. The county enforced a moratorium on building until a new supply of water was found. Ten years later, Avila Beach finally connected with the California State Water System, and plans to build in the business district were put back on the schedule, only to once again be put on hold because of the discovery of oil on the Rudd property. It was another in a long list of twists and turns that prevented the town from moving forward.

A 1998 *Los Angeles Times* story described Avila Beach as "a working man's paradise, happily frozen in time, circa 1960." The statement was only partly true, because while some of the residents loved it as it was, others called for changing the town while still retaining its unique character.

In the 1990s Avila Beach was a *Happy Days* kind of town, in an oily beach setting, with one foot in the past and the other in muck. And it was then that Evelyn Delany came away from her first meeting with Unocal with a bad taste in her mouth. She had the distinct feeling the company did not take the problem seriously and wondered if that were because the area was perceived as being populated solely by rubes and rustics. She had served on the planning commission prior to her election to the board of supervisors, and her experience with attorneys had been less than positive. She found that they could not always be counted on to provide clear communication or complete information. She also believed that they treated the local people like a "bunch of yokels."

"I['d] think, oh God, they are really up to something again," she said. "You know, it was like [they thought], 'we'll just tell them anything. What do they know?'"

But Unocal underestimated the population of Avila Beach, because the region had a high percentage of educated people, many of whom were retired and active in community service. Delany herself was a resident of Pismo Beach and a California Polytechnic State University faculty wife at the time. She had a master's degree and was representative of many citizens, with intellectual curiosity, an active interest in her surroundings, and the wherewithal to put two and two together. She also looked like a country gentlewoman without guile or the capability of subterfuge. Unocal attorneys mistook her round, smiling face as that of someone who could not possibly understand the complexities of the oil business.

Not only did the oil business have its own jargon and shorthand references, it was also in a state of rapidly expanding technological advancement. Delany recalls that when the Rudd property contamination came to light, it seemed as though Unocal came out with a new map almost every week, contradicting previous information and revising what they thought was the full extent of the plume. Delany believed that a thorough investigation could not be accomplished without an Environmental Impact Report.

To initiate preparation of the environmental document, the county is required by the state to oversee the hiring of consultants, and the EIR must be accomplished according to mandated standards. However, the applicant—in this case, Unocal—is required to pay for the work. Delany was not entirely satisfied with the contractors Unocal had hired for parts of the testing that had already been done, and she was reluctant to allow the company to select a contractor to do the work, without some input from the board of supervisors.

Additionally, in an unusual arrangement, the county became coleaders with the Regional Water Board for the EIR, something that is rarely done. Joint leadership was deemed necessary because the Regional Water Board set the cleanup standard levels that would drive the project, requiring their expertise in testing, and the county was responsible for the permitting process that would follow. Both the water board and the county continued to press for the EIR to be done, but Unocal steadfastly insisted that the air wells would work for the Avila Beach spill. Delany and the county disagreed.

At one time during these negotiations, the company sent a check to the county for more than half a million dollars, just out of the blue, according to Delany. "They had a corporate meeting and decided this was enough, here's the money, you can clean it up. They expected us to indemnify them after that and that [would be] the end of it."

Although everyone at the county offices was in awe of the amount of the check and marveled at so many zeros, the counsel told them not to do anything with the check, and especially not to deposit it into an escrow account, because acceptance would mean agreement with Unocal that the money would take care of the Rudd property problem. Delany laughs about the situation, saying, "Our mothers always told us get it in the bank fast, and here he was saying not to do anything with it!" The check was returned to the company.

As meetings dragged on without agreement, tension increased at the county agencies. When corporate lawyers arrived in groups to the meetings, county personnel confided to Delany that they felt a certain amount of intimidation.

Unwilling to dig out the contamination, Unocal proposed biosparging, a relatively new technology that uses petroleum-eating bacteria to clean up the products underground with a minimum of disruption to the surface structures, as a sure solution to the problem, but the Regional Water Board expressed reservations. The board believed the process would work well only for one year, during which time most of the volatile vapors from the gasoline could be pumped out, leaving the liquid underground. Documents uncovered in the legal discovery process would later not only confirm this notion, but also the fact that Unocal was aware of the shortcomings while continuing to insist the procedure would work well for remediation.

Scientific estimates at the time projected that using petroleum-eating bacteria to clean the spill to water board specifications could take more than twenty years, if it worked as expected. Twenty years of waiting to develop a property or add a bathroom, twenty years of waiting for a clean beach, twenty years of wondering if there would be another explosion, all the while hoping that biosparging would actually work. There were no guarantees.

Although California law had legal demands in place for Unocal to clean up the environmental damage, the company took a hardline stance with the agencies and managed to hold off on compliance through use of delay tactics, numerous challenges, and threats of appeal to Sacramento. There was no agreement in sight, until Rizzo's court action set the stage to bring *all* the key players together on the same stage at the same time.

3

THE LITTLE DIG—THE PERIL BELOW

COUNTY Planner David Church became involved in the Unocal contamination when Mike Rudd discovered oil under his property, six years before Saro Rizzo entered the fight. Church is a quiet-spoken man who resembles Rizzo in that he is young and intensely dedicated to public service. Both men are disarmingly open, and both are often initially mistaken as naive.

Church was thrown into the controversy at a time when new testing revealed that high levels of gas vapors under the Rudd property—for the most part from gasoline and diesel fuel—were potentially explosive. Unocal insisted that the most logical remedy for the problem was to install a soil vapor extraction system, consisting of a series of wells to vacuum the gases out for safe combustion.

"The vapor extraction system may have done its job that way, but it didn't deal at all with the rest of the contamination," Church recalled. Rudd's property was a block away from the 1977 apartment explosion, and Church was certain the gases came from the same source—pipelines under the street.

Once wells were installed to deal with the immediate danger, Unocal suggested biosparge, a prolonged process with limited application, as a permanent solution to the problem. Using biosparge, bacteria with an appetite for petroleum have to be introduced through additional wells and fed nutrients on a regular basis. As time passed, researchers in the field gained new information about the bacteria, which, by the mid-1990s, led them to revise estimates of the time it would take for the bacteria to partially eliminate the contamination to more than eighty years.

From the beginning, Church was sure that Unocal knew that biosparge was useless as a means to eliminate the contamination. "We knew when they proposed the idea," he said, "that it would not come anywhere near the levels people needed for their property to be freed from the contamination so they could get loans or sell their properties."

Biosparge was the least intrusive and the least expensive way of attacking the petroleum problem, which made it an obvious choice for Unocal. It would not destroy any homes or businesses like excavation would, but excavation was the only way to clean up the contaminants to the satisfaction of lenders and the Regional Water Board. That was not something anyone took lightly.

By 1994, and facing public disclosure of being responsible for major contamination problems in two adjoining counties, Unocal began a public relations offensive by partnering with First Bank of San Luis Obispo and offering five-year loans to businesses in Avila Beach that were impacted by the contamination. They also began buying the property of those people who were unable to wait for a resolution of the problem. For example, the company acquired the historic Avila Grocery Store when the owner was unable to expand, but leased it back to him to continue operations. Owner Marvin Dee was not entirely satisfied with the deal, but said he had no better options. The company also helped Avila Beach resolve the construction moratorium by purchasing five years' worth of water rights from the California state water network.

With a good supply of water back in the picture, the building moratorium that was put in place in 1977 was lifted, and permits could once again be issued, but new construction was still not permitted for those properties with soil tests showing contamination. Other properties located nearby were similarly impacted even if they were not atop the plume. Instead of helping residents, the Unocal-backed five-year loans did not offer much assistance to people, because without a traditional thirty-year loan, the program was merely a stopgap measure with a balloon payment looming in the near future. Even the company's five-year gift of state water appeared to be a ploy to avoid actual cleanup.

During his frequent walks around Avila Beach, Church found a great deal of confusion among residents, and he was unable to give them much comfort, which added to his own frustration. One of the eighty-year-old residents affected him deeply. "Gladys Misakian was a person who I got to know pretty well," he said. "She'd have me in her house for soup, and we'd talk." He was able to answer at least some of her questions about the problem and how it could affect her directly. That kind of open communication was destined to be the strongest weapon in the arsenals of both the county and the people of Avila Beach.

For the next two years, from 1994 to 1996, Church and Supervisor Evelyn Delany poured their hearts and souls into working out a solution for Avila Beach, without much measurable success. The possibility of excavation was brought up by scientific experts, but the idea was too much for most people to handle at the time. Unocal questioned every bit of evidence and testing done by both the county and the company's own contracted experts, unless it was to their advantage. Unocal also voiced doubt about the quality of the regulators' experience, especially in view of their youth, comparing it to the company's own century of accumulated familiarity with science and geology as they related to the oil business. Every water board and county decision not to Unocal's liking was appealed to the point that numerous legal actions were in the regulatory system at any one time.

Unocal also questioned the integrity of the water board, when the board set 100 parts petroleum per million as the requirement for a satisfactory cleanup. The company filed suit in Sacramento under the Brown Act, which requires meetings be public, claiming the meeting at which the standard was adopted had not been open and was thus illegal. Company attorneys asked that the standard be voided (because the meeting at which it was adopted was originally scheduled only for discussion) and asked Sacramento for further study, a tactic that left both the standard and the future of the cleanup in limbo.

Opening an additional front in their public relations campaign, Unocal established an office in downtown Avila Beach and formed a group to work on the question of health risks. On the surface it sounded like a good way to proceed, but the reality was that the standards for health risk were substantially lower than those of water quality. Nevertheless, the company teamed with representatives from the water board, the Avila Alliance, Avila Valley County Water District, State Department of Toxic Substances Control, Port San Luis, and San Luis Obispo County's Air Pollution Control District, Planning Commission, and Environmental Health and Planning Department.

The company asked for a one-month answer to the health risk question, claiming that establishment of a cleanup standard was premature until health risks were determined. David Church wondered whether they were laughably optimistic for resolution or knowingly determined to delay any action. Unocal contracted with a private company to do a preliminary health study. The report found that there was contamination beginning at five feet below the surface of the beach, but it did not appear to be moving. The test did little to expand the knowledge base, but it made Unocal look as if it were taking an active role in solving the health-risk question. Church and the county felt it was important to find the extent and content of the plume as well as to determine if the underground spill was in danger of *daylighting,* a term used to describe the escape of petroleum products or vapors into the air or surface soil.

Negotiations dragged on, and in late 1994, Unocal threw discussions into a turmoil by announcing it was relinquishing all of its long-term working facilities in the central California coast region to concentrate on independent oil exploration and production, mostly in the Gulf of Mexico and Asia. Tosco Oil Corporation bought out most of Unocal's California assets, including the Santa Maria refinery, pipelines from the central valley to Santa Maria and Avila Beach, plus 1,350 gas stations in six states (Tosco retained the Unocal 76 logo), three oil tankers, a fleet of trucks, terminals, and refineries, for $2 billion. The deal did not include ownership of the company's pier and some land it owned in Avila Beach that was heavily contaminated, in some places with crude oil a foot deep. Unocal announced the sale was necessary because profits were slipping due to environmental demands. The deal was enthusiastically applauded by Wall Street, because it accompanied Unocal's major plan to reorganize and streamline.

The divestiture was of no small consequence to the residents in Avila Beach, many of whom feared the sale would put Unocal out of reach for cleaning up the town. For two years Unocal had touted biosparge as the cure for the contamination. Many of the residents wanted to believe that the science was reliable and efficient and had supported the company's position until the California holdings went to Tosco. Then their confidence in biosparging took a decided downturn. The sale fostered a deep division in the town, with loyalists on one side and a small number of people perceived to be alarmists on the other.

Legally Unocal was still responsible for the cleanup, but, since the biosparge process took so many years, many people doubted the company would be around to do something else if it did not succeed, which meant they would be left with a multimillion-dollar problem to take care of themselves.

When more testing revealed additional contamination under the town, David Church found that a lot of public confidence in the water board and Unocal had been lost. The desire for a complete cleanup was gaining strength, and Church realized it was incumbent on the agencies to pull together for the good of Avila Beach. He also became aware, in talking with the residents, that if the agencies didn't join forces, the people were going to get the project done on their own.

"We had a job to do as far as pulling ourselves together," he said, "and to get on the same page at the same time." Although Delany and Church had been working together on the problem for a long time and shared an understanding about what was going on, over the same period of time, three different people had handled the project part-time at the water board.

Tensions moved to the fast track on a brilliant fall day in October 1995 when a member of California Fish & Game discovered an oily sheen on the water in Avila Beach. Oil had begun to day-light from a source below ground, and the water board ordered an immediate emergency cleanup along the San Luis Obispo Creek, a location where a mere 2.5 feet of sand covered the contamination.

San Luis Obispo Creek is one of the last waterways in central California to support salmon and steelhead spawning runs, and contamination of it by released petroleum would destroy a year's generation of sea life that depended on the stream, as well as threatening existing marine life in the bay. Engineers for the water board called it an imminent threat to the ocean and human health and claimed that children digging in the sand could be in danger.

By November, additional testing again showed that the plume was larger than had been estimated. Alarmed at the news, Church and the water board wanted an independent consultant to deter-mine exactly what the status of the plume was and to draw up a plan to deal with it. Unocal objected, and Jim Bray, a Unocal spokesman, claimed that there were actually two separate plumes, not one large one. He said that the two plumes just touched each other and, relying on reasoning and logic that escaped most peo-ple, claimed that the discovery was not a particularly significant increase in information, it was just a better definition of the situa-tion. He also insisted the plume was not moving, and that it con-sisted of weathered, old product that was actually a solid mass of old crude oil called "asphaltum," which is like the material used to pave streets. He went on to claim that it presented no danger and that digging it up would be like digging up old pavement.

In response to the water board's demand, Unocal presented a plan to excavate 4,500 cubic yards of old sand, about eighty feet wide and thirteen feet deep in some places. They would put in con-tainment walls to keep the petroleum from reaching the ocean and put clean sand on top of the Front Street plume. The plan was ap-proved, and the cleanup was set for November 13.

The county tried to get a brief Environmental Impact Report (EIR) approved, because the information available about the con-tamination was so uncertain. Unocal disagreed vehemently, saying it sounded like the report the county wanted was the kind usually done for a shopping mall construction. Company experts expressed the opinion that should the project need one, it should cost no more than $200,000–300,000. In the interest of getting the job done quickly, before it "daylighted" dangerously, the county postponed the question of an EIR.

At a community meeting in early November, Avila Beach residents expressed dissatisfaction with Unocal's plan for the cleanup, claiming it was too limited. Unocal was willing to dig up the beach, but not Front Street or the parcels directly north of the beach. One of the parcel owners was attorney Roger Lyons, who was initially active in attempts to get the cleanup done. However, at the last minute, Lyons sold his property to Unocal, and the water board lost some of its leverage in getting Unocal to move. Forced to defer the major cleanup until a later time, the water board instead pushed for the emergency cleanup along the San Luis Obispo Creek, referred to by many as the "Little Dig." With each additional bit of information, the problem seemed to grow dramatically from being a simple spill under the Rudd property to one that undermined nearly the entire town. Without expert consensus, people were fearful that no one knew what they were doing, and they requested more outside scientific help. However, Unocal continued to insist there was no threat to public health, other than the possibility that the pollution might cause a rash and nothing more.

At the meeting, Unocal's estimate of the extent of the excavation grew to 5,000 cubic yards to be removed, and their estimate for replacement sand grew correspondingly to 10,000 cubic yards, provoking one disgusted resident to declare that he would be long dead before Unocal made a move to begin the excavation.

The meeting was intended to concentrate on the Little Dig, but in light of developments at Guadalupe Dunes, the rapidly escalating estimates of the extent of both contaminations, and Unocal's reluctance to clean up either place, the San Luis Obispo County Board of Supervisors indicated that they were considering legal action against the company. Evelyn Delany was particularly angry and said that every step of the way Unocal had protested every proposed action as too expensive. One irate environmental activist resident called for Unocal to be declared a legal public nuisance, and another said Unocal's credibility was less than zero.

An attorney in the audience presented three Unocal maps, dated 1993, 1994, and 1995. The first map showed one large plume, the second showed two separate plumes, and the third again showed one plume. Nothing was clear except that oil was coming up from the plumes below and that Unocal was not demonstrating an eagerness to deal with the problem. The company suggested that the board call in a third party to evaluate both positions and mediate a compromise solution.

With tempers rising, Planning Director Alex Hinds asked, "Would the *district attorney* be acceptable?" The meeting in an uproar, the board asked county counsel if they had legal redress to force Unocal to pay for the EIR and learned they didn't, because that was up to the water board as lead agency.

After two months of acrimonious debate, the Little Dig began in November 1995 along the San Luis Obispo Creek. Contractors installed containment walls deep into the beach sand, and the digging began, even as Unocal representatives wrote in the local newspapers' opinion pages that some Front Street business owners no longer even *wanted* their properties cleaned up. Subsequent letters from residents were quick to point out that Unocal's claim was true, because the company had bought those properties outright, and the former owners had been bound by a confidentiality agreement not to say a word about it. Unocal continued to insist that the contamination was asphalted, and company spokesmen were quoted in the local newspapers as wondering why it was necessary to dig up Front Street pavement only to remove pavement beneath it.

Work continued on the dig, and on December 14, diggers hit a gusher, but not just water as they had expected. Asphalted oil was nowhere to be seen, instead free crude product floated in the murky water in an ever-widening lake. One Unocal official claimed that the digging had shaken and squeezed the petroleum product, separating it from the soil and causing it to become liquid. Ignoring arguments that solid asphalt was not capable of yielding free crude in the manner described, Unocal announced that they had always expected to find some liquid petroleum and had said so publicly.

County and state officials were stunned by Unocal's pronouncement and countered that the company couldn't have expected liquid since they had no cleanup booms or other devices at the site to handle liquid contaminants. The two sides bantered back and forth, ultimately accomplishing nothing. County planners wondered if the company had misled them again and whether or not their experts really knew what they were doing. Unocal shot back that the water board knew they could not clean it all up at the time, a comment that appeared to be pitting one agency against another. What was clear to everyone at the site was that the company was surprised, despite what they said to the media.

Regulatory agencies were scrambling to make the best of a bad situation that had suddenly turned critical. The water board now demanded Unocal do more testing. California Fish & Game announced they had told Unocal to be prepared for free-floating product, even though the company said there would be none.

At the dig site, workers spread absorbent pillows and used skimmers to soak up the oil that was floating on top of the water. The estimate of sand that had to be removed went up to 6,000 cubic yards. In another surprising turn of events, after 4,000 cubic yards of sand had been removed, tests showed the top two to five feet of sand to be contaminated with 35–750 ppm of petroleum products (the standards required no more than 1 ppm in the water and 100 ppm in the soil near the water table). This time even Jim Bray said he was surprised.

Two months later, the beach reopened, after 7,500 cubic yards of contaminated sand had been removed. The Little Dig had prevented the oil from reaching the creek, but the job was not finished, because a major storm was headed for the central coast. Remaining oil-soaked sand was covered over, but the crisis had been averted.

News of the oil lake on the beach spread to papers in San Francisco and Los Angeles. Jim Bray told a *San Francisco Examiner* reporter that he was surprised at finding the oil, apparently forgetting that he had previously told a *Telegram-Tribune* reporter he had expected it. The story about Avila Beach was picked up by wire services and sent around the world. The picture of bright yellow HAZMAT jumpers, black with oil from the waist down, and the little boat floating in the middle of a black lagoon, from which oil soaker pillows were spread to absorb the mess, made the front pages of publications around the country, causing a public relations nightmare that changed everything but Unocal's stance. The company continued to hold that biosparging was a reasonable solution to the problem, but suggested two new proposals for the beach cleanup: solidification and permanent containment.

Solidification is a way of cementing pollution in place by digging wells just above where the pollution lays and pumping in tons of concrete to keep the pollution isolated. Permanent containment is accomplished by pile driving the sixty-foot-long metal sheet walls used in the Little Dig into the soil to keep the oil from migrating. What these two new "solutions" did not address was the real possibility that the oil could still get into the freshwater aquifer under the town, making it difficult for both residents and regulators to take these suggestions seriously. It appeared that Unocal was grasping at straws and digging itself deeper and deeper into the quagmire.

The public reaction was expressed in a banner headline that read, "Well, Well, Well." The *Telegram-Tribune* called the dig a "huge pit of stinking petroleum." It was Avila Beach's worst fears realized. A cartoon in the *New Times* showed a Christmas tree with a gift under it, sitting in a puddle of black oil oozing out from the bottom of the package. Its caption read, "From Unocal to Avila, Merry Christmas from Your Good Neighbor." Another cartoon showed Unocal executives behind bars. Its caption read, "The Perfect Containment."

CONFLICTS IN
TECHNOLOGY

THE Regional Water Quality Control Board and San Luis Obispo County held key responsibilities to set the standards for cleanup and to issue permits to get it done. Soon after the Little Dig was complete, the Arthur D. Little Company was hired to begin work on a preliminary study of the expected impacts and to provide scientific information about the contamination in Avila Beach. Although the Arthur D. Little Company was hired by the county, the cost of the study was to be borne by Unocal, and the oil company was not willing to officially approve the contract until it was satisfied that all avenues to find a solution had been exhausted. Unocal's position in the middle of this controversy is emblematic of how complex an environmental problem can be and how difficult it can be to find a solution agreeable to all sides and stakeholders.

Consultant Steve Radis of Arthur D. Little's Santa Barbara office had a history in the region, having been hired by Santa Barbara County to look into the Guadalupe spill in 1995, more than a year before Rizzo filed his suit. It was hoped that some of the information he had gathered for that site would be helpful in getting the Avila Beach problem addressed.

Once again, the two locations shared agency interest and public scrutiny. The Guadalupe Dunes were emotionally connected to the Avila Beach legal action in geographic proximity, by the actions of the accused Unocal Corporation, and by the enormity of the two sites' underground spills. While the Avila Beach pipeline problem was smaller by far in terms of total gallons riding under the town, the socioeconomic impact was huge. There, lives, homes, businesses, and community identity were at considerable risk. The petroleum spill at the Dunes was one of mammoth proportions—one that could destroy a major agricultural area for a hundred years by contaminating an immense aquifer.

The Guadalupe spill, although larger than the Avila Beach contamination, was much easier to assess, given that it was located in an uninhabited region. However, Guadalupe was home to many endangered species and diverse biota as well as being an unusual ecological location—the only shifting sand dunes in California left intact other than those in Death Valley. It also has a storied past in a region that esteems history.

The Guadalupe Dunes are incredibly quiet and serene most of the year, but when the winds blow, the noise is deafening. Within a short walk from the last stretch of paved path, the world of the shifting sands is completely enveloping. Immense dunes are constantly shaped and reshaped by wind that is both friend and enemy, depending on how strong it chooses to run, both on and off shore. The Dunes are mysterious and serene, and for many years were the private domain of a band of independent squatters calling themselves Dunites. Creative and artistic, the Dunites lived free and easy until civilization and county regulations drove them away. One by one their shacks succumbed to the elements, until the last one was moved inland for preservation.

The Dunes rise suddenly from the beach, where one can feel as lost as if one had been transported to the great Sahara. It is completely out of touch and utterly foreign from any habitable, farmable land. To live in the environment of the Dunes, it is necessary to be one with the earth and completely willing to coexist with it. There is no compromise with the earth here—there is only a firm realization that you bend, conform, and accept nature as it is.

In 1923, Cecil B. DeMille came to Guadalupe Dunes and built

the largest movie set in history for his epic, *The Ten Command-ments*. There were a million pounds of statuary in the set that re-quired fifteen hundred construction workers to erect. The finished film set was 120 feet high and 720 feet wide. When shooting was over, DeMille ordered the set struck and buried in the dunes.

A boy playing in the sand in the summer of 1993 stubbed his toe on an artifact from the set, initiating a hunt for the rest of what had been buried. Cryptic clues in DeMille's autobiography have been used as a treasure map to unearth part of a statue of Ramses and a lion's face, among other items that are nearly a century old.

Suddenly, this incredible niche in nature along with one man's creation was under attack from below by a petroleum spill nearly the size of the Exxon Valdez disaster in Alaska. As it did with the Avila Beach contamination, Unocal proposed that the Guadalupe Dunes spill could be partially remediated with biosparging. While that choice of remediation promised to take much longer than ex-cavation, it presented the best alternative for the area, because it would leave the surface of the dunes relatively untouched and its expanse of wildlife undisturbed. There was no economic impact at Guadalupe Dunes for anyone but Unocal.

Despite this compromise to a very big problem in the Santa Bar-bara County location, Unocal would not pay the San Luis Obispo County for the A. D. Little Company contract to address Avila Beach until it was satisfied with the direction the cleanup would take. Radis wrote and rewrote the proposal several times over the year, but the main sticking point was that Unocal insisted that bi-osparging was the solution to the town's problem, since it was the primary cleanup effort underway at the Guadalupe Dunes, even though the impacts on the people and economics of the two areas were vastly different.

"The county wanted us to look at anything we could think of," said Radis, "but Unocal wanted us to concentrate on just what they were proposing to do, which was biosparging." The trouble was that science didn't back up Unocal. In biosparge theory, mi-crobes introduced underground consume hydrocarbons. The proc-ess works well on light hydrocarbons such as gasoline, but does not work well, if at all, on crude oil and diesel, which made up most of the Avila Beach spill. Radis said that although Unocal didn't have much real power to decide how the study was to be done, they did all they could to influence it.

For Saro Rizzo and his Avila Alliance suit, the delay that continued was both good and bad. It allowed more time to accumulate test results, and the delay in getting an EIR gave the county and the state attorney general's office more time to decide to intervene in the legal action.

While he waited for the EIR to be approved, Radis performed what the industry calls a "characterization study" of Avila Beach, describing the situation from both a physical and a human point of view. He also did additional test borings and found evidence that there was more pollution under the beach than previously thought. "The county knew about the plume close to Front Street, but not the one that goes out into the ocean," Radis said. In an interim report to the county, he recommended that further studies be done on the beach and on other areas he suspected might contain more contaminants.

Unocal argued that the newly discovered area of petroleum deposits was the result of a spill that occurred in the 1920s, when oil had flowed into the ocean. It apparently didn't occur to them to acknowledge that that spill had been their responsibility as well. They also argued that the earlier spill had been a natural oil seep, but Radis said tests showed that the sand above and below the thick layer of oil was clean, which wouldn't be the case with a well of oil pushing up from an ancient deposit.

Radis also studied the historical reports of the vapor extraction wells that had been installed following the 1977 Avila Beach explosion. It was clear that the vapor extraction devices that Unocal installed solved the problem at the time, but Radis suspected that dissolved total petroleum hydrocarbons (TPH) had migrated underground to the ocean, verifying the hunch that restaurateur Pete Kelley had had nearly twenty years previously that the contamination prevented from accumulating in one area would surely move to another. Radis's test contractor predicted that the plume's path would be shown by finding a region of "dead" sand. Further borings verified that the sand showed few living organisms in the area where the explosion had occurred and along the way to the new plume found under the beach.

Radis did not expect to find any serious health risks to people, but at one point, the test borings did reveal water with a concentration of hydrogen sulfide in samples taken from groundwater under Front Street. "We pretty much stunk up the town by pumping this water out," he said. "Nothing was going to hurt anyone, but it smelled really bad."

Another problem Radis faced in dealing with Unocal was that the company was unwilling to do complete testing—meaning they accepted test results based on fewer drillings and only estimates of the size and contents of the spill, instead of continuing to look for the actual limits of the plume. This shortcoming was one reason the company was repeatedly caught unaware like they were when they insisted there were no free petroleum products at the Little Dig site. Radis said that if they had done more thorough testing, they would have been aware of the presence of the petroleum.

"We faced this problem with Unocal for two to three years on the project. We felt there was a lot of liquid hydrocarbons." Radis referred to this liquid contamination as "free product," meaning that it was not absorbed into the soil and moved through it somewhat like water would. His tests of one of the groundwater wells in fact revealed slight contamination by liquid hydrocarbons, just as he had suspected. Radis's evidence showed that mobile free product was minimal; however, dissolved petroleum trapped in soil grains was a much bigger issue.

Unocal's testing began to appear questionable just before the Little Dig, when all Unocal wells were reported to have free product in them for the first time. Radis said the amounts of the free product in the wells varied—"six inches here, a foot there"—and he felt the variance was a result of the company purging the wells, which was the right thing to do. However, after each purging, a well is allowed to stabilize, and water returns to the well before the slower moving petroleum product. Apparently the company had taken samples before enough time had elapsed for the slower oil and hydrocarbons to flow back into the well, skewing their results.

Unocal maintained that the plume was not moving, but that was only part of the problem, because while the *soil* plume was stable, dissolved TPH was moving toward San Luis Bay and the ocean. Tides and the water table are integral parts of shoreline testing, because of the dilution and variability factors. It appeared to Radis that the company really believed their claim that the plume was stable, because they were clearly surprised and unprepared to deal with the problem when the Little Dig revealed the existence of free product.

Responsibility for the contamination was established once and for all when chemical fingerprint testing showed that the oil under the tank farm was the same as the oil under the town and the beach and in the intertidal plume. Radis ordered nearly one hundred test samples and found a far greater amount of oil products than anyone else had found or even estimated.

While the amount of spill discovered was a revelation, that there *was* a spill was not, because Radis said tanks are as notorious for leaking as pipes are—it is rare to find one that doesn't leak. Unocal's hard-line stance on culpability was hard to fathom. At one point Radis was given a corporate memo from 1977 that revealed that the company knew the gasoline leak that had caused the explosion next to Pete Kelley's restaurant was from a Unocal pipeline. Radis found other evidence that Unocal knew about the leaks and had replaced pipelines many times. At one time the company had actually raised the level of Front Street when they installed new pipes.

The flow of leaks toward the ocean continued unabated. Biological surveys showed a predictable dead zone along the path of the plumes, with high concentrations of hydrocarbons and diminished numbers of intertidal and beach organisms from what would normally be expected.

As the evidence accumulated, the greatest barrier to settling the question of the cleanup rested with the numbers—how many parts per million (ppm) of total petroleum hydrocarbons would be allowed to remain once the job was done? Because biosparging could not be expected to bring the level of contamination to anything less than thousands of ppm, Unocal stubbornly fought for a standard no less than that. The tracks of company heels that dragged through the sand toward a solution grew deeper and deeper with each level of confrontation. Finally Unocal did a tidal influence and mobility study, which confirmed the existence of TPH in the wells near the ocean.

By the time Saro Rizzo filed his suit to force Unocal to clean up the beach above and below the sands, recent battles in other parts of the country between environmentalist organizations and commercial businesses had served to harden positions on both sides. The war to clean up the spill under the beach town heated up, and Unocal's stalling strategy raised the rhetoric on both sides.

While the oil company had the resources to wait out legal meanderings through the appeals process with regulatory agencies, Rizzo and the Avila Alliance, having extremely limited funds, could not compete very long. There was no way to avoid the necessity of hiring experts and building the case. The Exxon Valdez court battle had already been in the appellate courts for years, costing the plaintiffs millions of dollars by the time the oil companies involved were convicted. The same fate faced Saro Rizzo and his partners in their lawsuit, until they evened the playing field with an ingenious legal approach and the help of smoking-gun evidence coming from an unexpected source.

PARTNERSHIPS DRAW
A LINE IN THE SAND

NOT long before Saro Rizzo filed suit against Unocal, the water board put Gerhardt Hubner in charge of dealing with the Avila Beach pollution threat to underground aquifers. Finally realizing that the problem required a full-time dedicated staff member, the board had reassigned Hubner from another job to the cleanup project.

In country parlance, Gerhardt Hubner is a "tall drink of water." Well over six feet, he has a way of communicating with his entire body, bending slightly toward you, clearly showing his interest in what is being said. He is also similar to Saro Rizzo in having close family connections in Europe—Hubner's in Germany, Rizzo's in Italy. In his voluminous files concerning Avila Beach, Hubner has two vials, one filled with water and black oil, the other with oil-soaked sand. They serve to remind him of the enormous challenge he faced when he took on the Unocal team.

With his expertise in groundwater and technical issues, Hubner began working on the project immediately following a visit with family in Europe. "We had a board meeting the second day after I got back. There were a number of community members there and they were pretty upset," he said.

Following the emergency Little Dig and all the coordination

that had to be worked out among the agencies, Hubner realized the best solution to the problem of dealing with Unocal was to co-ordinate the responsibilities of all of the state, federal, and county agencies together as a team. As Unocal talked with various regula-tors one-on-one, it became obvious they were shopping for an-swers that suited them regarding the problems in both Guadalupe and Avila Beach. For this reason, it was important have a working committee where regulators could talk through the issues and present a united front.

Hubner joined the Multi-Agency Coordinating Committee (MACC), which had been formed to meet the challenge of cleanup at Guadalupe Dunes. With members from the California Coastal Commission, California Fish & Game, San Luis Obispo and Santa Barbara Counties, EIR consultant Arthur D. Little Company, U.S. Army Corps of Engineers, U.S. Fish & Wildlife Service, and the Regional Water Quality Control Board, the team was able to speak with one voice and to avoid Unocal's attempts to pit one agency against the other. Avila Beach was miles away from Guada-lupe Dunes, but the contamination issues were similar.

The active agencies that signed on with the MACC met once a month, while many other responsible entities and departments re-mained in the background, but in the loop, in order to meet their jurisdiction mandates as necessary.

Hubner called the group the "MACC Coalition" in direct refer-ence to the media description of the Gulf War allies, and the com-parison was not far off the mark. Each agency was accustomed to dealing with problems in their own way, which made stepping on each other's toes a given. The MACC presented a formidable part-nership for dealing with Unocal, but it was a difficult group to co-ordinate. Sometimes it took months of meetings to get even the simplest things accomplished. To complicate matters, few of the agencies negotiated with full awareness of the power they had to force the cleanup. The case had little precedent, and none of the agencies had dealt with a commercial enterprise with the magni-tude of legal influence that Unocal commanded in world com-merce.

Well trained in environmental cause and effect, the team was highly educated and had some experience with smaller cleanups. However, this case differed in its scope and complexity, including the intertwined jurisdictions of the county, the state, and the federal government and their various responsibilities to the U.S. seashore. This may have been familiar territory to the oil industry, but it was new ground for the agencies of the central coast of California.

One of the greatest strengths of the MACC Coalition was the close and effective relationship the county had built with other agencies. Hubner, well aware that San Luis Obispo County Planner David Church had been working on the Unocal contamination for nearly seven years, saw himself as a kind of relief pitcher. He recognized that Church had a very good rapport with the community people and felt early on that sort of communication was critical to success.

Other agencies, accustomed to addressing problems on their own, found it more difficult to work in a partnership. For example, the U.S. Army Corps of Engineers had a satellite office in Ventura and a main office in Los Angeles, both some distance from the central coast, and they did not feel strongly about local issues. More importantly, the Army Corps was not governed by a board that community members could contact directly, and as a result they received very little public pressure. Hubner said, "We had to emphasize to them how important these issues were, that we needed their help to find their concerns and to reason out how we could resolve them."

In spite of the fact that a coalition had been formed, Unocal continued to pressure individual agencies and the community and continued to resist excavation, claiming it was technically and logically not feasible, uneconomical, something that could not be done, and even if it could, it would take a minimum of five years. In addition, the company mercilessly questioned Hubner's qualifications and every one of his reports.

There was one more part of the partnership that made a difference. From his perspective, Hubner felt it was the citizens who promoted action on the issue when they organized to become a vocal force at community gatherings. The water board, accustomed to quiet, routine meetings, found many meetings dealing with Avila Beach matters were noisy, abrasive, and hostile, especially when residents became frustrated at the slow pace of negotiations. Hubner knew people had been vocal in other information meetings held by the county government, and some meeting rooms were jammed beyond the numbers allowed by the city fire code. When some latecomers were asked to leave, they did so after accusing the board of deliberately circumventing the public's right to be there by meeting in so small a room. Eventually the meetings had to be held in large facilities to accommodate everyone who was interested. One very active resident, Perry Martin, became such a thorn in Unocal's side at meetings that one company official dreaded his in-your-face approach to getting answers. He observed that every time Martin opened his mouth at a meeting, it felt like getting a root canal.

One of the things that helped the MACC Coalition in Avila Beach was that the younger members understood what was going on in town, mainly because they made an effort to find out. David Church had been meeting regularly with the townspeople and had been passing on their concerns at the MACC meetings. One of the first things Hubner did was to follow Church's lead concerning public communication. He put together town hall meetings in conjunction with the county and spent long hours on the telephone and walking the streets of Avila Beach, talking with and getting to know the people. Like David Church, he was out of his office as often as he was in it, and his efforts bred community confidence in him and established a water board presence in town.

Learning from the company's annual report that it had an enormous remediation account set aside to meet corporate liabilities in Avila Beach and other sites, Hubner believed Unocal's delay strategy would work in the company's favor. "If the cleanup were to be a hundred million dollars, at five to ten percent interest," he reasoned, "that's five or ten million to support a lot of attorneys and a lot of consultants." With just himself at the agency and his counterpart David Church at the county working on the cleanup, Unocal could bury them in paperwork and reports, a strategy that in reality had worked to do just that.

However, Hubner refused to be worn down. He set out to establish a public presence with a professional mien and uncommon grace under fire. While it dealt cavalierly with the county, Unocal appeared to respect the water board—likely because it had primary jurisdiction over water issues, and petroleum is clearly identified in California state regulations as a pollutant to groundwater. The board also has fining and enforcement authority and could have levied fines of as much as $10,000 a day against the company. The original Cleanup and Abatement Order, which identified a time schedule for Unocal's compliance, was still in effect, although the company had tied it up in the appeals process to Sacramento.

Although the community-agency portion of the partnerships was building momentum toward the settlement of the cleanup problem, Hubner remembers that it was an even shakier venture than the MACC Coalition was. Successful actions made on behalf of the community, followed by Unocal's ever-present delay tactics, caused residents to be torn between feelings of elation and despair.

The water board made a bold move when it set the cleanup level at 100 parts per million in 1994, because it determined the type of cleanup to be done. Even the best scientific estimates of biosparging could not come close to that standard. That left excavation alone able to meet it.

Unocal reacted as expected. They objected and appealed to the state water board in Sacramento. Hubner felt he was in the middle of a stalemated chess match between his regional office and the head of the agency. But it wasn't the cleanup standard that Unocal protested in the appeal. Instead it attempted to have biosparging approved as the means of cleanup, which would prove to be a critical error.

Hubner said Unocal chose to play the stiff-arm, keeping people at a distance for a very long period of time, but the strategy backfired to the point the company was looked on as a pariah in the community. "People were livid," he said. "That made our jobs easier, because Unocal was looked upon as a kind of Evil Empire, and we were seen as being helpful."

Six months after Hubner entered the picture in early 1995, a court case came to trial that had substantial impact on the Avila

Beach cleanup. Motel owner Sharon Morrison sued Unocal for the 1992 Pirate's Cove spill, claiming that it had ruined her business and put her on the brink of bankruptcy. The trial opened in June, and Morrison told the court that her thirty-two-room motel was the only one in town. She testified that, following the spill, people began to cancel reservations out of concerns about the oil-soaked sands.

The spill had covered the beach in front of her motel in August of that year, one of the biggest months for beach business. She had owned the motel for nearly twenty years, and the two summer seasons following the spill were disastrous. She said it was the first time she had had trouble filling her rooms. She testified that she attempted to get compensation from Unocal but was unsuccessful and then tried refinancing, but the lender refused to loan her more money or to take the property back, once it found out about the contamination. Morrison told the court the bank said her property was "redlined" as a poor economic risk.

At Morrison's trial, Mike Rudd testified that Unocal was attempting to buy out the town. Rudd had not signed a confidentiality agreement when Unocal had purchased his property and was, therefore, free to speak about it. He told the judge that, while he was happy with the sale and agreement at first, he had since had second thoughts about it, in light of subsequent events. Unocal made no comment about Rudd's charge, but Judge Kenneth Andreen nonetheless imposed a gag order on the trial.

Morrison's attorney, Ilan Funke-Bilu, told the judge privately that he was having trouble getting other people to talk about their settlements with Unocal, which made it impossible for him to prove to the jury what the oil company was doing—attempting to compensate some people while ignoring others. During the trial, Unocal claimed that seventy-seven years' worth of its records, including those that discussed seepage from pipelines, had been destroyed in a flood and storm that had damaged the wharf. It strained the imagination to think the company would have stored decades' worth of records in a small building at the end of a pier, but that was their testimony, nonetheless. Funke-Bilu told the press that it was like Avila Beach was dying, and no one was transferring the patient to Intensive Care.

The Morrison case was watched very carefully by many people, including an army of attorneys that were gathering from Los Angeles and San Francisco in search of clients as the result of publicity about the Little Dig at the edge of the creek. Unocal claimed that since Morrison could not sue the weather or the economy for her losses, she had chosen to sue Unocal. Ignoring the impact of the oil-soaked beach on Morrison's business, Unocal claimed that there had been no evidence of a leak since 1977. Carefully omitting any reference to their ongoing negotiations with the county and the water board, they claimed there was no health risk, no moving plume, and no liquid oil on the plaintiff's property. Morrison never claimed the oil had tainted her property, she only claimed that the oil spill had negatively affected her business.

After a week of deliberation, the jury awarded Morrison $1 million, and after the trial, they said they would have given her more if she had presented more financial evidence. Jurors suggested she should have considered other spills, such as the one in 1977, but because her attorney had only presented information about the 1992 spill, the jury's determination had to be based solely on that evidence. Adding insult to Unocal's injury, the jury granted Morrison the award in spite of her having filed after the three-year statute of limitations had expired. They based their decision on the fact Morrison had been unaware of the full ramifications of her dilemma until new evidence surfaced showing how the underground spill and redlining impacted her property.

A week following the verdict in mid-1996, Unocal proposed four cleanup options at a community meeting without mentioning the water board's 100 ppm cleanup standard. The company said they had considered about forty possible cleanup options before settling on the following four: 1) covering the contamination with more sand, 2) biosparging, 3) introducing solidification concrete below the sand, and 4) excavating the area. The proposal estimated that it would take seven years for biosparging to clean roughly 30 to 60 percent of the pollution, but omitted the fact that it could never even approach the 100 ppm standard. In addition, testing now estimated the contamination to be at about a 25,000 ppm level, which put the effectiveness of biosparging even farther away from the water board standard.

Once again, Unocal pushed for "acceptable" levels of cleanup before they would pay for an EIR. David Church protested that nowhere in Unocal's proposal did it address the socioeconomic impact to residents who would not be able to get loans or building permits during the years the biosparge process would take. He said the plan was merely an attempt to forestall paying for the EIR. County Supervisor Evelyn Delany promised that the economic liability of Unocal's contamination would *not* be ignored.

When the company presented solidification of the beach as an alternative solution for the pollution under the beach, Gerhardt Hubner distinctly remembers laughing. He couldn't believe they were serious. But, ultimately he did give it a fair analysis on a technical basis. While residents saw the Unocal proposal as a new spin on an old theme, Hubner believed the company's technical people were serious about solidification. He felt that they had offered it because they had no alternatives to clean the beach other than excavation. Hubner did his level best to give the company's offer a fair appraisal. When new assessments estimated that solidification would take hundreds of thousands of gallons of concrete to cover the contamination, not even Unocal's allies were in favor of solidification, and, with zero support, the offer was removed from consideration.

Undaunted, Unocal entered into a new public relations spending spree, sponsoring an event they called "BeachFest '96" to promote Avila Beach. The promotion offered family events, including rides, a petting zoo, a fishing contest, live radio broadcasts, beach swim events, sand sculpture competitions, and entertainment, all scheduled to occur on weekends all summer through September. The promotion was successful in bringing out families as well as protesters dressed in HAZMAT suits that appeared to be stained with oil and were covered with orange balls, representing Unocal 76 logos. Environmentalists were outraged that Unocal would party on the beach instead of cleaning it up, and residents felt that the festivities mocked previous community events that the town had held.

Unocal spokesman Jim Bray countered the protests, saying that the public had a misconception about the contamination and the event was a part of the company's efforts to be part of the community. He reminded reporters that Unocal had been a good neighbor, having purchased state water for the town and offering a loan program to affected residents. He added that the company had paved a Port San Luis Harbor District parking lot and sponsored a summer jobs program for young people. Bray said people who came out could see there was not a floating reservoir of oil in Avila Beach. The plan worked in Unocal's favor, with many people saying the spill had been an accident, and after all, everyone makes mistakes.

The PR blitz continued. Unocal applied for a permit to build an expansive boardwalk and public gathering place on one of the properties they had purchased downtown. Described as what would be a beautiful addition to the business district, the boardwalk was well designed and would have been an asset to any beach town. Unocal's nemesis, resident Perry Martin, was angry because he believed Unocal wanted to build the boardwalk over the contamination in a thinly veiled attempt to eliminate excavation as an option for cleanup.

At the county planning board meeting slated to consider Unocal's building permit application for the decking, the plan was denied on the same basis that faced residents: no building permits would be issued due to the question of the underground pollution. Jim Bray objected to the building ban, saying if anyone wanted to add a deck to their house, they'd first have to see if it impeded cleanup efforts. His remarks stung and appalled residents who had faced the same prohibition for years.

The idea of cleanup meant different things to different people in Avila Beach. To Saro Rizzo, it meant cleanup of the beach; to Evelyn Delany, it was a major threat to the drinking water aquifer; and to Archie McLaren, it would be an opportunity to remodel the business district.

In a town with a large population of so-called characters, Archie is unusual. He is a small package of electric energy, and his black beret is a trademark. His house on the hill overlooking the bay is painted in brilliant shades of pink and purple with soft green trim. When asked about his choice of colors, Archie smiles enigmatically and says merely, "It makes me happy."

As chairman of the Front Street Enhancement Project, Archie had been involved in the cleanup crisis since the early 1990s. His group worked to develop a plan to upgrade the downtown business area for what was hoped would be a renaissance after the acquisition of state water. Pushing for a dramatically improved public walkway, the group hoped to make Avila Beach tourist-friendly, while it cleaned up some of the less desirable parts of the "funky" image it was so proud of.

As part of the Unocal PR campaign, the group had received a $100,000 grant for design, and Archie worked optimistically with the company until the announcement of their planned deck and boardwalk. Belatedly he realized that to the company, cleanup meant covering over the contamination. "They did *not* want to dig it up," he said. "What they did was to throw out this carrot, creating a nice promenade area on paper and covering the contamination, assuming that the community would say, 'this is nice enough, we can allow them that luxury of not digging it up.' They would be spending millions of dollars to create this enhancement zone," he said, "but basically they wanted to just pave it over."

As a professional fund-raiser for nonprofit organizations, Archie was accustomed to dealing with corporations. When encouraged by Unocal representatives, he simply assumed the company was of the same mind as the Front Street Enhancement group. Innately optimistic, he took a great deal of criticism from townspeople for trying to work out a compromise. When the negotiations reached critical mass and tempers were hot, some of the residents openly suggested that Archie was a spy for the corporation. Negotiations for the cleanup were now at a complete standstill, termed a *chess game* by one water board member: no EIR until Unocal paid for it, which they refused to do until a new standard for cleanup was set; no cleanup plan possible without an EIR—Unocal waited for a new cleanup level to be set, which couldn't be set before the EIR was done.

Sharon Morrison told the board the EIR would have helped her case enormously. She described herself as a sad individual who had to take on the corporation alone, risking everything to make the company do the right thing. In all the years of talk and conferences, the only time Unocal had lost anything was with the Morrison case, a fact that was not lost on Saro Rizzo. With the idea of getting a beach-cleaning machine still nagging him, he finally admitted to himself and to his brother that it looked like the only way to get the attention of the oil company was to file suit.

While Rizzo worked all summer to put the suit together, Unocal was busy lobbying in Sacramento. Company attorneys were able to convince the State Water Resources Control Board to accept the concept of containment zones as a solution for the Avila Beach problem. Pile driving huge sections of steel sheet deep into the sand would form an underground wall to keep the contaminants in place, but would not address how to get rid of them. This alternative was seen as a way to make biosparging look more palatable.

Hubner and the local water board were against containment and argued that leaving the pollution in the ground was an open invitation to contaminating the aquifer, not to mention that the option would leave Avila Beach residents twisting in the wind economically.

Meanwhile, in the midst of the turmoil on all fronts, Saro Rizzo put together his petition to the court. His suit on behalf of the Avila Alliance was unique because instead of filing a class action suit, which required the involvement of approximately thirty similarly affected people, he chose to file under an unused section of California's Proposition 65, a law that had been passed by initiative ten years previously. While a typical class action suit reflects only a segment of the population, Rizzo filed on behalf of *all* of the people of California, on the grounds that water belongs to everyone.

The Avila Alliance was passionately concerned with getting a clean beach. The small group of fewer than ten people represented a cross-section of the town, from surfers to doctors, and they established plaintiff status in what was considered a relatively minor suit. It is safe to say than no one, including the young attorney himself, had any idea that this action would lead to a major confrontation in so short a time. Rizzo's decision to include the entire state of California in his suit had the effect of making it grow like a forest mushroom after spring rains.

Proposition 65 is called the "private attorney general statute" within the legal community. "This is what's called a citizen's suit," said Rizzo, "where you can have one person, or a small group of people acting on behalf of everybody in the state. Our point was that the contamination underneath the town affected public property—the beach—which belongs to the state of California and therefore belongs to all the people of California."

In his extensive research, Rizzo also found a section under the business and professions code, Section 17200, called the Unfair Businesses Act, the genesis of which goes back to the 1930s. The basic concept behind that law is that anyone or any entity conducting business in the state by doing something unlawful, unfair, or using deceptive practices, can be enjoined from continuing that practice. Moreover, that person or company should give restitution of any profits gained because of its actions. The basic philosophy behind the law is that people should not be unjustly rewarded by breaking the law.

Proposition 65 is popularly considered a toxic warning statute. The first part of the law has led to the ubiquitous posting of labels throughout California, warning the public that a product known to cause cancer is present. Gasoline stations, grocery stores, factories—any place that sells or has toxic materials on the premises—must post a warning label at the entrance. The second part of the law protects water, especially drinking water sources, and it was that part of the law that Rizzo tied to the citizen suit action and that was ultimately the main strength of the court action. "The law," said Rizzo, "gives you the power to enjoin the action and order a cleanup." That part of Proposition 65 had never been used before as a basis for a legal action.

Once he filed his suit there was nothing more to do, except notify the California state attorney general office that the suit had been filed. If that office did not intervene within thirty days, the suit could proceed. The attorney general's office did not object to the suit, and Rizzo recalled that it was curious to have no response from the state to the action. "I think it sort of fell below the radar, because Guadalupe Dunes and the eight-million-gallon diluent spill was a much larger case at the time," said Rizzo.

Rizzo related that his friend Mark Masada, a well-respected environmental attorney who had done work for the Sierra Club, had filed a similar suit against Unocal on behalf of the Surfrider Foundation. In that case, the California attorney general had intervened on the twenty-ninth day, and because of that action, the Surfrider Foundation lost legal standing and couldn't bring the suit forward. Rizzo had reviewed the details of that action before filing his own suit, and used the basis of that complaint for his own.

"The people weren't being served while we had a continuing contamination leak under the town," Rizzo fretted. "It had been happening for a long time, and every time Unocal was asked to provide a study, it was delay, delay, delay. Why spend the money today if they could stall it out and get a better deal later on?" Rizzo reasoned, after talking with various staff levels of the involved county and state authorities. The more he learned, the more obvious it became to him that the agencies were getting nowhere with traditional governmental negotiations.

The suit was electrifying, because when Rizzo stepped up to the plate, the agencies that had been scattered in the outfield were able to join him in the infield. "There was good communication at the lower levels of staff, and we are lucky to have some very high-quality professionals in the county. David Church from the county planning department was excellent, and Gerhardt Hubner from the water board, too."

When he first met Church and Hubner, Rizzo said they appeared to be overwhelmed, pressured by Unocal and their many attorneys. They told him that no one actively represented the state's legal interests. Rizzo felt the environmental lawsuit had the effect of empowering them, perhaps because they were no longer alone in the fight.

Although it happened without planning, three young men with

similar worldviews and comparable work ethics were destined to labor in separate arenas of the same fight. Church had the experience and an accurate picture of what had already transpired, and Hubner had science and state authority to act on his side, while Rizzo had put together—partly by chance as well as by choice—a legal partnership that would bring Unocal to the table as an equal instead of as a Goliath against the little guys.

Rizzo began to feel more confident about the likelihood of success for his suit when it was announced that Unocal had settled a suit in the San Francisco Bay Area. The company paid $80 million to plaintiffs because of a major release of refinery fumes at their Rodeo facility. However, Unocal continued with their public relations push in San Luis Obispo County, this time partnering with Mid-State Bank to set aside $10 million for traditional thirty-year loans for impacted homes and businesses in Avila Beach.

The special-circumstances financing was designed specifically as an interim measure to last until the contamination was cleaned up, and was meant to apply to the area between Front Street and Avila Beach Drive, a total of one hundred twenty-five impacted parcels. The action was seen by residents as another indication that Unocal was still expecting to use the lengthy biosparging for remediation.

The end of the crisis appeared to be nowhere in sight, and residents were becoming even more polarized, with some still loyal to the company and others growing angrier at the possibility that the pollution was there to stay. A glimmer of hope came in fall 1996, when, after a year of delay tactics and bickering, Unocal finally relented and agreed to pay for the EIR, still requesting that the socioeconomic part of it not be included.

The stage was set. The battle was to be waged between corporate attorneys with an accumulation of hundreds of years of legal experience on one side and three fresh-faced young men who believed passionately in working for the public good on the other. It would prove to be an arduous, uphill challenge, the outcome of which was never assured until the very last moment.

THE BATTLE FOR THE
PLAN—THE EIR

F ROM an engineering standpoint, the project Unocal submitted for the Environmental Impact Report (EIR) was
sound. From a human and economic viewpoint it was a disaster. Incredibly, the company again proposed solidification of the
beach on both sides of the pier to isolate the contamination as the
primary solution to the problem, plus biosparging and vapor recovery of the plumes under Front Street and north of the Front
Street areas. The project also limited excavation of the area immediately adjacent to the ocean on the east beach and one location
near Front Street.

Unocal suggested the drilling of horizontal biosparge wells to
reach the plume under Front Street and use of compressed air to
move vapors up to a facility at the tank farm on the bluff. The
bacteria needed to be fed to stay active, and the wells necessary to
drop nutrients would be scattered throughout the downtown area
in order to facilitate accessibility. The proposal asked for no action
in the intertidal plume by the pier.

Steve Radis's Arthur D. Little Company EIR team had to take
Unocal's proposed project and research the impacts of implementing it, as well as those of any other scientifically logical and economically feasible alternatives. That meant he had to work within

the parameters of the California Environmental Quality Act (CEQA), which provides a long list of guidelines to direct the process of determining impacts as well as a detailed description of the format for the resulting report.

Unocal was correct when they claimed very few EIRs have been done on a contamination remediation project. Usually an offender does the remediation as a cleanup or improvement, which is not normally viewed as something that would trigger a CEQA review. However, because the scope of the Avila Beach project was so unusual and complex, the county and the water board felt the only way to meet the challenge was to commission a thorough study. Normally, only the proposed project is subject to research concerning its expected impacts, but, in the Avila Beach case, Radis had to include impacts for each alternative outlined, which, of course, increased the size of the final report.

Unocal was adamant in their claim that the EIR was overkill, but it was the only way to visualize what was going to happen and the best way to approach the cleanup with some measure of control. Subcontractor to Arthur D. Little, environmentalist Chris Clark helped determine the effects of each alternative proposed as options to the Unocal proposal. Clark said, "An interesting thing about CEQA is that the alternatives you look at are those that would solve environmental impacts resulting from the project. You start with what the proponent, in this case Unocal, wants to do and we add the alternatives or different ways of doing that with fewer or different environmental impacts."

Only a handful of similar projects were found around the state to compare what should be analyzed, and those were landfills. It was helpful that Radis's company had also done the research on those projects.

Unocal's proposed project turned out to be the biggest surprise for the EIR team. "We thought they were going to have a project of biosparging and wells, with typically very little impact from that. What they came up with was to take the beach and turn it into a giant concrete wall—solidification of the beach. We saw that and realized that we could certainly derive alternatives with less impact than that," Clark said.

The primary solution of Unocal's project was essentially to create a concrete dam under the beach to stop the migration of groundwater into the ocean. By containing it, engineers could then capture and clean the plume as it moved toward the wall, by way of wells, where the contaminated water could be pulled out of the ground and purified. The EIR team was able to come up with seven alternatives, by making alterations to Unocal's proposal. The alternatives ranged from biosparging only one portion of the area, to partial digging, to complete excavation. Clark felt the error in Unocal's thinking was that their solution might have made sense from an engineering standpoint if the project were out in the middle of nowhere. However, in this case, it would destroy the most valuable piece of beach property in all of San Luis Obispo County by essentially creating a concrete shoreline covered with a layer of sand that would vanish every winter.

Part of the charm of the Avila Beach business district is that it runs parallel to the beach in the manner of eastern coastal towns, whereas most other towns in the west are positioned so their streets head toward the strand, perpendicular to the beach. This difference in layout gives Avila Beach unique ambience compared with other West Coast beaches. "We made jokes about the concrete wall to relieve the tension," said Clark, "by saying we could turn it into something like beach chairs with beer holders on it, where people could sit and watch the ocean. We called Unocal's project the 'Beach Plug.'"

It was Unocal's responsibility to present the project, and the water board did not tell the company how to clean it up. Instead, they simply ordered Unocal to do it and set the level they expected to see when it was completed. In a very real sense, an EIR is a rebuttal to a proposed project, and this particular project demanded an extraordinary amount of engineering followed by thorough analysis, by both Unocal and the EIR team. It took a great deal of negotiation between Unocal, the county, and the water board to determine the limits of the EIR. One of the greatest stumbling blocks was the question of socioeconomic impact on the residents of Avila Beach. Clark said he got a sense that the company was concerned that if questions about socioeconomic impact were included in the investigation, it would result in extraordinary costs for Unocal that would go far beyond those of the physical cleanup. He said that it appeared Unocal feared that even the discussion of economic impacts could lead to speculative demands for compensation from businesses and individuals who would be affected by the project. Socioeconomic impacts would include such things as potential business losses incurred, should they be closed for years as the town was cleaned and then rebuilt. It also meant defining the costs of disruption to the people who lived there. Economic impacts had to be included.

On a broad scale, the economy in Avila Beach was another unknown. Would a tourist want to come back to vacation in town if they knew about the contamination, even after it was cleaned up? "We dealt at length with the issue of stigma," said Clark. "Would there be a decline in business that was perceptible or measurable as a result of this, or could it be the other way around?"

From a strictly technical standpoint, Avila Beach was deteriorated. With no banks willing to grant property owners improvement loans, buildings had not been refurbished for years, and many of them were dilapidated, some in serious need of repair. Clark and his team had to project what the new Avila Beach would look like upon completion of the cleanup project, and their assessment that it would most likely result in a positive change was included in the report.

Calculating costs and impacts of physically doing the project was uncomplicated. If the dimensions of a hole to be dug are known, then the number of skilled people, the number and kinds of equipment, and the number of days required to complete the task can all be calculated. "That was the easy part," said Clark. "When you deal with a reality like long-term stigma or disrepute or blemish, that's hard to capture."

A tremendous amount of research time and effort went into trying to put a dollar value on the economic and social impacts. Not surprisingly, it was difficult because of the broad spectrum of opinion. Market value of real estate was also readily ascertained with the help of local real estate experts. The science of appraisal is well established, as anyone who has transferred real estate will attest.

The basic dollar value of the area could be determined, including not just the value of the real estate, but also that of the businesses over time, based on past performance.

When discussion moved into the areas of stigma, especially the long-term taint that might be associated with the contamination of the area, determining impact was much more difficult. The resident of Bakersfield or Fresno who is looking to escape the heat of the central valley for a week in the summer might question whether or not to go back to Avila Beach and instead head for another less controversial spot. "Their decision would likely be based on recalling the big mess in Avila and not wanting their kids playing on the beach there," said Clark. "That's the kind of question we were probing, and it's the hardest thing to put a handle on, because people's decisions are based on public information or their personal perception of an area."

One of the team members, environmental psychologist Dr. Sara Kocher, had experience in both economic and social analysis, and she designed a study to look at the physical impacts of the proposed project and alternatives, including their social and economic impacts on the people in Avila Beach. A comparable example would be the construction of a freeway that divides a community in half. That kind of change leaves people with the necessity to drive miles to reach what was once a few steps away. The child who was a neighbor and played with your family is now four miles away for all intents and purposes, as is the little store and the theater that were once within walking distance. Kocher looks at people and their relationship with their environment. Her task was to pull together the available literature and collect information regarding the reactions of business owners and residents in Avila Beach. That involved conducting door-to-door surveys of residents, telephone surveys of business owners, and in-depth interviews with others in the community to determine their expectations and concerns. The task was made more complex by the fact that there was no demographic data available to provide a baseline.

"Avila Beach was not a census-designated community, so we had to compile our own demographic. We also asked if residents thought the cleanup would impact them," said Kocher. "By the time we finished that we had a pretty good idea of which issues kept coming back up and what people's concerns were."

Kocher found that people were worried about the disruption of business and community life, especially during remediation, with the expected noise, dust, traffic, and beach closures it would cause. They were also concerned about the drastic reduction of their land values and if there would still be difficulty in obtaining loans.

Some people voiced concern that the public outside the region didn't know about the problem, and that a high-profile cleanup like excavation would announce to the world that Avila had been contaminated. They wondered if it was a good idea to draw that kind of attention to their beach.

Most people did not use the word *stigma*, but they did express concerns about how others viewed their town. Some told the survey team their relatives were uncomfortable bringing their children to the beach anymore. Others wondered whether, since their own children had grown up there, they should expect to have health problems in the future.

"*Stigma* is a pejorative word, and I tried to be objective and considerate," said Kocher, "not adding to their worries. Some people talked about being sad when they looked out, and instead of seeing well-maintained buildings, they saw the deterioration. A planner might call that blight, but that's not what they called it. They just felt bad it was happening in their community."

Despite the problems, people in Avila Beach had a wonderful place to live because of tourism. Kocher said that under normal circumstances, a town the size of Avila Beach would not have a grocery store, good restaurants, and live music on the weekends, were it not for the influx of tourists. "We looked at that as part of the good things tourism brought to the town," she observed.

The most telling connections Kocher made for the EIR involved the description of other beach communities and the changes that were occurring in them, such as increased development or the replacement of older buildings, that were not occurring in Avila Beach. The survey also revealed that more than 70 percent of Avila Beach houses were rentals. By comparison with other beach communities, this represented a much higher percentage of renters to owners living in the town. Kocher said the data suggested that people were aware of the contamination problem and had chosen to move out. "I think knowledge of the contamination was eroding people's loyalty to their home, and that's sad," she said.

What Dr. Kocher found surprising was the notion that Unocal's proposed project would leave high levels of residual petroleum products in the area for such a long time. With biosparging, it was estimated to take seven years to remediate gasoline, and at the end of that time, there would still be 1,000 ppm of the gasoline-related hydrocarbons, 10,000 ppm of diesel, and 15,000 ppm of the crude. To reach 100 ppm gasoline would take ten years, seventy-five for diesel, and after one hundred years, significant proportions of crude oil residues would still be left. After reviewing the time line projected for remediation by the scientific team, there was no question about the choice of alternative in her mind.

It seemed odd that Unocal had chosen to meet its cleanup obligations with the alternative that presented the greatest amount of unknowns. Unless the company was banking on research in the field to make bacteria work better, faster, and more thoroughly, its proposed alternative would keep the corporation married to the problem in Avila Beach for a century. At the same time, from a psychological point of view, they probably didn't want to be the one to suggest the destruction of the town.

Exchange of information was vital to the writing of the EIR, and sometimes Chris Clark noticed something he called "corporate behavior" coming from Unocal during the year it took to write the document. "We could almost tell what division was responding to a particular issue," he said. "We don't know how much of a big deal this was to Unocal overall, but when mention of Avila Beach showed up as a sentence in their annual stockholder report, we took that to mean it had some consequence."

Clark attended many meetings before he experienced reasonably open exchanges with Unocal. "It was always that we would dig deeper and present evidence, and they would acknowledge it. Then we would repeat the same thing, and they would acknowledge the newer stuff, especially as the information about the plume got larger, because we did more exploration," he said.

There were meetings where Clark felt the two sides had come to an understanding. He specifically remembered feeling this way about one meeting dealing with the scope of the socioeconomic report, but a week later, a letter arrived from Unocal that announced that the company was going off in a completely different direction than had been agreed upon at the meeting. "We knew that the people we had been dealing with hadn't written it, and it had to come from the legal department or maybe the PR people. There were other times when their letters were very positive and glowing, and they just couldn't have come from the same person. It's speculation on my part, but you can see the difference in tone and message from correspondence to correspondence. It was difficult to know who had the actual authority to make decisions."

Clark terms the situation *classic*. One person apparently having authority participates in a meeting and takes part in a discussion where things appear to get resolved, but is later revealed to have no authority within the corporate structure to make final decisions, rendering the meeting's resolution worthless. One asset the EIR team and Unocal representatives had around the table was the realization that the problem had been caused by another generation of people, not those at the table, and it had been done in a vastly different time.

From a socioeconomic perspective, all seven alternatives developed by the EIR team would have some impact on the community, but although excavation was growing in acceptance, it was not the selected choice from the start. Neither Kocher nor Chris Clark and the rest of the EIR team thought excavation was a foregone conclusion from the start of the work. In the end, when the scientific numbers were gathered and verified, it was not surprising that biosparging was the least desirable choice. That made the choice of excavation look much better, although still not the best alternative. But when the length of time necessary to get the job done under the other alternatives was added to the economic hardships they would cause, the entire team was startled to find one choice stood out from all the others. "My God!" exclaimed Clark. "The best alternative is excavation!"

RIZZO LOADS HIS SLING WITH SMALL ROCKS

S TAND facing the ocean on nearly every beach on the West Coast and the sun will rise behind you and set directly into your eyes. Do the same at Avila Beach and the sun comes up on your left and sets on the right in a magnificent arch across the heavens. Sheltered from winter storms that originate in the Alaskan north, south-facing beaches are warm and sunny when most others in the region are overcast and cold.

Old-timers chuckle about the oil tanker captain on his first run from San Francisco to Avila, who complained bitterly about the dense fog that covered the coast completely, saying he'd never find the Union Oil dock in the middle of it. To his surprise and delight, the fog parted like the Red Sea at Point Buchon, and the dock waited for him in brilliant sunshine. It is no surprise that the only other California beach communities having the same geographic characteristics are well known: Santa Barbara and Santa Cruz.

Avila Beach has not been able to develop as a playground because it is confined by port traffic in oil. However, it has never lost the special aura of being on the Pacific, something Hawaiians call *hui pu moana*, or meeting by the sea. The mountains surrounding the beach hem it in, making it feel like an island far from civilization. With a population that had been remarkably stable, there were many settler families living in town when the Unocal problem surfaced.

Lucy Lepley married into one of them. At the time of the Unocal crisis, her husband worked for Port San Luis, but he did some fishing on the side. Shortly before Saro Rizzo filed his environmental suit, Lucy had business to conduct at the San Luis Obispo County Courthouse. "My husband had his boat then, and I had to do something at the courthouse for him," she recalled. Her mother-in-law, Dolores, came with her.

While Lucy was busy at the courthouse, Dolores got coffee at the stand in the atrium and waited for Lucy there. When Lucy finished her business and rejoined Dolores, Lucy could see that her mother-in-law's attention was riveted on a large gathering outside the nearby county supervisor's meeting room. "She said it must be something going on about Avila," said Lucy, "because she pointed out Perry Martin. She hadn't seen him in years, and they had gone to school together some sixty years before."

The women also recognized Jim Cummings from the Pizza Pantry and neighbor Tom Guernsey, so Lucy decided to find out what was happening. Lucy remembers Dolores telling her later that she regretted in some ways having mentioned the gathering at all, given the changes it would make in their lives from that point on.

What was on the supervisor's agenda that day was a building permit application Unocal had submitted for a deck on their newly acquired property in downtown Avila Beach. A few residents who found out about it were fighting mad, and they were successful in getting the permit turned down at the meeting. The incident left Lucy and Dolores very upset, wondering why in the world Unocal would be building a deck over the pollution unless they intended to avoid a cleanup.

When they got back into the car, the women looked at each other, both with tears in their eyes. Not realizing it was impossible at the time, Lucy asked if Dolores was ready to sell the house. The question was not meant to provoke action, but rather was an acknowledgment of the severity of the pollution they had been hearing about. It appeared to be really bad—bad enough to drastically impact the house Dolores's grandfather had built for her sixty years earlier.

Raised by her grandparents, Dolores had been protected as a child. She was born in nearby See Canyon and grew up knowing only the city of San Luis Obispo, Avila Beach, and her dolls. It was a small circle of awareness, and she thought of the citizens of Avila Beach as one big family living in an isolated farm community, lovingly protected from change. Her schoolteacher had been her aunt, known as Mrs. Rude in class, and World War II had brought the only great change she could recall.

She told Lucy about the excitement of U.S. Navy boats practicing landings on the beach and about blackouts that were very strict. The extent of her memory of the war was that during that time she saved money for ten-cent savings stamps that she would paste in a book, which, once filled, she could exchange for a war bond.

Grandfather Antone Rude was looked upon by residents as an important man because he owned much of what is now downtown Avila Beach. Dolores was one of his fifty-six grandchildren, and when her mother passed away, Grandfather Rude and her grandma raised Dolores. Dolores married early and remained in the comfort of the beach town that was the only home she had ever known.

By the fall of 1996, she had been widowed for three years, and after a long, happy marriage, Dolores was heartbroken and still grieving. Like her grandfather, her husband had taken care of her in all ways, in the manner of the times, and until he died, Dolores had had few decisions to make on her own. However, she would have to rise to the occasion and make some major decisions that would cause even strong people to falter.

Lucy realized that since the explosion in the 1970s, property values in town had been declining, but until the supervisor's meeting, she had no idea how serious the problem was. Information about the pollution had been around for a long time, but when she tied the decreasing value of the town's properties to it, the contamination became sinister. Learning this, it seemed to Lucy that Unocal spokesman Jim Bray, who had come across as a man about town, taking people to breakfast and making other plays for their attention, was in actuality only trying to get residents to support the company's announced plan for biosparging.

Both women recalled that when the emergency Little Dig was done the previous winter, it felt like black evil lived down by the bridge. "The smell was putrid," said Lucy, "I know what oil smells like, but this was putrid. One time we were in Mom's house getting something, and when we opened the door, the smell was overpowering. I talked with authorities about it, and of course they said it was nothing. Everything there was 'nothing.'"

Also, to their discomfort, they realized that the Avila Beach problem was portrayed in the local media like a little fight between the pro-Unocal residents and those wanting a cleanup, rather than a fight for survival. "Seemed like the rest of the world didn't care at all about it," Lucy said. "It was not worth the reporting." Adding to the misery was the division between Avila Beach families. Those who were still loyal to Unocal were incensed with the idea that the company was being demonized when they had brought a lifetime of prosperity to the town. The division of opinion did not keep Lucy from learning. She attended every meeting scheduled and brought home the news to her husband and Dolores. Gradually the older woman shook off her lifelong shyness and took an active interest in the Unocal crisis.

Saro Rizzo found the town's divided mind-set frustrating during his public meetings of the Avila Alliance. There were meetings where residents were openly hostile to the idea of excavation and the inevitable destruction it would cause. Opinion was divided about how serious the problem really was, even after the huge black lake emerged during the Little Dig, and there was disagreement about who was responsible for the precipitous drop in property values as well as about who should do something about it. For weeks Rizzo and his buddies made every attempt to encourage people to attend the meetings, to learn about the problem, and to take a stand against Unocal.

Rizzo had always pushed to get the beach excavated, and when it became known that the downtown was similarly affected, he thought long and hard about whether or not it, too, should be dug out. At the time, the extent of the underground plume was loosely drawn, and the amount of destruction that would result from excavation was not clearly known. It was a decision without any easy resolution no matter which way he looked at it, but he came to the conclusion that there was no alternative to excavation if the town wanted to live.

In an effort to build support, Rizzo got a friend to design a slogan that his brother suggested: AVILA BEACH . . . EXCAVATE, DON'T PROCRASTINATE! The creation made use of Unocal's bright orange and electric blue logo colors. With the last available credit remaining on his charge card, he had posters and a box of large lapel badges printed up. With all the aplomb of the Keystone Kops, Rizzo, brother Marco, and their friend Matthew Farmer spent the wee hours of a starlit night putting the posters up all over town and leaving the buttons around for people to wear. They concentrated on the area adjacent to the Unocal office downtown, so that no one could enter or leave the building without being faced with the command in Unocal's colors.

The midnight foray turned out to be a stroke of PR genius that not only made an impression, it got people talking. Rizzo did not immediately admit to the deed, instead allowing the mystery to ride in order to extend the impact. It got people thinking differently, and at least one of these people was moved to action. Dolores Lepley filed suit against Unocal because of the drastic decline in the value of her home and the fact that she couldn't sell it if she wanted to.

She paid a high price for her bravery. Neighbors nearby, some of whom had known her for forty years and were clearly pro-Unocal, stopped talking to her. Others castigated her for "biting a hand that fed the town." Even though she was shunned, Dolores stood her ground, because she felt strongly that Unocal was trying to "pull a fast one," as she put it. Worst of all she felt they were making fun of her concerns instead of taking her seriously. "I was raised there," she said. "I raised my kids there, and it was important to clean it up."

Many older people in Avila Beach had much more to lose when

the value of their property dropped, because their entire personal wealth was tied up in their homes. To the surprise of many involved, they also had the vision to see the fight through. They were more emotionally invested, and no matter how many times Unocal said everything was okay, they knew it wasn't. They knew the media had to tread lightly because of advertisers and the "cocktail network" of Cal Poly professors who had their research money to protect. It was particularly galling to Avila Beach residents that they were made to look silly, and the disagreement was painted as just a little squabble.

The increased interest from residents had a positive effect on Rizzo's suit. Unocal set a date with the court for a hearing to dismiss his suit. Rizzo knew he was breaking new ground, and in preparation for his first court appearance, he went to great lengths to ensure that his arguments were well founded. He prepared himself personally as well, wearing a brand-new suit, which he purchased specifically for his debut. That particular outfit became his lucky suit, and it always had a lapel pin that held special significance for him.

"When I graduated from law school, my friend Mike Hayashi's mom gave me a little scale of justice—a pin with two diamonds on it. She had been through a lot and had been interned during World War II. The family lost everything. I made sure I wore that pin the first time I put a suit on and went to court—and every time after that." Rizzo felt the pin helped energize the strong sense of justice he carried from his father, especially when the going got tough.

In court Unocal legally demurred to Rizzo's lawsuit and asked that the case be thrown out, but the judge refused the request. Rizzo had heard nothing from Unocal attorneys until after they lost the demur, at which time they called to ask if he wanted to meet with them. It would be the first of a series of settlement conferences the two sides would hold over the next year and a half.

"We talked, and it was clear they just wanted me to go away," said Rizzo. "But I wanted a beach-cleaning machine, and I wanted the town cleaned up." When that failed, Rizzo was not deterred. The Avila Alliance sought no monetary damages, only cleanup. "It was a very simple thing. Unocal obviously made a mess and they needed to clean it up."

At an Avila Alliance meeting in the spring after he filed the suit, Rizzo was approached by representatives from both the Environmental Law Foundation and Communities for a Better Environment. Both organizations had been following the case ever since the publicity reached the Bay Area the previous year when the Little Dig at San Luis Obispo Creek found oil. The environmental groups were keenly interested in seeing the suit go forward and offered to join the action. The offer came as a relief to Rizzo, because the case had grown considerably more complex, and he had maxed out his credit cards paying for legal necessities and travel.

Rizzo amended the suit with input from his new environmental partners to allege that Unocal's releases of crude oil, gasoline, and diesel had violated the Clean Water Act 5,478 times and the Federal Resource Conservation and Recovery Act more than 3,652 times. Each violation could cost the company $25,000 in penalties for a total of more than $228 million, not including the cost of cleanup.

The three partners to the suit divided the work, with the Environmental Law Foundation doing the heavy work in litigation, motions, discovery, and negotiation and the Communities for a Better Environment using the local membership of that organization to mobilize grassroots support for the case. Rizzo's role was to deal with the local political front, which meant dealing with the agencies and the MACC Coalition.

Emboldened by the court's decision to deny Unocal's plea to dismiss the case and with the backing of his growing constituency, Rizzo upped the ante, adding the Front Street Enhancement Project to his demands. "Archie McLaren had been working on this forever," he remembers. "It was sort of the dream of Avila Beach to have their community organizations try to get the town cleaned up and fixed up. They had spent countless hours on this plan, but it seemed to us there was no way to make it a reality. There was also no way the town was going to be able to come up with the money to do the actual construction themselves, even if Unocal subsidized the design."

Although Archie's group was hoping that somehow Unocal would pay for the entire project, everyone readily admitted that companies don't just hand over $4 million no matter how often or how nicely you ask. "They'll dribble it out in hundred-thousand-dollar increments," observed Rizzo, "but not in one lump sum. They were willing to give the group a hundred grand toward the project, but I think it was only to placate them. The project was basically dead in the water."

Rizzo's observation proved to be true, as more Unocal money was spread around. A grant of $100,000 went to Bellevue–Santa Fe School for a new discovery-type museum. The hands-on display was set in a brand-new set of portable classrooms that also housed a computer laboratory. The one hundred Avila Beach students in the school were the envy of the entire district. Unocal had a very positive public profile in San Luis Obispo County, with the exception of Avila Beach. Even the city of Guadalupe seemed to be more concerned about jobs than a cleanup.

The MACC Coalition began to work well together, and Unocal was not as able to get around one agency at the expense of another. In Santa Barbara County the company was also told by the water board to rewrite its plan for the Guadalupe oil field cleanup. Extending the directive, Unocal was told in no uncertain terms that a plan would not be approved before testing showed the actual extent of the plume, meaning both its quantity and its mobility. Regulators made it clear that their decision was made mainly because the testing on which they had previously relied for the Little Dig was outdated and did not show the true extent of all the hydrocarbon plumes.

In response, the company got Cal Poly, San Luis Obispo, involved in a continued push for bioremediation. Professor Niropam Pal at the school was featured in the *Telegram-Tribune*, pointing out that digging destroys habitats and exposes toxins into the surrounding air and water. The professor claimed bioremediation was a permanent solution because bacteria convert the petroleum into CO_2 and other benign molecules.

Professor Pal pointed to a Lawrence Livermore National Laboratory project that concluded that natural attenuation was a more effective way to deal with contamination from underground storage leaks from gas stations. Chris Kitts, another professor in the same department, also pushed for bioremediation as the preferred method of cleanup, but others in the research community countered that a biosparge cleanup was very slow, admitting it could take decades or even longer to work. However, it was Professor Pal who got the bulk of publicity at the time.

Gradually, those in Avila Beach who were most vocal seemed to back away from their condemnation of Unocal. Perry Martin was outspoken with his opinion about payoffs, saying Unocal was making cash settlements to people who then stopped talking about the problem. Some property owners admitted in public to accepting an undisclosed amount in settlement for the decline of the value of their property. The agreements required them to sign away any right to sue Unocal, but they were still allowed to keep their property. They also had to sign a confidentiality agreement. The so-called Disappeared Ones increased in number and were notable by their absence at community meetings.

The news that Unocal was buying out protestors reached the supervisors, and at the end of another vigorously debated meeting, county staff were instructed to get a list of Unocal real estate holdings so supervisors could see just how many actual parcels the company had purchased. The total would not show how many others had been merely given settlements not to sue, but it would give some indication of the number of buyout deals that had already been consummated.

Before he had time to savor his court win, Saro Rizzo received a surprise—a summons from the California State Bar Association claiming he had violated the Bar Code of Ethics by talking to the press about his suit. It was claimed that he had tainted any potential jury pool by making intemperate remarks. The charges were made anonymously, and required Rizzo to take precious time away from the suit to prepare a lengthy defense that would satisfy the California State Bar Association that the charge was false. Few people doubted the complaint originated with Unocal.

The company complied with the directive to do more testing, and machines replaced people on the beach, while winter storms eroded the beach over the contamination area again. Unocal was given a permit to cover the area with more clean sand to keep the plume from daylighting again. The company's PR push continued unabated, as Unocal project manager Bill Sharrer told the *Telegram-Tribune* that, although the company was concerned about the contamination, he still brought his children to Avila Beach. He blithely added that the risk to children existed only if one were to eat a pound of sand daily for six months.

Business owners wavered between "dig" and "let it be," but one resident who could not grow anything in her yard said, "Bulldoze the town, clean it up, and start from scratch. The future of our children deserves it." Another said, "Do it now or endure a slow death of the town." Unocal's PR painted a bleak picture of the destruction of downtown properties that would occur as a result of excavation, explaining that it would require thousands of truckloads going in and out, a rerouting of utilities, and removal of the seawall, accompanied by a great amount of noise, dust, disruption, and air pollution.

In a commentary by Paul West of Unocal, published in the local daily paper, he appeared to take credit for everything that had been done, even though Unocal had to be coerced into taking any action. West pointedly said that Unocal could not take any remedial action without permits from a number of agencies, and they had to wait another year for the EIR to be finished as well. He also touted Unocal's "talented, experienced people on staff" and attacked the credibility of the water board staff at meetings, blaming any negative impacts on the negotiations with regulatory agencies. West wrote that Unocal was committed to deal with Avila Beach in a responsible and efficient manner as well as committed to doing the right thing for the company's neighbors, customers, and its community.

It was not surprising then that many people in the rest of the county thought the Avila Beach people were being petty and obstructive to any settlement of the problem. Once Unocal agreed to fund the EIR, the company embarked on yet another huge PR offensive.

In an open letter published in the daily paper, the company declared, "Perceptions regarding underground contamination from previous Unocal operations on the central coast are of great concern to us because we are the new stewards and managers assigned to clean up contaminated sites." The message went on to say, "We know the trust of the community must be restored."

Writing for *New Times*, reporter Jeff McMahon invited readers to meet the new Unocal. He wrote, "Unocal jumped into a phone booth as an oil company this week and emerged as an environmental remediation firm," reflecting the Avila Beach attitude that it was all subterfuge.

In November Unocal announced a gift to Cal Poly of $1 million in cash and $350,000 in equipment for a joint three-year study to find environmentally sensitive ways to remove soil pollution, meaning bioremediation. Expenditure of the money was to be directed by Raul Cano, the first scientist to extract dinosaur DNA from amber, whose research is widely believed to have been the impetus for the book and Hollywood blockbuster *Jurassic Park*.

Cano headed up a team of five teachers and eight students to work at the Guadalupe oil field, learning how to enhance remediation and concentrating on three locations there, two of which already had functioning wells on site doing just that.

Unocal's image was on the upswing, but still the company's reputation was tied to pollution. Shortly after the announcement about the donation to Cal Poly, a Unocal-contracted truck, carrying rainwater that had been pumped off a company building in Santa Maria, broke down in Avila Beach. The water needed to be tested for oil before it could be dumped, and when the truck's diesel line broke, a small aboveground spill poured onto two streets in town. The incident was reported widely in the local media.

The idea of concreting the beach was meeting with stiff opposition. At a meeting in early December, Unocal was asked if children could stub their toes in beach sand underlaid with the concrete barrier they proposed for permanent containment. The baffling answer was, "You may see the actual cement body during a storm event."

When the discussion turned to biosparging, Mike Rudd sat shaking his head in disbelief and asked why, since in eight years

Unocal could not get rid of the mess by excavating it, they were now saying they wanted another seven years to do a part of it with bacteria. Unocal's reply was, "Excavation is not the cure-all for this town. You cannot remove all the contamination. It's that simple." Residents wondered aloud if the term *company town* meant they were moving to a new level of ownership resembling a fenced-off Love Canal or Times Beach.

After so many rewrites of the description of the plumes and their content and location, residents were dumbfounded to learn that new pollution was discovered near the company pier in the intertidal zone, with the greatest concentration found so far: 61,000 ppm. Jim Bray again put a spin on the news by saying the existence of the new plume was not totally a surprise and had no effect on the cleanup proposal. On the other hand, Gerhardt Hubner said that it was significant, and important, and he declared a need to find out how the newly discovered pollution was related to the rest of the plume fifty feet away.

Unocal remained low-key about the newfound leak. Local regulators were left to wonder if the company had any idea of what they were doing. In a company press release it was announced that the new discovery was about two feet thick at its deepest and that surface erosion was highly unlikely. It was suggested that surface erosion would happen only in a *100-year storm*, a weather term meaning an event that occurs once in a century. The announcement completely ignored the fact that the biggest El Niño ever recorded was expected to hit the west coast that winter. Satellite measurements of the recurring warm water current showed a monumental plume of warm water spreading across the entire Pacific Ocean, making a 500-year storm a very good possibility for Avila Beach.

The year 1996 ended the way it began, with Unocal-contracted trucks hauling sand once again to cover the beach where the company had previously held the risk of petroleum daylighting to be very low.

SMALL TOWN FIGHT
IN THE BIG LEAGUES

MATTHEW Farmer grew up on the beach in the shadow of Unocal's tank farm. He was one of those kids who put on a swimsuit as soon as school closed for the summer and didn't take it off until the day before classes started again in the fall. A longtime friend of Saro Rizzo, Farmer returned home after getting a degree in aquaculture from the University of Hawaii, just in time to learn about the crisis issues in Avila Beach. "Sar told me about coming across Proposition 65 and some cases where it was used as precedent," he said. It didn't take Farmer long to join in the action.

Rizzo also brought Farmer up to date about what was happening with Unocal and shared information he had been getting from tenants and property owners at home about the suit he wanted to file against Unocal. Farmer's education in aquaculture biology would prove to be especially effective in dealing with biological issues and the complexity of documents. With dueling experts on both sides of the controversy, paperwork was fast becoming something akin to the daily newspaper—a large one at that.

Farmer was elected head of the Avila Alliance, a group of individuals who had grown up in Avila Beach plus others who lived elsewhere in the county but spent a lot of time there. A member of the Yacht Club and a lifeguard for ten years, Farmer swims with a group of people every Sunday morning, rain or shine, every week of the year. Some laugh that they have seawater in their veins, but the draw to the ocean is irresistible for many, and they all agree that Avila Beach ratchets up the drive another notch to be there with the best of them.

Farmer and the Avila Alliance quickly realized it was unlikely their suit could move successfully against so powerful an opponent without public support, and members agreed to meet the challenge with a grassroots campaign among people who enjoyed the beach. They held meetings where they hoped people would sign up and become members, but mostly the forum was used to disseminate information to the whole community.

With the fast pace of events, many more residents were getting involved, both personally and politically. It was important for the Alliance to ensure that everyone had a chance to voice their concerns and to get clear information in return, and especially to counter the wild rumors that circulated faster than a wildfire in a tornado. The Alliance quickly became a place for the community to ask questions about every issue and every agency involved, as well as to get the latest spin from Unocal.

Prior to the partnership with the Environmental Law Foundation (ELF) and Communities for a Better Environment (CBE), the work went slowly, dealing with people one-on-one, but with the addition of new financial resources and ground troops, information began to be disseminated in earnest. ELF had extensive contacts with technical experts and the money to pay for their services, while CBE brought in local members to canvass the entire town to give and receive information.

Farmer was a partner in the midnight poster foray that pushed for excavation, which subsequently drew more people in to investigate the issues and sort through fact, fiction, and heavy science. "Sar brought in legal people," Farmer remembers, "and I brought in people from the community who had been around a long time, both those who lived here and people who came to use the beach. That's how the case got started."

As the official representative of the Avila Alliance, Farmer became the chief executive officer, and, although it seemed a fanciful title for the leader of a group of beach denizens, as more information was disseminated and meetings proliferated, he was also called on to deliver testimony at hearings for agencies such as the California Coastal Commission and the local water board on behalf of the people in the Alliance.

To further the people's participation, the Alliance brought in Cotchett and Petrie, a premier environmental legal firm from San Francisco. Joe Cotchett was described in the *San Francisco Examiner* as a multimillion-dollar super lawyer with a client list that reads like a Who's Who of the poor and victimized. Cotchett has successfully defended the rights of children abandoned in war-torn Bosnia and the Philippines by the U.S. military, oil-damaged sea life, and families of murdered civil rights workers.

In addition, some of his courtroom adversaries have been equal to or greater than Unocal—the FBI, the savings and loan industry, big tobacco, and major movie studios in Hollywood. When Cotchett's firm came to the one-horse town of Avila Beach, Farmer thought it would send a major signal to Unocal corporate offices, but it did not change the company's stance at the settlement table.

To add to the community's confusion, attorney Ed Masry and his assistant Erin Brockovich also came into town looking to represent residents. Fresh from their success in Hinkley, California, with a major Pacific Gas and Electric settlement, the Masry team did not join those offering environmental representation, but instead chose to build a case for health risks and signed up people who feared they were being poisoned by the toxic mess. In January 1997, Masry appeared to be on the right track when traces of oil were again found in the ocean off Avila Beach.

Samples taken from surf and sand matched samples taken in the previous July, and since no natural ocean cleaning was normally expected at that time of year, scientists said it had to be coming from a continuing source. New pollution discovered near the pier in the intertidal zone consisted of an astounding 61,000 ppm. True to form, Unocal declared that it was premature to draw conclusions, because the new samples were from heavier diesel and crude. Despite the company's claim that the plume was not moving, the natural movement of underground water from the tank farm and inland, along with natural tidal action, suggested the plume was leaching into the ocean as a mixture of petroleum products and water.

Unocal experts doubted the initial assessment. "It doesn't take a rocket scientist," Gerhardt Hubner said firmly at the time, "and Unocal will debate it to the death. However, it is still a threat to water quality, and that's the board's position." There had been so many petroleum leaks, it was difficult even for scientists to keep track and make sense of them.

After the water board showed Unocal the data they were given from the latest testing and recalculated the percent breakdown and quantity of the plumes, the company released an updated map showing that the plume was estimated to contain 80 percent diesel, 14 percent crude, and 6 percent gasoline, with some areas being mixed and others having a single petroleum product in pockets. Also, the company increased the estimate of the volume by more than 30 percent of the water board's figures, to nearly 400,000 gallons. They also said they had found a finger of a plume that connected it to the Front Street pool that followed the pier to the ocean. Residents were amazed that the company still did not admit that what they described was the underground pathway of the pipelines from the tank farm to the end of the pier.

The best chance the residents had of getting good information and having their views heard was at the community meetings held by the Avila Alliance, the county, and the water board. They turned to Peg Pinard, who was elected supervisor to the Avila Beach region, when Evelyn Delany's health problems became serious and she declined to run again. Pinard chaired a citizen's forum in January 1997, and when the room filled to overflowing with angry residents, she leaned over to Gerhardt Hubner in shock and surprise, asking what was she had gotten herself into.

Initially the meeting had been called to discuss the draft EIR process and to take public comments, but it turned into a health issue circus. The meeting room was already jammed with people when Ed Masry and Erin Brockovich walked in.

"The movie hadn't come out, and we hadn't heard about that

case," said Hubner. "They made it a big spectacle and commandeered the meeting, sitting front and center." During the meeting Masry told the crowd that he had information that proved that the beach was toxic and needed to be closed immediately.

Masry came representing several property owners and claimed the beach was contaminated with considerably higher concentrations of petroleum products than either the county's or Unocal's testing had revealed. He told the crowd that those tests failed to include standard surface tests, which showed the beach to be carcinogenic, and said his office had conducted tests showing disturbing results, including the presence of MTBE, meaning the leak had to have happened in the last four years, because that product had not been in oil products prior to that time. He added that chroma 6, the most carcinogenic form of chromium, was also present.

Masry vigorously claimed that no one in government was looking out for the people's interests except his law firm. Erin Brockovich also addressed the group, saying she was the law firm's scientific director and that she had collected samples from the contaminated beach. In answer to a community member's question about her scientific qualifications, she replied that she had taken the forty-hour Hazardous Waste Operations Training (HAZWOT) course.

Insiders to environmental issues know that the HAZWOPER course, as it is commonly known, is a basic health and safety training course, dealing with the risks and precautions necessary for doing fieldwork. It introduces some of the basic equipment used, but it does not offer instruction in sampling, sample handling, quality assurance and control, chain of custody, or laboratory procedures, which are all basic to good science. Gerhardt Hubner had good reason to know that in the environmental business, HAZWOT was meant for aides and assistants, not for scientists or scientific directors.

When Hubner asked to see the results of those tests, Masry replied he was expecting final results soon and would supply him with copies. He added that if the water board or any agencies had really been concerned about health issues, those tests would have already been done. Hubner felt the meeting was getting out of hand, but although it appeared to accomplish little and generated a lot of heat, it did serve to introduce him and others to the public who had been affected by the problem.

Three hours later, the only thing settled was that the county should make the final EIR readable by everyone and, to mollify Unocal attorneys who were pushing to exclude economic factors from the EIR, that matter was moved to a separate committee with their findings to be incorporated into the final EIR. The meeting ended with residents wondering what new disaster would befall them next.

However, the health issue had been raised, and the Masry-Brockovich team had set into motion a wild orgy of testing, dueling experts and public controversy, suspicion and confusion, over the health aspects of the contamination. They also helped delay the settlement for another year, which Unocal used to expand its public relations campaign.

People were again justified in their suspicions of Unocal, as lobbying in Sacramento continued unabated. The State Water Resources Control Board (SWRCB) in Sacramento adopted containment zones as a policy, meaning that Unocal could use the system to isolate the plume in Avila Beach. The local water board officially commented on the proposed policy, vehemently disagreeing with it.

At the same time, Unocal commissioned a brochure describing cleanup efforts in Avila Beach and Guadalupe Dunes and sent one to each resident in town. They also mailed one to John Caffrey, Chairman of the State Water Resources Control Board, a highly inappropriate action, because that body was about to review four separate Unocal appeals from local water board actions.

The eight-page brochure was supposedly intended to be a "guide" to the EIR. County planners found it was misleading and inaccurate. It gave a rough history of Avila Beach, a summary of Unocal cleanup proposals, the cleanup as outlined in the EIR, and a timeline for the EIR process, which allows time for public comment before final approval. However, since the brochure bore no Unocal logos or any suggestion that it came from the company, it looked like it might have come from the water board or county environmental health or planning office. The brochure also contained inaccuracies and was weighted heavily in favor of Unocal alternatives. The EIR information in it misled people into thinking that they had ninety days to respond to the EIR instead of the sixty that they really had.

When questioned about the brochure, Unocal expressed surprise at the county reaction, describing them as "courtesy copies" and said that subsequent copies would have the company logo, along with a letter clearly explaining the brochure had been generated by Unocal.

When the State Water Resources Control Board responded to the brochure blunder by citing Unocal for "inappropriate contact," no one was fooled by the slap on the wrist the state regulators administered. Residents and local agencies believed the State Board thought of it as just another case of a small rural area that was out of sight and out of mind.

Unocal spokesman Jim Bray announced that the company only meant to provide information with the brochure. "We just think in order to move the process along," he was quoted as saying in the *Telegram-Tribune*, "there's got to be communication and dialog." The damage was done, and the already low public opinion of Unocal slipped further into oblivion in Avila Beach.

State Senator Jack O'Connell was as upset about the proposed containment policy in Sacramento as was the local water board. He proposed legislation to prevent the official adoption of a containment zone policy. In July the O'Connell bill passed, effectively preventing the State Water Resources Control Board from allowing Unocal to get out of cleaning up Avila Beach or Guadalupe Dunes.

The Masry confrontation at the public meeting had a strong impact on people, generating fear and promoting suspicion in the community that local agencies were partnering with Unocal, and undoing much of the trust David Church and Gerhardt Hubner had worked so hard to build. Behind the scenes, the company continued to bewail their blighted public image. In Cal Poly's *Mustang Daily,* Jim Bray said that Unocal had already spent nearly $50 million cleaning up Guadalupe and Avila Beach, as if to suggest that they had the problem in hand and were taking proper action to see it through.

Money continued to flow in every direction except toward Avila Beach. When fishermen discovered oil in waters immediately off the Avila shore, Unocal was found to be at fault again and was fined $1.2 million for it. The Land Conservancy was appointed to spend the money, and not a dime went to the town where the spill happened. When the Avila Beach Advisory Council protested that no one from town was represented at those negotiations, Unocal replied accurately that money had been transferred, and the company had no say in who spent it or where it was distributed.

The Pacific Gas and Electric (PG&E) settlement was very important to Avila Beach, because it happened within very close proximity to the downtown and amplified the fears that residents had with trusting those in government who were responsible in a very large degree for their own future. The event appeared to be a dress rehearsal for the town's crisis and, incredibly, set the stage for more public controversy to come, this time from within the San Luis Obispo County Board of Supervisors.

Although they were a united front to get the contamination cleaned up, the SLO Board of Supervisors disagreed among themselves on how to see it accomplished. Supervisors Bud Laurent and Mike Ryan were not in favor of the dig, because it would destroy the town. In addition, Ryan was uncertain about any health risks that might threaten people should the contamination be exposed.

The controversy was set into motion when Laurent participated privately in an action against PG&E dealing with Diablo Canyon nuclear power plant on the basis of fish entrainment. The power plant is within the geographic curve of the bay that makes up Avila Beach, and while not a part of the town per se, it is certainly economically and emotionally tied to it, as if the entire bay is one town family, especially for fishermen.

The PG&E settlement took on the same suspicious aura as private Unocal deals with individual property owners, because it was done quietly, without public input. It was a legal matter between government and the energy company, of the type that had always been done quietly in the past. However, this time it was accomplished in an arena already seething with emotion. For Avila Beach residents, it was bitter medicine.

The controversy erupted when it became known that sea life was being pulled into the nuclear power plant by a gigantic impeller and being destroyed in large numbers. Infant rockfish, anchovies, cabezons, and croakers were being sucked in with ocean water used for cooling. Many of them were eaten by barnacles and mussels living on the walls of the plant intake. Beyond that obstacle the fry were subjected to a temperature increase of nineteen degrees after cooling the reactor before getting dumped back into the ocean. Most did not survive the gauntlet.

PG&E self-monitored the entrainment, but turned in selective data to the county. Missing from their reports was the fact that there was a problem. The complete data showed that up to 90 percent of larval fish thus ingested were killed in the system. PG&E said the utility withheld data because of errors, but the U.S. Environmental Protection Agency and the water board said in effect, "too bad, the law requires you to send it all."

PG&E's illegal activity was revealed when an anonymous whistle-blower sent supervisor Laurent the missing pages of data. The ensuing settlement sent $2 million to the Federal Treasury and $7.1 million to be split between the U.S. Environmental Protection Agency and California's Attorney General's Office. Another $6.19 million went to the Bay Foundation to fund the Morro Bay National Estuary Restoration Plan, and $750,000 to attorney's fees. Governmental press releases said it was one of the largest settlements of its kind for the Clean Water Act. Instead of some of it coming to Avila Beach close to Diablo Cove, where the entrainment happened, all the money went elsewhere, mainly to Laurent's district, which includes neighboring Morro Bay.

Feeling like lightning had struck the same place twice, Avila Beach residents led by the Avila Alliance were irate that they had been ignored again. Many expressed their outrage publicly that PG&E was let off too easy when the *New Times* newspaper reported that at the time the energy company generated $14 million in less than thirteen hours each and every day.

While the PG&E settlement had nothing to do directly with the

Unocal contamination, other than the fact that it happened so close to Avila Beach, emotions in the little town were at a crisis level because the little trust that was evident in negotiations the agencies had with Unocal suddenly became a major rift in any communication. Residents felt the state and county attorneys who handled the suit and settlement against PG&E had not taken them into consideration at all, and they believed that history was bound to repeat itself when Unocal finally agreed to the cleanup. In addition, the perceived intrigue that surrounded the PG&E settlement put any hope for a citizen-friendly closure with Unocal into limbo, if not out of reach entirely. It felt like all the months and years of negotiation and budding trust had been destroyed in a heartbeat.

The *New Times* gave the story lengthy coverage, detailing that PG&E paid nearly $4 million to the Morro Bay Estuary, marine biologist Laurent's district, and $30,000 to SLO Land Conservancy as a management fee to disburse the funds. It appeared to Avila Beach residents that even if they ever were to reach a good settlement, the management of the money would not be entrusted to them. They called the assignment of funds management to the Land Conservancy a gift, not a fee.

Supervisor Peg Pinard was angry and vocal about the settlement, saying four out of five supervisors knew nothing about the deal. According to the *New Times,* Laurent had unusual connections to the winners of the settlement. He had helped launch a monitoring program to determine the impact the Diablo Canyon plant had on larval fish. When he received the plain brown envelope with the missing PG&E data, he gave it to the local water board for investigation. Later Laurent signed the part of the settlement for the Morro Bay National Estuary program, as interim chairman of the organization's Local Policy Committee. He had been appointed to that position the same day because of a reported internal upheaval in the organization. The water board was connected to the estuary program and appeared on their flowchart as an integral division.

The *New Times* article went on to say that the Bay Foundation had close ties to PG&E, from which the organization received donations enough to raise a red flag for the Internal Revenue Service.

Further, a PG&E employee sat on the board of the Land Conservancy, and Chairman Ray Belnap, who had been given the responsibility to see that the received funds were spent in the community's interest, was a former treasurer of the Bay Foundation. No matter how logical it was to assign the responsibility for the distribution of funds based on expertise, it had the appearance of a backroom deal to residents in Avila Beach.

When the story broke, Rizzo tried to get the money redistributed, but found it was already assigned. Outraged Avila Beach residents formed a new organization to ensure it would not happen again. They hoped the Fair Share for Avila group would keep a close watch on the deal makers to ensure that the people's interests would be heard and taken seriously. The PG&E settlement added fuel to the fire of advocacy and fed the people's determination to be a part of the solution.

The board of supervisors met and tried to calm the growing outrage, drafting a resolution to be sent to the state to ask for funds to go to Avila Beach ventures, including help for the local nonprofit Salmon Enhancement Project, to plant abalone in the ocean, to improve the Avila Beach sewer system and drainage at Port San Luis. Their action was fruitless, because the settlement was written in stone, and all efforts to change it were ineffective.

Only in retrospect would it become apparent that the furor over the PG&E settlement was key to getting the Avila Beach contamination addressed as the people hoped. Two of the country's finest environmental attorneys who worked that case were destined to join forces again for the benefit of Avila Beach—one from the state attorney general's office, and the other from a prestigious private law firm in the eastern part of the country.

There was little time to grieve over their indignation in town, as new events within the Unocal controversy began to unfold quickly. Ed Masry filed suit on behalf of a group of Avila Beach residents, claiming negligence on the company's part because the spill created a public nuisance. Unlike Rizzo's suit, which sought only cleanup, Masry's legal action was the first to ask for punitive damages.

Reporter Jeff McMahon of *New Times* reported that Masry

said, "The government agencies put the fox in the henhouse," and that was why he said their testing was suspect. "Of all the corporations that we encounter," he continued, "Unocal has the least regard for human life and the environment. They've been pulling the wool over these government agencies and the people of Avila Beach for years." His suit sought unspecified damages against Unocal for "the toxic contamination and destruction of a seaside resort town and the poisoning of its residents."

In McMahon's article, Masry took credit for shaking up the long confrontation with Unocal, something few people would dispute, but for reasons that differed. McMahon also wrote that county officials were still waiting to see the results of Masry's testing, which he claimed to have had at the meeting more than a month previously. When the agencies finally received the data, it was poorly organized with no narrative description of the data results. Furthermore, the chain of custody forms Masry submitted showed that the samples had been collected the afternoon of the citizen's forum where he and Erin Brockovich made their public Avila Beach debut, making it impossible for Masry to claim he had data to prove that the beach was toxic at that time.

Unocal now faced half a dozen suits. They shifted their PR campaign to show company concern for the environment. In another mailing of slick brochures to Avila Beach residents and responsible agencies, the company now took responsibility for the contamination and promised to clean it up. The message was clear: "We are corporately responsible." However, given the history of the controversy, there was more suspicion than acceptance of Unocal's change of heart, with people wondering aloud if legal action from the California District Attorney's Office was at the root of the transformation.

Actually, the company had been on probation for three years because of violations stemming from concealment of documented problems at Guadalupe Dunes. As part of a plea bargain agreement in 1994, prosecutors dropped nearly three dozen criminal charges in exchange for Unocal's plea of no contest to three violations at the Dunes. Even though Unocal paid $1.5 million to settle the charge as well as agreeing to clean it up, the state continued to pursue a civil lawsuit that was scheduled for trial.

The informal probation was to expire in a month, and as the appointed probation officer, the local water board turned up the heat when it told local District Attorney Barry La Barbera that Unocal had not lived up to the agreement adequately. The legal move was just one more indication of escalating tensions on all fronts. The company protested, saying they had drilled 615 monitoring wells and tested the soil with nearly 1,400 borings and eight pump tests to determine water capacity and sustainability.

However, the reality was that the Santa Maria River had shifted in winter storms, and with the added pressure of constantly reshaping dunes, there was reason to believe that a major release of diluent into the water table and ocean was a real possibility. An emergency dig at the Dunes began soon after widespread media coverage of the continuing controversy.

Despite the uproar over health concerns, other matters could not be ignored. The draft EIR and possible solutions to the problem of the pollution were discussed at another community meeting. It was from this particular meeting that the California State Bar Association charges against Saro Rizzo stemmed. When the meeting ended, a reporter from the *Telegram-Tribune* had asked him a question about the draft EIR and subsequent cost to Unocal, and Rizzo had replied, "If it costs them $50 or $100 million, I really don't care. They have got to give back to Avila Beach what they have taken." The Bar Association said he was being investigated based on that comment. Four years after the fact, remembering the incident still made him smile with a mixture of modesty and bravado.

The particular section with which he was charged was new at the time, having been added following the O. J. Simpson trial. Rizzo said he guessed the legislators, in their wisdom, and prodded by the State Judiciary Committee, had decided that they didn't like to see Johnny Cochran on TV all the time and may have felt they had to do something about public commentary. Their recommendation to the State Bar Association Rules Committee resulted in a rule to bar attorneys from talking about their cases. The ruling is seen by many as a First Amendment violation.

By the time Rizzo was charged, he had formed a friendship with James Wheaton of the Environmental Law Foundation. Wheaton is considered one of the top First Amendment attorneys in California and teaches the subject at Golden Gate University.

A Berkeley activist from the 1960s, Wheaton was more upset about the charge than Rizzo was, and he wanted to use it as a test case. His belief was that the U.S. Constitution protects people when they comment about something of public concern. The anonymity tactic used in the complaint against Rizzo protects whistle-blowers, but also is seen as equal to a "slap suit" to discourage a plaintiff. It is extremely rare for anyone to use this tactic for leverage, but it appeared that someone didn't like Rizzo or his suit and had used the process to intimidate him. One had to have inside knowledge to know how the system works.

Rizzo responded to the charge with a three-page letter explaining what had happened and showing that the Avila Alliance suit was a matter of public concern. "We were taking on a multinational corporation that had left pollution all over the place and violated all these different laws. Our citizen suit was holding them accountable. I told the Bar in the letter exactly what I said, and if I had to, I'd do it again. I didn't take anything back." The investigation was dropped.

"Here I was two years out of law school," he said, "and being investigated by the State Bar Association. The ink wasn't dry on my diploma!" It was a no-holds-barred welcome to the big leagues.

9

CORPORATE COMING
OF AGE

BEFORE it reached such a contentious point of confrontation, the oil industry in general and Unocal in particular
had written a history rich in lore and economics. The discovery of oil made a profound difference to the entire U.S. economy, almost as dramatic as that of the Gold Rush. It began in the
eastern United States, when the first commercial oil well was successfully drilled at Titusville, Pennsylvania, in 1859. It took only
twenty years, including the duration of the U.S. Civil War, for
John D. Rockefeller to corner the entire industry from discovery
wells, to transportation and, ultimately, the entire market. Rockefeller's Standard Oil manipulated the market and drove away
nearly all its competition, including Lyman Stewart, a gifted man
with a "nose for oil." A successful independent oil broker dealing
in leases, Stewart experienced one too many blows to his business
at the hands of the eastern financial mogul and sold all his holdings
in 1880.

Stewart took his money and moved west, settling in the Santa
Paula area north of Los Angeles. He left the quiet of an office and
entered the fledgling oil production part of the industry, where
down and dirty was the norm for a workday. At the time oil was

selling for twenty dollars a barrel, and petroleum was moving to displace both coal and whale oil as the lantern fuel of choice.

While eastern oil fields harvest a "sweet" crude that is easily refined, California crude is vastly different—thick and sulfurous, with a mixture of "impurities" such as gasoline. The volatile fuel had little if any use at the time and caused many unexpected explosions. It would take ingenuity to devise a new refining process for this western crude before it could be used in homes and businesses. Not many years would pass before gasoline coupled with automobiles would give rise to another giant step forward for oil companies in general and Stewart's oil company in particular.

One of the many inventions Stewart's company brought about to promote the industry was a nozzle invented by employees. Boilers used to power oil rig engines were coal-fired at the time, but by using oil pumped on-site instead, the advanced power system made a major cut in what it cost to bring petroleum products to the surface. That small item also ushered in a new use for oil in manufacturing factory machines and transportation engines. It was one of a number of revolutionary firsts attributed to Stewart's young enterprise, which a few years later became Union Oil Company. It also helped advance a new Gold Rush—the Black Gold Rush.

Most wells at the time were shallow and did not erupt with any force, but in January 1888, near the present-day city of Ventura, a drilling rig hit oil at 750 feet. Oil spewed out of the earth and shot up a hundred feet. The well set a new record for production with eight hundred barrels a day. It also signaled the downside risk of production, as oil poured downhill into the Santa Clara River. The one new well out-produced all the rest of the company's holdings combined.

Not only did Stewart have a talent for successful oil wildcatting, he also knew how to run the business competitively. When railroad transport costs escalated to one dollar a barrel, Union Oil devised the first seagoing oil vessel by retrofitting a freighter to make the run from southern California wells to markets in San Francisco. The threat of a new transportation method had an immediate effect—Southern Pacific Railroad reduced the cost to transport a barrel of oil from one dollar to thirty cents. Even despite that concession, oil transport by sea had been firmly established.

Stewart faced challenges everywhere he went, and he met them all. To be able to send crude by ship took an act of Congress because of a law passed the previous year following an oil-fired ferry explosion in San Francisco Bay that killed nearly thirty people. The law prohibited the use of petroleum engines in the marine environment.

However, Union Oil was able to get a special exemption to that law for the oil tanker to sail as an experimental vessel without passengers. The ship made only six round-trips before burning to the waterline at dock in Ventura. The cause was not attributable to a flawed idea, but rather to a flawed employee who had attempted to check the level of oil in a tank by lowering a lantern into it.

By the early 1900s oil wildcatting was rampant in the West, owing to expanding use of petroleum products. A 1900 *Los Angeles Express* article said, "The state has gone oil mad. A feeling of speculative unrest is abroad. Los Angeles operators just in from Kern County say that a large number of people in that county appear to be actually oil crazed." Speculative drilling moved north to Santa Maria, twenty miles south of Avila Beach.

Santa Maria was the site of Old Maud, a spectacular oil well discovered by chance. As a wildcat crew neared the location where they were to drill, a large piece of equipment slipped off a wagon. Rather than take the time to hoist it back onto the wagon, the crew chose to drill right where it landed. Not expecting much, the crew was openmouthed to find that following an indescribable roar, the well erupted in a geyser more than 150 feet high and eventually pumped out 12,000 barrels a day—one million in the first one hundred days.

The new oil fields in central California ushered in an era of pipelines to move crude oil more easily to a central point for further transport, and by 1906 Union Oil completed a six-inch line from Old Maud and other wells in the Santa Maria area to the Port Harford area at Avila Beach. It was the start of a company town that Union Oil built, which included a tank farm on the bluff south of town. By 1910 California was producing one-third of all U.S. oil.

Pipelines would prove to be a frequent source of continuous spills, as lines wore out or ruptured because of earthquakes. Union Oil used slow-flying, small planes to check their lines, and in one year, pilots found more than two hundred leaks between Bakersfield and Santa Maria. However, old-timer oilmen on the ground were unconvinced that a pilot high above the lines was able to accurately locate leaks. That criticism led one of them to "plant" a leak by dumping five gallons around a pipeline in a remote area to see if it could be detected. Within a short time, the observer reported the leak and added, "By the way, you left your oil can under the sagebrush on the west side of the line."

Gushers became the norm. The ultimate one occurred in the Bakersfield area in California's San Joaquin Valley. It was 1909, a time when drillers were accustomed to any number of well surprises, or so they thought until this one. Each time the bailer was drawn up from the casing, the crew saw oil on it at an ever-rising level, until finally crude began to bubble out of the ground in a steady stream. Within a short time oil was roaring several hundred feet into the air, steadily building thrust, until it created a depression so great the entire derrick and all the accompanying equipment vanished into the chasm. It was estimated that 125,000 barrels were lost in the first day alone.

The company crews created earthen dams to contain the oil, but the banks were overwhelmed by the continued flood of crude. The gusher continued for seventeen months without letup until a sixteen-acre oil lake had been formed. Unfortunately, another disaster was in store when a powerful earthquake hit the area. The earthen dams were destroyed, and accumulated oil was released to flood any and every place downhill. A year and a half later the flow slowed to a trickle and was contained when the giant well quieted as suddenly as it had exploded to the surface.

In the movie *Boom Town*, starring Clark Gable and Spencer Tracy, one of the most memorable scenes depicts the men with a disheartened crew looking at what they thought was a dry hole. The roar began softly, before it exploded, covering the cast and everything surrounding them with crude, as they joyfully danced in the oil. That Hollywood depiction couldn't begin to replicate the actual destruction that faced the Bakersfield area. Homes, barns, fields, people, businesses, crops, and animals in a fifteen-mile radius were covered with crude oil. Union Oil faced a massive cleanup and a barrage of lawsuits in a strange preview of what would occur at Avila Beach ninety years later. That Bakersfield disaster site is now a state historical location.

The cost of doing business hit Union Oil other times and in other ways. The 1926 lightning bolt that hit the company's San Luis Obispo tank farm about a dozen miles from Avila Beach set off a colossal sequence of disasters. The explosion damaged thousands of windows in the city of San Luis Obispo, and while firemen used Foamite to suppress the fire, volunteers worked with picks, shovels, hammers, tractors, and plows to build dikes to contain the released oil. Smoke was so thick it felt like night to those fighting the fire and those living in the surrounding area. Heavy rain in Santa Margarita sixteen miles away was a dirty black because the smoke rose far into the sky and then returned to earth mixed in the rain. Flames from the conflagration could be seen in Pismo Beach, which lies immediately south of Avila Beach.

People from all around rallied to help with the catastrophe. Lawmen from neighboring cities and counties as well as members of the American Legion and Boy Scout troops directed traffic. Residents brought sandwiches, coffee, and sweets to feed exhausted firefighters, and the Salvation Army organized a first aid station. In an effort to reduce the amount of fuel in storage, Union Oil sent a flotilla of oil transport ships to drain the remaining crude by way of the pipeline to Avila Beach. Crews were able to load three tankers, but there still remained a huge amount of oil that was unable to be contained. San Luis Obispo Creek ran black with crude, and the sands of both Avila and Pismo Beaches were deeply coated with it.

Flames backfired through gas absorption pipes that had been installed on the tanks to pull dangerous vapors from the tanks. A second explosion happened in the afternoon and blew the tops from tanks. Cyclonic winds from the impact uprooted trees and demolished buildings. The roof of one home was crushed like an eggshell, according to the local *Tribune* newspaper, and the impact of the blast killed two people at the W. F. Seeber home.

At her nearby home, Doris Seeber had just let go of the front doorknob, when flames suddenly shot into the air. She was hit immediately with the concussion from the explosion and tossed fifty feet away. She landed near a small bridge, which she crawled under for protection from raining debris. Both her father and grandfather died in the house. She struggled back to find the surrounding area strewn with household furnishings and dead chickens.

At farms surrounding the San Luis Obispo tank farm, schoolchildren were thrown from the breakfast table by the impact. Terrified, the families were torn between remaining in their houses, which were badly shaken, or racing outside into torrential rains and constant thunder and lightning.

Two men fighting the fire had to race for their lives when burning oil crept over the sides of an earthen reservoir. One of the men could not start his car and had to make a run for it. Unable to outrun the flames that ran toward him like lava from an eruption, he was saved when the oil hit a low area in the earth and pooled there. At one point oil poured out from an underground reservoir within the tank farm compound with such force it ran uphill.

For seventeen hours, firemen were unable to get close to the conflagration and could do little more than let it exhaust the petroleum accumulation on the ground. Burning oil overflowed into another reservoir, igniting a million more barrels. In all, fifteen huge tanks were destroyed, with their contents and the fuel burning for several more days. The single winter storm that started it all dumped nearly the annual average rain total for the region in one pass. The same massive storm continued to move south toward the Los Angeles area, where disaster continued to batter Union Oil. Lightning hit the company's Brea tank farm, setting off three reservoirs and engulfing the refinery. Three thousand men from the oilfields were rushed to the scene to help fight the second inferno by building earthen dams to hold the oil. Finally the fire burned itself out.

The weather catastrophe destroyed more than eight million barrels of oil, along with twenty-one steel tanks, miles of pipeline and fittings, as well as other adjacent property. The oil was insured, but not its containers. The company received $9 million as compensation for their losses. The insurance industry listed the San Luis Obispo/Los Angeles Unocal fires as the second greatest single natural disaster, behind only the San Francisco earthquake and its resulting fires. As a direct result of this terrible calamity, Union Oil established a laboratory to investigate prevention, containment, and scientific study of firefighting. That lab is still in existence today and shares its findings with fire departments across the United States.

Union Oil has a history of progress and change over the last hundred years. They pioneered the use of oil for locomotive fuel and were the first to move fuel by custom-built tank cars for railroads and by ship. They also established the five-day workweek for employees three years before it became a part of President Franklin D. Roosevelt's New Deal. In 1932, the company developed an improved gasoline they called 76, after the U.S. Spirit of 76 of Revolutionary War fame. That corporate logo achieved such strong public recognition that a letter addressed simply to 76, Auburn, California, was promptly delivered to a company substation in that town.

In Avila Beach, Union Oil became a dominating presence, making the little town the world's largest oil port just before World War II. Two weeks after the attack on Pearl Harbor the Montebello, an oil tanker, sailed from the little town and was torpedoed by a Japanese submarine while still a short distance from shore. The ship went down quickly, but every member of the crew reached shore safely in lifeboats, despite having to duck a hail of bullets from the surfaced sub. Nearly the entire Pacific war effort was fueled from Avila Beach, and Army Chief of Staff George C. Marshall was quoted as saying, "No plane has failed to fly, no ship has failed to sail for lack of oil."

Following the war, however, relations between the oil industry and the public began to sour. Oil-company-owned property was increasingly surrounded by growing communities, and the sight of oil derricks as well as the smell of petroleum was not consistent with suburban living. Any new drilling was met with protest, and the company tried to conform with some grace. When new wells were planned on leases already owned, the company still negotiated with homeowners in spite of the fact that they owned the rights to drill. When one of the pipelines was being laid in southern California, a Miss Arabella Mays, age eighty-seven, asked the crew to go around an old oak tree she had enjoyed as a child. They did.

The company tried to be a good neighbor, and, in 1952, painted one of their huge tanks in the Los Angeles area a brilliant orange (taken from the company logo) and then added the features of a jack-o-lantern. Company employees gave out candies to trick-or-treaters who came to the office. Lit up at night, the "pumpkin" garnered so much public pleasure it was continued for a number of years. The Los Angeles Mirror featured the tank on the front page, estimating that if it were a real pumpkin it would make twenty-seven million pies.

In 1965 the company painted another tank to look like a giant baseball, honoring the Dodgers as world champions, and again in 1988, when the team beat the Yankees for the baseball championship. It was effective public relations, but it could not counteract the myriad growing problems concerning petroleum contamination.

In 1967 the Torrey Canyon, an oil ship subchartered to British Petroleum Company for a voyage from Kuwait, was about a hundred miles from the shore of Wales when a navigational error drove the supertanker aground on Seven Stones Reef. An attempt was made to salvage the oil from the tanker, but the spill was overwhelming. Eight hundred thousand barrels of oil were dumped into the sea. The world was aghast at pictures of oil-covered birds and a slick that covered the sands on Cornish and French beaches. An estimated 40,000–100,000 birds were destroyed, and intertidal marine life was devastated by both oil and the detergents used to disperse it. Surprisingly, areas afflicted by the oil recovered faster than those hit with detergent.

Two years later, the oil industry was rocked by another spill, this time not from a tanker, but from a Unocal offshore oil platform within sight of Santa Barbara. A huge blowout in one well erupted under natural pressure, and although the well was sealed within fifteen minutes, the continued pressure found ocean outlets in the surrounding waters. Oil blew out from underwater natural fissures for eleven days before enough drilling mud was pumped into them to seal the leaks completely.

Strong winter tides and winds drove a gigantic slick ashore, covering beaches, seawalls, and homes. The spill came on the heels of a particularly devastating winter on the West Coast, making the disaster more compelling to the people who lived there. Tempers ran red-hot, and this time the pictures in the media were in color. Union Oil came into more than its share of criticism when company CEO Fred Hartley was quoted in top newspapers in New York and Washington, D.C., as having said, "I'm amazed at the publicity for the loss of a few birds." What he really said was, "I think we have to look at these problems relatively. I am always tremendously impressed at the publicity that the death of birds receives versus the loss of people in our country in this day and age. When I think of folks that gave up their lives when they came down into the ocean off Los Angeles (in a plane crash) some three weeks ago—and the fact that our society forgets about that within a 24-hour period—I think relative to that the fact that we have had no loss of life from this incident (the oil spill) is important."

The story was retracted by the media but the damage had already been done. The Santa Barbara spill galvanized the environmental movement, leading to the National Environmental Policy Act the year following the spill. A line was drawn in the oily sand, and the battleground moved to the courtroom, pitting oil companies against the public, whose escalating use of oil continued unabated. The battle between oil interests and environmentalists seesawed for years, with cautionary tactics achieving delay of new oil field production, notably at Prudhoe Bay. Public opinion reversed in times of crisis, for example the oil embargo of 1973, and the oil industry gained momentum back toward production as a result of congressional action to meet shortages. Court actions served to push the cost of oil upward by escalating the cost of the Alaskan pipeline from the original $1 billion to a final $9 billion.

Overseas exploration was no easier for the oil industry. In Indonesia, Union Oil purchased a site for a company town, only to find it was riddled with unexploded World War II munitions. The very first day of bulldozing uncovered a live five-hundred-pound bomb. None of the old armaments could be defused, instead they had to be exploded on-site. Invested so heavily in the development, Union Oil chose to become a partner to the region and even found architecture suitable for the culture there. It built the town out of local materials to fit the climate and surrounding neighborhood.

By the mid-1980s Union Oil Company was merged as an operating subsidiary into the company's Unocal Corporation. Newly reformed Unocal was represented by a new orange and blue corporate insignia, but it did not require capital outlay to put it in front of the public. T. Boone Pickens did it for them, when he attempted to take over the company. Worldwide press coverage made the new logo instantly recognizable without any paid public relations effort. However, Unocal spent $10 million fighting the battle to retain control of the corporation.

The company appeared to have weathered the storm again, but the battles left little room for negotiation when evidence of underground contamination surfaced at Avila Beach at about the same time.

10

PADLOCKS ON THE PIPELINES

-- -- -- -- -- -- -- -- -- -- -- -- -- -- -- -- --

AFTER it was over, 1996 felt like a watershed year to Avila Beach residents, but while unfolding, it was a blur of meetings, challenges, disappointments, and surprises. Those who had a background in technical expertise helped others understand the blizzard of material that it was necessary to wade through nearly every day. Archie McLaren continued to negotiate with Unocal to bring the Front Street Enhancement Project (FSEP) to reality. The job was extremely difficult, especially when Mc-Laren learned that some people in the community thought he was selling out the town in his efforts to get the money for construction of the design.

The very idea brought tears to his eyes, because his group had labored long hours for the good of the town, and without support of the community, McLaren felt there was a good chance Unocal would pull out completely. He was convinced that what he was doing would result in the right thing for Avila Beach. At times he felt he was treated shabbily by some of the townspeople, but he still defended them, because he reasoned they had no idea what was in his own mind.

Residents each had a different measure by which they gauged the sincerity of neighbors. Some thought it was important to have longtime roots in the community, but the amount of risk faced by each one mattered a great deal. Those who had all their money tied up in a personal residence garnered more sympathy than those with investment properties scattered around the area. All had conflicting loyalties, some with relatives having worked for Unocal or dependent on them for a business.

Others felt the environmental damage should be grandfathered in to any settlement and did not want to believe that leaving the pollution in place could be harmful. The reality of losing the entire downtown business section pressed like a painful heartache, and it left many with physical and psychological maladies. The illnesses residents began to experience were directly related to the pool of contaminants under the town, but not because the volatile mix was inhaled, eaten, or absorbed through the skin. It was because the circumstance tore at the hearts and souls of the town.

The worst part of dealing with the EIR was that, of the options presented, from partial excavation to biosparging, none of them were palatable. It felt like they were being forced to choose among a number of evils. Solidification of the beach to seal contamination has been done in ports such as Long Beach, Los Angeles, and San Francisco. It is fairly common at industrial wharfs, but not engineered for recreational areas. Moreover, county staff described it as a poor choice of alternatives from both visual and public safety standpoints.

San Luis Obispo County engineers agreed, telling the supervisors that concreting Avila Beach would enhance erosion and increase potential overflow of water into the town from rain runoff and extraordinary high tides. There were also concerns that the sand cover would simply vanish in winter storms, leaving an ugly concrete beach that would require annual replenishment of sand. Natural cycles in weather at coastlines deplete sand in the winter and then gradually return it in the summer, but with a man-made barricade to natural tides, which vary widely at times throughout the year, some experts expressed concern that it was unlikely any summer replenishment would occur.

A greater danger was what concreting under the sand would do beneath the barrier. Engineers felt it would serve to block the natural movement of groundwater that normally flows through the town toward the ocean.

Although it was unpopular, Unocal's proposal was not ignored entirely. As part of the eventual Environmental Impact Report, the Arthur D. Little Company did some computer modeling to see what would happen if the beach were concreted under the sand. Their results showed clearly that since First Street is a low area and floods each winter, the concrete would raise the water level in that area and leave standing water on Front Street or in businesses or residences.

Archie McLaren said Unocal made what appeared to him to be very strange suggestions for ameliorating the contamination and avoiding excavation. Although he did not succeed in the way he had expected, the group he started became one of the established resident cadres ready to put the cleanup money to work in town, when the settlement materialized.

At meetings, some longtime residents who had family on the Unocal employment rolls continued to support the company and criticized those who pushed for the complete removal of the contamination. According to McLaren, people who spoke up for Unocal in the early stages were respected because of Unocal's longtime connection to the town and what they already had given to the community. "On the other hand," he said, "the opinions of those people changed when Unocal was doing its shuck and jive and dancing around the issues."

No one in town was able to separate their connections to the past in order to deal with the present. For some it was easier than others, but all were in some way connected in ways that defined their responses. White-haired octogenarians Gladys Misakian and Evelyn Phelan had been across-the-street neighbors in downtown Avila Beach for more than four decades. They looked on the looming crisis with a mixture of trepidation, curiosity, and interest. Both educated themselves on the problem and attended many of the meetings. "We had no idea it was going to be as drastic as it turned out to be," said Phelan. However, she still felt all the planning and publicity about it was very educational.

Gladys Misakian had lived in Avila Beach all her life, and one of the landmarks in town was the model boat she had in her window. Her front door faced the front door of the motel across the street that Evelyn Phelan and her husband had purchased in the 1940s. The two women became immediate friends and remained close over the years.

Phelan and her husband had come to Avila Beach for a holiday and quickly fell in love with the place. As soon as possible, they sold their property in Pasadena and moved permanently to the beach. After her husband passed away, Phelan ran the motel for a few years, but the seven-day-a-week demands of motel management were too difficult for her. She switched to monthly rentals instead.

Life in Avila Beach for the across-the-street neighbors was comfortable, because of the strong sense of belonging to their neighborhood. "There were five couples here," Phelan said, "and they called us the Frantic Five. We raised funds for the civic building with cake sales and even had a carnival in the street, played Bingo there, and had street dances. That must have been thirty-some years ago. We had a great time doing that!" Any time one of the neighbors hadn't been seen for a while, Phelan said that someone would check up on them to see if they were okay. "You can't buy that [kind of concern], and it's so important," she said.

The community in those years included Union Oil, and both women felt the company had been very good to Avila Beach. "They supported the fire department and made donations," said Phelan. "Several years ago they donated one of those Jaws of Life, and they purchased five years of state water for us." The water issue was a knotty problem, which she knew well, having served on the Avila District Water Board for nineteen years.

Although it was not a town in a legal sense, Avila Beach was well organized in a variety of venues, partly because County Supervisor Evelyn Delany revitalized the Avila Valley Advisory Council in the late 1980s. She felt that when the building moratorium was about to be lifted, following the town's connection to state water, people needed to know what was going on and how they could participate in decision making that affected them all. The advisory council served as a means of understanding issues before they were brought to the board of supervisors, especially concerning the anticipated boom in development.

When the Unocal controversy arose, the advisory council became another forum for distributing information. This was especially important because emotions over the contamination fostered wild theory and rampant rumors. Having a direct link to county government close by was serendipitous. Although few people realized it at the time, those strong lines of communication proved to be one of the best weapons residents had in their meager arsenal.

At regular meetings in whatever venue, everybody knew each other, from working people living in the trailer park downtown to professionals at the pricey resort north of the business district. The town consisted of very wealthy people and some who were on welfare, but they all came to meetings in their Levis, and if you lined them up, you couldn't tell who had money and who didn't.

When it came to learning about the cleanup, alternatives about how to get it done, and planning the reconstruction of Avila Beach, residents and agencies had to juggle scores of balls at the same time. Copy machines ran overtime, and information came in streams, then cascades, and, toward the end of the controversy, in torrents. It was common to see groups of residents sitting in front of the Avila Grocery Store or on the seawall, paperwork in hand, shuffling pages, while they waded through the buildup of information.

There was so much information coming to light at the same time in various locations that no one could be expected to know all the answers or, more importantly, which questions to ask. Each new report brought new anxiety about what it was the people faced and what could be done to meet the crisis, all of it focusing on Unocal and science, which was first presented as fact and then rebutted as nonsense.

Archie McLaren said that in retrospect he felt that one of the things that appeared to get Unocal's attention was the feature article published in the *San Francisco Chronicle* about the Little Dig. He said the timing was perfect, and the fact that a former Cal Poly graduate had come back to do an in-depth story that was exceedingly critical of Unocal had had a major impact.

"We told Unocal that was just the tip of the iceberg," McLaren said. He added that it was the first big event, and the rest were on the way—a confluence of small events gathering steam to push for a moral and righteous solution to the problem, instead of the ludicrous things that Unocal had proposed up to that point. "They were spending thousands, tens of thousands, maybe hundreds of thousands of dollars on PR when they could have spent that money to do something beneficial to the community."

It would be years before it became obvious that the company was spending millions to polish a very tarnished image. However, from a deposition taken in a similar environmental suit against Unocal in Arizona, Gerhardt Hubner came into possession of clear evidence of the company's stance to "spend no dime before its time." The document confirmed what everyone already had known or suspected, but it was gratifying to see it in print.

In addition to the behind-the-scenes spending, Unocal was putting millions into the region to counter bad media coverage. In a thinly disguised attempt at redemption, company CEO Roger C. Beach, along with supervisor Peg Pinard and Bob Carr of the California Regional Air Pollution Control District, ceremoniously padlocked and chained the valves connecting the pipelines leading into town. Carr installed tamperproof seals on the locks and kept the keys.

CEO Beach claimed it was a visible commitment to clean up the *beach*, and he apologized to the people of the town, promising to clean it up. He said, "Excavation of the beach clearly reflects commitment sentiment." His failure to include the town as part of the proposed cleanup was not lost on the listeners.

CBS anchor Dan Rather featured Avila Beach on the evening news, and while widespread attention to the plight of the town was welcome, the only real difference it made was that tourist trade in town dropped dramatically. Despite his public announcement, Unocal CEO Beach still opposed cleaning up under the town. To draw tourists to counter the tarnished image of the dangerous beach the company funded a series of weekend summer celebrations at the beach called "Family Fun Days." The events drew people and more coverage, as well as the protesters in oily HAZ-MAT suits covered with bright orange balls.

The company gave $100,000 to a new group that called itself the Avila Business Association (ABA). The organization was able to attract a few new businesses to rent beach paraphernalia out of trailers and the beds of pickup trucks. The ABA leased a visitor center, and a Unocal representative sat on the nine-member board. Promotional materials were done in brilliant orange and blue company colors, and banners waved from lampposts in the ocean breezes. It was seen by residents as a brazen attempt to buy the voices of "businessmen" who were favorable to the company. Unocal countered by saying it participated on, but did not direct, the board.

For a little while, the summer of 1996 appeared to be calm. However, although the lid may have been on the potboiler, the fire was still fierce below.

11

SHOOTOUT STALLS—SHERIFF COMES TO TAKE OVER

WHEN the suit was first filed, the Avila Alliance's Matthew Farmer and Saro Rizzo had to run through some major stumbling blocks to get over monumental hurdles, all without benefit of prior experience. They were flying by the seat of their pants and constantly adjusting strategy to meet Unocal's legal offense. In the early stages, essential power rested with the accused.

By the time Rizzo was first approached by Unocal to discuss the possibility of settlement, the company's legal policies had been in place for years. The Avila Alliance was not only dealing with formidable company opposition, they also had to adjust their own tactics to incorporate new information about the extent of the plumes as revealed by additional testing.

At his first few settlement conferences before the Environmental Law Foundation and Communities for a Better Environment joined the suit, Rizzo was alone in the fight for a machine to clean the sand and a commitment from Unocal to dig up the pool of petroleum below the beach. "They said they wanted to settle, but they had no viable solution," he remembers. "Unocal's first remediation proposal to clean up the beach was downplaying the idea of any threat, and did not address the question of whether or not the mass of contamination was moving."

The latter was a huge legal question, because if it were mobile, the plume constituted a continuing nuisance. The suit's position was that, given the underground water table and how it flows—moving from the valley underground to the ocean—the plume certainly *was* moving. That meant there was no question that it represented a threat to both the groundwater quality and, eventually, the ocean. By contrast, Unocal's position was that it was not moving, claiming the contamination was stable and should be left alone due to the fact they were certain it was a low-level product that would eventually just go away. The company claimed that if the contamination were to be dug up and exposed, it would be more dangerous. Rizzo was astounded by their position, considering Unocal had already been ordered to do the Little Dig by the creek when it was about to daylight. The record was clear. A torrent of water from heavy winter rains had washed down San Luis Obispo Creek and removed much of the top layer of sand. If the contaminated layer were to be uncovered by more rain, people would be exposed to the toxins, and the oil products would be washed into the ocean where they would destroy marine life.

"I lived in Avila for ten years and remembered that Little Dig," said Rizzo. "I remember walking or running by and seeing this pit, and what was there was amazing! So I used that as an example and called for an excavation of the beach." He also requested that Unocal work with the local boards to figure out the best possible solution for cleaning up the plume under the downtown area. "We premised it on the fact that they had already done an excavation a year ago at the creek and went around saying what a great success it was. It looked like everything worked out very well, so I said why don't you do that with the rest of the beach and apply that same logic?" He reminded Unocal attorneys that the company's own Internet site touted what a great success the Little Dig had been, and, therefore, it was logical to just continue the same approach in dealing with the rest of it.

Unocal's answer was to cement the beach. "Initially, hardly any residents went to the meetings," said Rizzo, "and [the company] may have thought they could pull it off. They went public with this idea of solidification and must have thought people would actually buy into it." For the rest of the pollution under the town, Unocal held fast to biosparging as a means of cleanup.

To Rizzo and the Avila Alliance, the suggestion was ludicrous and environmentally bizarre. "My question was, why do you want people to live on a petri dish that you don't know will work?" Rizzo said. "They wanted to experiment with people's lives. If this were a field out in Timbuktu where you don't have humans in the equation, it might be different, but Unocal wanted to pump air into their homes for seven to eight years, then likely have to come back and say, you know what, it didn't work, and you still can't sell your house or build that second bathroom."

Reason and common sense appeared to have no effect on settlement negotiations even after the Environmental Law Foundation and Citizens for a Better Environment joined Rizzo at the table. The Pacific Gas and Electric settlement did not move Unocal toward a path of a more reasoned stance as Rizzo had hoped, and instead seemed to etch the company's position in stone. Rizzo was unwilling to wait for the regulatory agencies to try to convince the company to accept responsibility. He was impatient to get the job done.

After a series of particularly frustrating meetings that went nowhere, Rizzo reached into his arsenal and pulled out a big rock. He announced to the media that he was going to file the suit in federal court under the Federal Clean Water Act. The effect was electrifying, but not on Unocal.

The water board and California Fish & Game sat up and took notice, because if the suit were to be put in the hands of the federal government, state agencies would have to cede primary legal responsibility to them. In the world of legal priorities, Washington, D.C., is top dog, and state interests would have to fall in behind a legal entity even farther away than San Francisco and Los Angeles.

It also meant that any settlement would also have to include federal government agencies, meaning that less would end up in the State of California. Federal involvement meant that Avila Beach had an even better chance of being left out again, although it could ensure that the cleanup would actually happen.

State agencies immediately called the California state attorney general and requested he intervene. When word reached the central coast that Deputy Attorney General Ken Alex was assigned to represent California Fish & Game and the water board, Peg Pinard was quite upset, particularly about what she perceived as the history of the Diablo Canyon settlement. However, she was not the only one who believed strongly that the state's participation was a bad omen for Avila Beach. To anyone who knew even a little about the complex interconnections of state agencies and their different legal mandates, the ramifications were clear. With the same agencies coming into play, residents were fearful that the results would to be the same. Avila Beach would not be the beneficiary.

The PG&E settlement that Pinard felt might be repeated in Avila Beach actually turned out to be the catalyst for change. Ken Alex was assigned to the case, and, remembering the public outcry over the previous action, joined in Rizzo's suit, instead of intervening in it. A key player with considerable power had entered the fight and made a huge difference.

When the state joined in Saro Rizzo's suit, the legal issues had already created a bit of a quandary, but not for the Avila Alliance and their group partners. As evidence continued to pile up delineating the extent of the plume under both the beach and the business district, the small suit for cleanup and request for a beach-cleaning machine that Rizzo had originally planned was forced to expand to encompass a vast ecological disaster, with Avila Beach sitting at ground zero.

"We wanted to do what was best for the environment," said Rizzo, "but also we wanted what was best for the residents, because we had a major social factor to consider in town. It was a delicate balancing act, because the Avila Alliance did not want to see people lose their businesses or homes."

The group also felt people would not be better off dealing directly with Unocal or dealing with the various individual agencies, because every office had its own unique set of requirements set out by state law. Furthermore, the company had already earned a bad reputation in terms of their conduct in dealing with individuals. The Avila Alliance took the stand that the best avenue for progress was to empower people to take action on their own behalf. They knew best what they risked personally and what they were willing to yield in the quest for cleanup and closure.

For the first time Rizzo felt uncertain in his situation, not knowing exactly how his role was evolving, because of Ken Alex's position in the suit. While he was working alone, he could make decisions based solely on his client group, the Avila Alliance. With two environmental organization partners in the action, his status changed to something like senior partner. When California Deputy Attorney General Ken Alex entered the action, Rizzo lost that status and was left to wonder where he fit in at all, even though he felt Alex was the top environmental prosecutor in the state.

While the addition of the state to the suit's partners made a significant change in the legal pictures, it did nothing to alter the residents' resolve to get the contamination cleaned up. Public feelings exhibited at meetings had begun to show that the townspeople were gaining strength in purpose. No matter how complex the science was said to be or how many different methods were considered for cleaning up the various parts of the plume, Avila Beach residents stood firm: Clean it up, and do it now!

There was never a question of selling out, as had been the case at Times Beach and Love Canal, where the companies responsible for the widespread contamination bought up the tainted properties and simply fenced them off. No longer hesitant about speaking up to any entity, townspeople were very direct in telling Unocal that anything short of a complete excavation was not acceptable. While some of the attorneys representing individual property owners indicated they might consider a lesser solution, Rizzo and his cohorts emphatically refused, especially in view of what appeared to be a change in Unocal's stance. Company attorneys appeared to be taken aback by the growing unity of the town. Rizzo was emboldened to draw his own line in the sand, saying that any settlement offered other than full excavation would just serve to continue the litigation. The problem now was that the young attorney was no longer captain of his own ship. The scope of the suit had grown, as had the involvement of others, in ever-widening circles. Most important for the moment, he felt he had little continuing impact on the very settlement negotiations brought about by his own initiative. Ken Alex was in charge, and while he invited the Avila Alliance and partners to continue at the table, Rizzo felt the change in power structure was sure to give Unocal the idea the shift was in their favor. The highly disputed PG&E settlement over fish entrainment had been a team effort led by Ken Alex, and a great deal of rancor remained in the community over that settlement.

Rizzo felt the deputy attorney general was inclined to make a settlement offer that was considered his best expectation and remain committed to it in order to achieve cleanup and financial redress for the damage caused by the contamination. The private attorneys involved on behalf of Avila Beach felt it was preferable to work in alternative ways to arrive at a settlement that would reach the best cleanup and most reasonable dollar compensation. It appeared that the private attorneys were well advised, because until this point in settlement conferences, Unocal had lowballed their offers at absurd levels.

The apparent disinclination of the company to compensate at a reasonable rate moved Rizzo's team to ask for millions more than they expected to realize, especially since the scope of the contamination picture was still clouded. Any settlement would indemnify Unocal from further legal action over the Avila Beach problem, and while Alex had been successful in his previous negotiations, Rizzo's partners had been successful as well. The difference was in the details. By comparison, the private attorneys managed to obtain fairer compensation for damaged plaintiffs, and judgment in their cases was harder on perpetrators.

In the case of the PG&E settlement, even though it was the largest of its kind in U.S. history to date, the perception that the power producer had been let off easy left many people very upset. The secrecy of the final outcome and the fact that Avila Beach had been left out of the distribution of funds put Alex on the spot. He was the subject of bitter recrimination in the press, on television, and at meetings. Rizzo recalled that at one point Alex wondered aloud why he was so hated.

As the dust began to settle into new legal patterns, Rizzo did something that had a major impact on the Avila Alliance's suit. Determined not to be a minor partner in the legal action, he decided that to stay involved, he would need to enlist the help of an 800-pound gorilla—he called on the internationally acclaimed law firm Milberg Weiss to participate with him.

Perhaps the largest plaintiff's attorney group in the United States, Milberg Weiss is a household name in legal circles for winning huge suits, including the Exxon Valdez case, obtaining German reparations for Holocaust victims, mitigating the savings and loan fraud, and winning tobacco litigation. The firm sent attorney Steve Crandall to Avila Beach as their representative. Crandall had gained experience in the San Luis Obispo area when he helped to resolve the PG&E case with Ken Alex two years earlier. That case may have been old by the time Crandall arrived, but the wounds in Avila Beach that had been inflicted by the distribution of the PG&E settlement were still fresh. Crandall was the perfect partner to Rizzo, and the two immediately became good friends as well as forming a professional team.

The details of the legal battle remained behind closed doors, but the public debate took center stage in the local media, especially in the daily newspaper. Adding to the town's misery, the *Telegram-Tribune* announced the results of an informal countywide poll, revealing that more than half of the people questioned opposed the dig. Some letters to the editor painted less than positive images of Avila Beach residents, and the criticism was terribly hurtful.

Avila Beach resident and property owner Cliff Branch observed that if the excavation wasn't done soon, it would probably have to be done years into the future. "This town is going to get raped," he said. "I'd hate to see it get raped twice." In a rebuttal letter to the editor in the *Telegram-Tribune*, Archie McLaren took the pollsters to task, accusing them of gross inaccuracy and proposing that they run another poll solely in Avila Beach, where the effects of the spill were felt most keenly. Resident Tom Harrington also wrote the paper, pointing out that the people in Avila Beach were the proper stewards for their own environment. It is "disheartening," he wrote, "to think people feel we should continue to float atop 400,000 gallons of crankcase oil."

The Avila Alliance was also lambasted in the media and called crazy environmentalists in California by conservative talk show host Bill Wattenburg, who declaimed the problem by making the observation that they were digging up the whole town just for a little oil. At the time Rizzo filed his lawsuit, the host of a radio show in San Francisco called the Avila Alliance "environmental nazis." Making light of the man-made disaster, it was suggested that people were in more danger standing on a paved street on a hot day, and that digging it all up was a scheme devised by Green Gestapo environmental attorneys trying to use bloodletting to cure a disease.

Rizzo was tolerant of the attacks, pointing out the paradox of people looking at environmental attorneys as wacko tree huggers, while at the same time supporting property rights. "When a big corporate polluter comes and damages their own property, then it's different and the environmental attorney is a friend," he mused.

Rising to Archie McLaren's challenge, the Cal Poly psychology department ran a survey for residents in Avila Beach. Results of that poll contrasted sharply with those of the one taken in the entire county. Residents admitted to having mixed emotions about the choices they were given. While they didn't like the idea of excavation, they felt it was the only acceptable solution to the pollution problem, because it was the only proposal that would rid the town of the public perception that it had a dangerously polluted beach and would return their rights to buy, sell, and alter their properties.

For comparison the same survey was given to Cal Poly employees and students. Not surprisingly, that group was less supportive of excavation than were Avila Beach residents, just as McLaren had predicted. The campus group was also more concerned about the effectiveness of the cleanup method than they were about the disruption of the town. The answers were effectively at cross-purposes: Respondents didn't like the idea of destruction, but felt it was okay if it would result in a better cleanup, no matter whom it affected. The previous, disputed poll from areas outside the beach town supported mitigation for residents who would be relocated or disrupted during the cleanup, as well as compensation and loans for anyone who was affected by it. Other than that, they still did not want Avila Beach to change, another distinction lost on the beach town's residents.

Daniel Levi, the Cal Poly professor who ran the poll, observed that the farther away psychologically people were from Avila Beach, the more concern they had about activities that would disrupt access to the beach and the town. In other words, it was okay for the townspeople to float on the pollution, as long as potential tourists to the town weren't kept from having a good time there.

Unocal would not even discuss the possible costs of excavation with media, but Silas Lyons of the *Telegram-Tribune* queried stockbroker Norm Rosenberg about the costs the company faced in Avila Beach. An oil and gas industry analyst for Standard & Poor's Equity Group, Rosenberg said the stock market could look at a very large liability and respond to it, but he didn't believe it would kill the stock. Although Unocal would not discuss a cost estimate publicly, in their financial report to the U.S. Securities and Exchange Commission, the company said it expected to spend hundreds of millions on the two projects, perhaps as much as $270 million.

At the time Unocal was a stock described with the moderate "to accumulate" recommendation by most brokers. Another oil analyst at a major brokerage house, who didn't want his name attached to a discussion of Unocal's legal responsibility, said the Avila Beach cleanup would have to break the $250 million threshold to even put a dent in the company's stability. Otherwise, he was quoted as saying, "I'd say it's a sneezer."

The town was pressed on all sides at once, and emotions were taking a serious toll on families, friendships, and businesses. The people's stamina and resolve were further tested when the health questions raised by Ed Masry exploded into a frenzy of testing, interviewing, and alarming rhetoric. It felt like a three-ring circus to townspeople. Testing of the plume was beginning to reveal a toxic soup of organic compounds. The most worrisome from a health standpoint were volatile organic compounds having benzene, toluene, ethyl benzene, and xylene, plus polycyclic aromatic hydrocarbons and organic lead, all of which are harmful to people if inhaled, absorbed through the skin, or ingested. Some heavy contaminants like lead are known to accumulate in plants, which required the testing of gardens and fruit trees in Avila Beach.

Incredibly, it was in the midst of this gathering storm that the *Telegram-Tribune* reported in July 1997 that a bubbly oily sheen had been discovered in the ocean off Avila Beach. Resident Perry Martin had spotted it and notified San Luis Obispo County Environmental Health Department. Coordinator Curt Batson came out to investigate and notified the California Fish & Game Oil Response Team, the Central Coast Regional Water Quality Control Board, and the U.S. Coast Guard.

Local fishermen were the first on the scene and hurried to contain the oil to keep it from spreading, until the response team could organize their equipment and set out cleanup booms. Avila Beach once again braced for another disaster settlement that would benefit everyone but the people who suffered from the leak, and the beach was closed in the middle of the busiest season.

The extent of the contamination remained small and was mitigated quickly. The *New Times* reported that Unocal's fine for the incident sent $1.2 million to sea otter support and to the San Luis Obispo Creek restoration project. In addition, another $1.5 million fine for Guadalupe Dunes was split among Cal Poly's Performing Arts Center, youth recreation, and ecology projects in San Luis Obispo County.

Each of the supervisors netted $65,000 for their district, most of which was reported in the story to have been spent on fax machines and computers, with the remainder being donated to libraries, youth recreation programs, fire districts, and historical societies. Avila Beach got none of the money, and it seemed that the town had once again been deliberately ignored. However, there was no upwelling of protest because of the democratic way the funds had been distributed.

Three hundred thousand dollars of the settlement went to an environmental trust in the county. Local rancher Harold Miossi was appointed to manage the "Unobucks," as they were called, to fund forty-three projects that were suggested by people from throughout the county. Schools, Little Leagues, and private organizations all received grants averaging $7,072. The public viewed the way the trust was divided as fair, and there was little complaint from anyone, including those who applied for and did not receive funds.

The war of words continued to be fueled by dueling experts and exploited by the media. Ed Masry sent $100,000 to a group called Concerned Residents of Avila Beach to sample sand on the beach. The money was to be used only as long as Unocal matched the funds. He was described in a local newspaper as unwilling to accept the results of the previous testing, calling them unreliable, since the tests had been done under the polluter's direction.

Unocal reacted to the challenge by announcing it was committing $200,000 to the San Luis Obispo County health study. There was even disagreement on the method the testing should take, with Masry wanting random samples rather than sampling of targeted areas. By May, an army of testers descended on residents, sampling the air outside their homes, each room inside their homes, and the crawl spaces underneath. Samples conducted at Avila Beach were compared to samples conducted at Pismo and San Simeon Beaches. Relatively isolated San Simeon Beach to the north was used as the control area, because it was thought to be particularly pristine. Instead, some unexpected tar paddies from offshore oil seeps were detected there, throwing the data into dispute, just as media representatives from the around the country and the world descended on the little town.

12

STRANGERS MUDDY PARADISE

IMMEDIATELY following the public meeting in January 1996, where Ed Masry and his assistant Erin Brockovich charged that Avila Beach was dangerous to humans, a dramatic change came over the Avila Beach controversy. Masry raised the question of the possibility that Unocal threatened the health of everyone who lived near the underground spill, including those who visited and played in its sands. Until that time, residents had been able to muster the courage to keep fighting to make the cleanup a reality, but suddenly every sniffle, rash, or memory of a resident who had died prematurely took on new meaning. Whereas before, the people were bonded by their anger and united in pushing to get the job done, now they felt uneasy and fearful.

Three months after announcing he had proof of health problems at the beach, Masry finally revealed his study results and continued to demand that more testing be done. He also hired the Response Team for the Chemically Injured (RTCI), an environmental firm located in nearby Atascadero, to do more testing. RTCI quickly claimed it was dangerous to play in the sand, especially to burrow into it. The claim was based on the findings of toxicologist Dr. James Dahlgren, a consultant who taught at UCLA School of Medicine at the time, and William Marcus, an occasional consultant for the U.S. Environmental Protection Agency.

Dahlgren was quoted in the *New Times* as saying, "skin rashes, respiratory irritation, and nervous system" problems were expected in people who used the beach. He added, "even local dogs are ill and die mysteriously." Masry's people suggested that experts with the county may have misconstrued their own data and made incorrect assumptions. Battered residents of Avila Beach felt they were at the mercy of dueling experts again.

Dr. Greg Thomas, Chief County Health Officer, along with Curtis Batson, County Director of Environmental Health, hired toxicology consultant Alvin Greenberg and Rick Krentzer of Environmental Health Investigations in California to examine the Masry study data in detail. Both disagreed with the attorney's conclusions. The group of professionals called the study poorly done, because it did not use standard sampling procedures and did not provide a scientific rationale, which is usually a part of a scientific report.

In illustrating how that disagreement was important, Alvin Greenberg quoted from the report for the media: "Please also note that the location of the sample 3877-9 is uncertain; it was assumed to be a 'tar ball' not beach sand. Also, it is unclear where samples labeled Beach #1 and Beach #2 obtained 12-25-96 were located and whether they were beach sand or 'tar balls.'" Dispute over whether the sample was a tar ball or not was crucial, because balls are indicative of natural crude working its way to the surface.

Erin Brockovich, who said she had directed the research for the Masry team, confirmed that the samples had been beach sand and added that benzanthracene measured beyond safe levels, as mandated by the U.S. Environmental Protection Agency. Masry said, "That beach is toxic and should be closed." When questioned about the economic impact to the residents, Masry said, "I have no motives for wanting to exacerbate the problem in Avila Beach. In fact, I'll make more money if they don't close the beach and people keep getting exposed to the stuff." Residents who once looked to Masry as a legal ally began to wonder if the attorney had any of their interests in mind at all. Instead of considering what a disaster it would be for residents to lose their homes, it seemed that the flamboyant lawyer had a more limited vision of financial impact—specifically how his own pocket would be affected.

Media coverage of renewed health questions spread well beyond the central coast again. The *Los Angeles Times* reported that Masry claimed that Avila Beach residents suffered from higher rates of cancer than did people living in other parts of the county, an allegation that was not backed by records of the Tri-County Cancer Registry. Masry also said he had proof that pollutants had migrated to the surface, which had resulted in the introduction of toxins into at least two residences, according to testing done by the Response Team for the Chemically Injured. Unocal was incensed at the charge and fired back, saying the attorney was alarming people without proof. In San Francisco, attorney Joe Cotchett severed his firm's connection with Masry.

At the local water board, Gerhardt Hubner was shocked by what Masry used as a basis for his charge of toxic surface contamination. Hubner remembered that, although Masry had claimed to have test results in hand at the December meeting, Erin Brockovich had later admitted to having collected the samples that same afternoon just before they made their dramatic announcement, leaving no time to analyze test results by the time of the meeting.

Worse, the samples had been collected next to beach fire pits, where the likelihood of finding PAHs (Polynuclear Aromatic Hydrocarbons found in fuels and oil) was a virtual certainty, because the compounds are also contained in charcoal, which has no connection to the spill beneath the sand.

Furthermore, Hubner was appalled at the differences between what the attorney publicly claimed and what was on the report. For example, although Masry said the tests had revealed levels of hexavalent chromium, another toxic compound, no mention of that chemical was in the report. "When I asked where it was," Hubner remembers, "Masry said it wasn't here, that [hexavalent chromium had been found in] another place where they had collected."

In March 1997, Unocal funded the *design* of the Front Street Enhancement Project, donating $300,000 for engineering and plans, not construction. Company spokesman Bill Sharrer claimed it was an example of Unocal's commitment; however, since the county building moratorium was still in effect and construction was not a possibility, residents, weary of the irregular public relations money drops by the corporation in the past, cynically looked upon the large gift as just another effort by the company to garner good press.

Dr. Dahlgren claimed negative health risks existed in town and said Unocal testing had failed to measure the extent of daily exposure to people who were in regular contact with pollutants. Also, new estimates of the plume made the two-year-old county health study outdated and irrelevant. Unocal gave the county health department $100,000 for the first phase of a new health study. The pace of new information, charges, and countercharges was dizzying to embattled residents, and showed no signs of letting up.

Little Dig—San Luis Obispo Creek 1995. Ribbons strung across the "Little Dig" by San Luis Obispo Creek prevent birds from landing in the oil. This smaller cleanup project proved that there was a serious problem and there could be no turning back from the challenge that lay ahead for the Avila Beach community. © *Telegram-Tribune/David Middlecamp*

Palamino Estates home. Located in a quiet neighborhood, this house is one of thirty-eight repurchased by Unocal because of erupting petroleum products from old oil sumps. The houses were built atop what had been an oil field. © *Barbara Wolcott*

Avila Beach, aerial view. A view of Avila Beach one month before the excavation began. The Unocal tanks are gone from the bluff at center right. There is no outward indication of the enormous lake of petroleum products under the town and the beach, both of which would be dug up in the coming year and a half. © *Dale Reid Ginder*

Downtown business district in Avila Beach with Unocal mural. In the last days of 1998, Avila Beach Downtown was a rapidly aging ghost town. The Café was boarded up, and the mural commissioned by Unocal was being prepared for transfer to Bellevue–Santa Fe Charter School where it was made. © *Dale Reid Ginder*

Demolition and rainbow. On the day before Thanksgiving 1997, the first buildings succumbed to the wrecking machinery. No one was left emotionally untouched by the unexpected rainbow created by sunshine slanting through the water sprayed to keep dust at a minimum. © *Dale Reid Ginder*

Avila Grocery closing. On the final day of its existence, the Avila Grocery Store was the site of a community potluck meal. Everyone was invited, including Unocal people. The old building and what it represented was honored with food, music, tears, and laughter. © *Dale Reid Ginder*

San Luis Yacht Club move. Moving the Yacht Club was complicated by its width, which is greater than the bridge over which it had to travel on its way to a temporary berth at Cherry Canyon. Experienced professionals had some anxious moments until the flatbed truck made it past the barrier without mishap. © *Dale Reid Ginder*

The dig begins. The Avila Grocery remains the only building in the downtown area as the beach is cleaned. Criss-crossed by coffer dams of sheet pile, the lovely beach vanished under a beehive of equipment, trucks, stockpiled material, and destroyed buildings. © *Dale Reid Ginder*

Inside the cofferdam. Inside the cofferdam created by sheet pile, two Jacobs Engineering crewmen round up surface oil in booms. Oil captured went to a recycling operation, and the water was filtered for secondary use. © *Dale Reid Ginder*

Demolition of a downtown business. Small businesses like the Ski Rental are not likely to be seen in Avila Beach ever again, because the cleanup resulted in a radical increase in property values. The fall of this establishment signaled the abrupt end of an era. © *Dale Reid Ginder*

Big Dig response to protect birds. Concern for the safety of shore birds moved students at Bellevue–Santa Fe School to build a unique scarecrow. A Jacobs Construction crew installed their project at the top of the sheet pile cofferdam where it moved with each ocean breeze. © *Dale Reid Ginder*

Ground Zero—no more town. On an overcast day with every building gone or relocated, and streets removed, Avila Beach lies completely destroyed. The ragged beach blended with the downtown area, and only the sidewalk in front of the foundation slab of the Grocery in the right foreground is recognizable. © *Dale Reid Ginder*

Avila Beach today. Two years after the last dump truck lumbered up the hill to the tank farm with the last load of contaminated soil, only one of three blocks destroyed had new construction. Representing a small fraction of lots to be rebuilt, Mr. Rick's, the Sea Barn, and Custom House form the nucleus of the new downtown along the Front Street Enhancement Project promenade. © *Barbara Wolcott*

13

HIGH NOON AT AVILA BEACH

AFTER changing at a snail's pace for a hundred years, Avila Beach had begun to move into high gear by the end of 1997. Unocal announced that the tank farm would be dismantled. As the most visible identifier that Avila Beach was an oil town, the tanks had dominated the area for so long it was hard to imagine they could disappear as quickly as they did. Tanks had been on the bluff for nearly a hundred years, and even though they were a comfort to some people, others cheered as three huge storage units came down over a two-week period.

The three-quarter-inch-thick, sixty-foot-high steel plates were cut into three-foot sections, causing a deafening noise that could be heard easily a mile away. Pieces were so heavy that only six could be put onto a truck at a time, making a twelve- to twenty-ton load. Old-timers had mixed emotions about seeing them leave, because the tanks had been so important in the World War II years. It seemed incongruous that the tanks that had held the fuel to fight the war against the Japanese would likely end up being made into Toyotas. One of the residents remembered feeling happy when he had seen the tanks from the deck of a U.S. Navy minesweeper during the 1940s, but now he was pleased to see them go, interpreting it as a sign of the town's success in bringing Unocal to recognize its responsibility for the contamination.

The battle lines were set in a last-ditch stand in the central coast region, which has a rich history involving independent, pragmatic people like the Cattaneo family. Avila Beach is an enclave of people, many of whom have a mind-set much like that of the Cattaneos. Charlie Cattaneo was the last lamplighter of gas street-lights in San Luis Obispo city. Occasionally, he would sleep past his appointed responsibility, and the job still got done on time. His father would take the lighting stick, which was a converted pool cue, and do the route on foot, since he was unable to ride a bicycle. By its own merits, that may not seem to deserve much attention in a century marked by computers and global markets, but the last gas street lamps in San Luis Obispo city were turned off in May 1941.

To the north of the central coast in the town of Watsonville, gas street lamps burned a few years longer, into the 1950s, and when they were finally taken down to make room for modern electric lights, they found a home in San Luis Obispo city at the world-famed Madonna Inn. Still in use, they are no longer powered by gas but were electrified when installed. The region has always been a waste-not-want-not kind of place. For example, when a boat went down offshore fifty years ago, residents salvaged bolts of material from it to make clothes and curtains. At least one restaurant in town was constructed of wood salvaged from an abandoned railroad trestle.

Nearly six decades after the converted pool cue was retired from lighting gas street lamps, the last bastion of an extraordinary can-do spirit was under siege in Avila Beach, and the public meetings continued. Lucy Lepley remembers that Ed Masry held one of the meetings at the Madonna Inn to give residents access to all the environmental experts at one time. "There was a huge turnout," she said, "and I remember one woman sitting up front who said her husband was healthy nearly all his life. The man had just died of cancer."

The woman went on to describe a big strapping man, hit hard and suddenly by disease, and recalled that he often worked on the beach shoveling sand. In retrospect she wondered if he got sick because he was working close to the chemicals. Masry's team assured her that his proximity to the chemicals probably had made him sick. Their reply came too quickly for Lucy Lepley, and instead of getting answers, she left the meeting with more questions.

While the battle was fought in the press and on television, the real work was being done behind legal doors. Deputy Attorney General Ken Alex called a meeting of the principals in the Rizzo suit to meet in Oakland late in 1997, along with representatives of all the affected agencies. He set the agenda by saying the State of California wanted a full cleanup, because that was what the water board wanted. He also let the embattled plaintiffs know that he was joining them, not taking over.

The partnership began to take shape, and prior to each meeting with Unocal, members of the plaintiff group selected one person to speak for their side. At one gathering in the Los Angeles area, Rizzo was in charge. It was the first gathering attended by the Milberg Weiss attorney team, and when they all sat down at the large conference table, Rizzo began immediately to conduct the business at hand. He was interrupted by one of the Unocal attorneys, asking who the six gentlemen seated with the young attorney were.

Rizzo apologized, as the six lawyers each reached into an inside pocket and laid their individual business cards on the table facing the opposition. The six cards containing the Milberg Weiss logo made a dramatic impact on opposing attorneys, and Rizzo could easily read the words on the lips of Unocal's legal team: *Oh f—k!*

At the same time, the day-to-day pursuit of Dolores Lepley's suit with Joe Cotchett was put into the hands of local attorney James Duenow. It was a move that would prove to have a major consequence for Unocal in the discovery process. Cotchett and Duenow had known each other for years and had worked on a number of other cases in the San Luis Obispo area. It was a comfortable partnership for handling cases so far away from the San Francisco office. Cotchett had the resources to get the expensive testing done, and Duenow had the local experience to meet the legal hand-to-hand combat.

Having sued Ford Motor Company and General Motors in the

past, Duenow was reluctant to take on the Avila Beach case, mainly because he knew how large corporations work. "They just bombard you with paper," he said. "Their attorneys, and they usually have lots of them, sometimes use a kind of scorched earth policy." However, with Cotchett's office having far greater resources to take up the slack, he was glad to get in on the action.

Word got out about the power behind Dolores's case. Other residents began to sign contracts with Duenow and Cotchett, so that the two lawyers ended up representing more than twenty parcels of land in Avila, concerning a total of nearly fifty people by the time the suit was settled. These suits were all based on damage to the real property because of the contamination.

In his initial meeting with Unocal attorneys, Duenow recalls the company's general counsel telling him "to take it to the bank: we will never, never, never, never remediate Avila unless the Supreme Court forces us." That put the pressure on Alan Bond. Hired to be the private investigator for the Cotchett and Duenow cases, he had a formidable job determining the genesis of the contamination, what it was, and when it happened.

Bond had spent summers in Avila Beach, and the parents of many of his friends had worked for Unocal. He began contacting people he knew, some in their seventies and eighties, especially those who had worked for the oil company. "They told me some amazing stories," Bond said. One man recounted to Bond that when he was young, he and his friends had gone to school in San Luis Obispo city, and, while they waited for the bus to take them there, they would sit on the curb and ignite gas coming out of a crack in the ground with matches. They were entertained by watching the fumes start tiny dancing flames along the street. The last time the man lit the gas was when his father caught him, and, in a tirade worthy of a U.S. Marine Corps drill sergeant, let the boys know that the gas was coming from breaks in the underground pipelines and their seemingly innocent activity could have "blown everything up from here to the central valley."

It was a story Bond could understand well. When he was in school himself, Bond remembered his mother always telling him that if he was going to the beach he should wear old cutoffs because of the oil. "On your feet, on your clothes," he remembered, "you'd be lying on the sand and all of a sudden there'd be oil." As he continued to investigate for Duenow, Bond found out that the product actually percolated up from under the sand.

As an investigator, having worked for years in the Santa Ana Police Department and handling thousands of private investigator assignments, he was accustomed to complex litigation. However, he was unprepared for the anger of the people who lived in Avila Beach. It took a while for him to realize that at the root of the condemnation they heaped on him was the previous connection between Cotchett and Masry. Not realizing that compact had been terminated, residents saw Bond as a part of the Masry team. People were fed up with that firm's scare tactics, and especially with seeing Erin Brockovich signing up clients in bars and leaving the impression that everyone who lived in Avila Beach was going to die from the toxic spill that was under the town.

Bond had to convince the traumatized residents that he did not represent Masry and merely needed to find out what had happened in the past. His exertions found the man who later proved to be a devastating witness, but not in the way he was accustomed to finding witnesses, by using his experience, skill, and ingenuity. The witness had been a Unocal foreman, and Bond's son met him at an environmental organization meeting.

By the time Bond got to talk with the oil company retiree, the man was not sure he wanted to be interviewed, because he had begun to fear it would cost him his retirement income and benefits from Unocal. Bond knew there were other people who would like to talk about the company's past handling of spills that hadn't been made public, but who also feared retaliation. He sensed that this particular man had something very important to say. The man was a highly decorated World War II veteran who had been well respected by his coworkers. Bond and the man sat down together, and Bond was able to convince him that talking was the right thing to do.

Whereas the company insisted they knew nothing about the pipeline leaks before 1977, Bond found out about ex-Unocal employees and laborers from different unions who had later talked about standing in oil up to their waists—not just in Avila Beach, but wherever there were company pipelines. Until they were forced to, by a change in laws, oil companies generally did nothing about leaks, because fixing them would require expensive shutdowns. During his investigations, Bond saw one three-foot length of pipe that had twenty-two repair welds in it.

While Bond was successfully uncovering evidence, a series of victories began to accumulate in the negotiations of the legal teams of Saro Rizzo, Ken Alex, and representatives of the various agencies. One particularly satisfying victory resulted from the quick reaction of alert agency lawyers during the testimony of Unocal's contractor, Dr. David Huntley, professor of Hydrology at California San Diego State University. Addressing the legal point of the plume's movement, Huntley presented an impressive scientific model of the contamination and his contention that it was not moving. However, biologist Melissa Boggs of California Fish & Game asked him simply, "Dr. Huntley, do you believe some part of the dissolved hydrocarbon plume is reaching San Luis Bay and the ocean?" His reply was, "There is at least some," at which point Ken Alex reacted quickly. He turned to Unocal attorneys and informed them that the company didn't have a permit to discharge into the ocean. Two sentences translated into a telling legal point made by the agencies with Unocal's own witness.

This movement, shifting in favor of the plaintiffs, was overwhelming in its importance to the suits, and the attorneys who had filed actions against Unocal shared their information, with the exception of Ed Masry. There was jubilation in law offices from San Luis Obispo across the country to the halls of Milberg Weiss in the East. The news would take longer to get to the people represented in the legal actions, but there was no doubt that when it did they felt an increase in optimism from their attorneys.

Alan Bond uncovered two other vital witnesses who were willing to testify about their Unocal connections. The statement of one concerned Front Street in particular:

I worked at Avila for approximately twenty years. Almost every Friday for years we had to repair broken lines that went down Front Street or the lines coming off the hill. In fact, by the Front

Street gate at the entrance to the tank farm, you would actually see oil coming out of the bank.

The pipe under Front Street that broke most was the ballast line. It was a clay pipe with metal bolts and rubber between the joints. The rubber would rot or the bolts would rust off. Also, when the ground shifted, the pipes would break. Lots of product would go into the ground—crude oil, seawater, gas, and natural gas. We didn't mind getting called out to repair the leaks because we would get overtime.

Unocal didn't think anything about leaks, in fact, when I was on the wharf, we had all kinds of oil and other product going into the ocean. The company knew it, so they always had a couple of tons of sand on the wharf. We would toss buckets of sand on the oil slick to try to sink the oil. Unocal also had a launch that they would run back and forth through the oil slick. They did this to break up the oil so people could not see the big oil slick from shore.

When asked for records of pipeline maintenance, Unocal said they had been lost in a flood. However, one former company employee gave the following testimony,

A lot of the records you would want regarding the gauge readings at the tank farm would be at the Unocal facility in Palatine, Illinois. We had to prepare typed certified copies regarding the oil, temperature, gravity flow, etc., and send them to Illinois.

"Regarding the records that were kept at Tank Farm Road (in San Luis Obispo City), they were not destroyed in the flood. I was part of a crew sent to save the records. When it was obvious the water was going to keep rising, we took the records out of the bottom drawers of the file cabinets and put them up high. They were safely stored until after the flooding. Then, after the water receded, the office was painted, fixed up, and we returned the files to their drawers.

After years of frustrating delays, denials, and stonewalling on the part of Unocal, in early 1998 there was light at the end of the tunnel for the litigants. Unocal sent word to Deputy Attorney General Ken Alex that the company was willing to accept the cleanup demand and discuss a settlement.

Saro Rizzo and his partners in the suit, combined with the State of California, County of San Luis Obispo, and the attendant state agencies, were elated by the change in Unocal's position. There had been other times when they were sure the company would capitulate under the press of overwhelming evidence, but until faced with the testimony of their own employees, Unocal decision makers had, much to the consternation of the plaintiffs, chosen to stand pat.

The company was now besieged with an EIR clearly pointing an accusatory finger at them for having caused the spill, the testimony of former employees who showed that the company *had* known about the problems many years before 1977, and the fact that internal documents garnered by the discovery process confirmed what witnesses were saying, including one report that indicated their own testing had proved that the explosion in 1977 had been caused by Union Oil Company gasoline. The company's board of directors indicated their serious intent to get down to business when they sent their top corporate attorney, Mark Smith, to take over the negotiations.

Unocal accepted the disputed EIR and went on yet another huge public relations offensive. In an open letter to the region, the company declared, "Perceptions regarding underground contamination from previous Unocal operations on the central coast are of great concern to us because we are the new stewards and managers assigned to clean up contaminated sites." The letter went on to say, "We know the trust of the community must be restored."

The offer to do the cleanup and settle claims suspended the legal discovery process, and in the interim Rizzo and Steve Crandall began to take tentative steps to get San Luis Obispo County counsel actively involved in the process. Securing the presence of the legal county representative at the table was not an easy accomplishment, since that department was willing to let Ken Alex do the job for them.

It was not an unreasoned reaction; it was comparable to letting the boss take over once the state became a partner in the legal action. However, Crandall and Rizzo felt strongly that their presence had a strong psychological impact on the union they had promoted, not only from a standpoint of strength in numbers, but also to show a unified front pushing for a fair settlement.

The two young attorneys worked long, hard hours convincing county counsels they had an important role to fill. Once that hurdle had been conquered, the next one was reconciling the difference between the dollar amount that Alex intended to ask for and the one that private attorneys felt was a more logical high-end number at which to begin negotiations for a settlement.

The first local settlement meeting with the legal principals was held at the water board in the early part of 1998. Word got out about it, and even though it was not a public meeting, people showed up and began pounding on the windows wanting to be admitted. The legal group was accustomed to having quiet conferences, with ten people attempting to make substantive negotiations; however, this one turned out to involve one hundred twenty people in a small room.

"There was no way we could do settlement negotiations," said Rizzo. "It was myself and our group of seven attorneys, Unocal's attorneys, Fish & Game. Before we knew it we were having mass settlement meetings where nothing got done [except for] a lot of yelling and screaming. However, it was still good because it alleviated a lot of the fear townspeople had."

The individual attorney groups had been meeting separately as well and knew going into the meeting what they were intending to ask for in settlement now that a cleanup was no longer at issue. However, getting to basic issues was impossible in front of a large public group. Attorneys from both sides did the next best thing, by tackling many of the concerns residents had about the type and the magnitude of the cleanup, without ever admitting it had been conceded by Unocal.

Rizzo knew the full excavation was going to happen, but was not able to tell anyone about it for months. He took heart in knowing that it had become a reality, in large measure because of the pressure his 800-pound gorilla had brought to the table. With Crandall and the Milberg Weiss powerhouse legal team on his side, he was no longer a small-town attorney who simply possessed a creative approach to law, with no experience to back it up.

The talents and experience of the entire team meshed well together, and, from the start, the legal partnership worked well together. The problems that came up had been dealt with honestly, with the realization that the team was breaking new ground, and everyone in the group worked hard to see it succeed.

14

THE COST OF A COMPANY TOWN

EIGHTY-seven-year-old Gladys Misakian's home sat atop some of the worst of the underground spill. As long as the petroleum products were unseen, the idea of cleaning them up was open to discussion, but when the health questions were raised, nothing else mattered for the moment. The pollution floated a mere eight feet below Misakian's home, a distance about the same as that from the carpet to the ceiling of her living room, which was unsettling to say the least.

While Lucy Lepley and the rest of the citizen army battled Unocal and worried about feeling assailed from all sides, Curt Batson of the San Luis Obispo County Health Department focused his attention solely on the question of health risks. As director of the Environmental Health Department, Batson had been involved in plans to conduct a health study long before Ed Masry and Erin Brockovich raised the red flag.

From the time the county was first notified that there was some contamination underneath Front Street, Batson had been involved, but not to monitor the cleanup. That responsibility remained with the Regional Water Board, but as testing continued, it was clear that the possibility of a public health impact existed. Early on, Batson recommended to the board that a health study was necessary.

Again, because so many agencies were involved, Batson became just one more partner in the growing investigation, along with the California offices of Environmental Health Hazard Assessment, the Environmental Health Investigations, and the Department of Toxic Substances Control. The local Air Pollution Control District also joined the team in designing the parameters of the study.

The group of agencies had no real problems, but as the project went on, they had to address new issues that were raised as information about the project escalated precipitously in 1996. What started out as an estimate of $250,000 to $300,000 to do the project ended up as a cost of around $750,000. The group had to identify all constituents of concern and to decide which areas needed to be sampled that had not been included in the original scope of the project. The changes arose from concerns raised during public meetings, and that input was included in the design of the project.

When Masry raised the ante in public disclosure, Batson said the project had to be done by an outside consultant to avoid any suggestion of bias. Toxicologist Dr. Alvin Greenberg of San Rafael was selected to run the study to determine what, if any, health impacts there might be. The proposed study evolved into an even bigger project, when it was determined that much of the existing data had to be gathered again because it failed to fit within the parameters decided, or to cover all the aspects determined to be necessary for scientific evaluation. The fault rested partly with Unocal for not reporting complete results of their own testing, and partly with the county, because their testing did not go far enough. With each test boring that was done, the contamination appeared in places not expected, making it necessary to drill more test holes until areas of clean sand were found. There was no other way to define the extent and limits of the spill underground.

Avila Beach residents had to learn a new vocabulary to understand what "significant health impact" and "significant risk" really meant. They also discovered they were now called "receptors," which was a variable that ranked children, adults, and visitors to the beach.

Cooperation from Unocal, which had been singularly absent

until that time, underwent a noteworthy change for the better. Batson felt it was because the company had conducted a similar health risk assessment of their own, the validity of which the community and various agencies had questioned, since that study had found no real risk to people as long as the petroleum products remained underground.

"I think they were anxious for us, as an independent third party doing an independent health study to verify or find if there was anything different from what they had found," said Batson. Given that Unocal's previous test results had been shown to be grossly inaccurate numerous times, it was a legitimate suspicion. Not only were the results reported by the company under suspicion, it was abundantly clear that dangerous information had been omitted from the documents. The water board had uncovered a number of errors in the testing reports submitted by Unocal, and that raised suspicion that remained in the minds of the local agency representatives. As long as Unocal selected the study consultants, the study was not going to garner much credibility. Although the company paid for the new study, it was the county that selected the contractor, and that degree of independence was necessary in the maelstrom of public opinion as well as to maintain the health department's integrity.

Masry's focus on tar balls made it difficult for him to be taken seriously, since local authorities knew that those ubiquitous annoyances to beachgoers have been floating up on west coast beaches for centuries. Tar balls are found up and down the coast, especially at Santa Barbara and Carpinteria, just to the south. Sometimes emerging as huge blotches of oil, they ooze up from natural cracks in the ocean floor and then float on the water until they are brought to land on rocks and sand by the action of waves and tides.

When Brockovich focused on that material, it appeared that she had found oil and then tried to characterize the entire beach by what she found in the tar balls. In order to make her case to the community, she would have had to prove that the entire beach had been covered with tar balls *and* that those particular tar balls had come from Unocal products. It was a legal stance doomed to failure, because it could not meet the burden of proof.

The health study had to be completed before final negotiations could be pursued regarding the level of cleanup that would have to be done. If significant health impacts were uncovered, a different level of cleanup would be required than if no health issues existed. The testing began, while ongoing studies continued to identify the materials, the depth and breadth of the compounds, and the concentrations of each. Testing was an evolving process that continued in all corners of the tiny town, and each piece of evidence helped to complete the puzzle.

Once people began to understand the unique language that each professional agency used, communication improved dramatically. The ultimate result was the increasing strength in the incredible partnership of residents, private organizations, responsible local agencies, the California state government, and federal interests.

Unocal finally realized they could not win with the tactics they were using. Digging in behind their line in the sand and demanding only bioremediation instead of immediate cleanup as a solution to the problem was not acceptable, and there were growing signs that the company was moving toward accepting its responsibility for the contamination and the necessity of cleaning up the town.

Batson figured the company had decided they needed to get into step with the health study if they were ever going to be able to put the situation to rest and move on. It was imperative that the health questions be answered. "You could feel the turnaround in cooperation," said Batson. With Unocal joining the agencies and the residents to find a solution to the problem, only Masry's team remained outside the united front of a resolute effort.

Residents who wanted to be tested were included in the study, and Gladys Misakian was one of them. She sat quietly, as a steady stream of reporters, toxicologists, and geotechnicians trooped through her small home. She answered a battery of questions about her health, as testers gathered samples to take to a mobile laboratory that was parked at the beach.

Outside samples were extracted from drilling into the ground, and samples were evaluated in terms of both their long-term effect on residents and the effects of the short-term exposure experienced by visitors. The contaminant levels were rated for both sedentary and active lifestyles, taking into consideration body size, body type, and varying inhalation rates. The equipment in the lab was able to measure as little as one micron per liter of air, according to Dr. Greenberg, and he told the *Telegram-Tribune* that if soil gas were present he would know it.

Beyond testing homes and businesses, Greenberg had to be certain of where to set his beach testing sites, since bonfires had been a part of Avila Beach for more than a century. It was important to avoid those areas where fire rings had been in use for a long time, because PAHs, natural products of combustion, would be found. The remains of fires had been washed deep into the sand in and around the fire pits, and those areas had to be avoided.

An important part of Greenberg's job was to determine which of the contaminants were Unocal's responsibility and which were from natural oil seeps or simply the by-products of civilization. The study had to sift through the effects of both toxic and non-lethal compounds. Even crude oil is a complex mixture of heavy metals and other elements, for example, sulfur and lead. Greenberg concerned himself mainly with two groups of volatile and nonvolatile substances, which contained benzene, toluene, ethylbenzene, and xylene. In particular, benzene is a carcinogen and is found in gasoline.

The second group, mainly PAHs, are also extremely hazardous. There are more than a hundred types of PAH compounds, and they are found more in diesel than in gasoline. Both gasoline and diesel made up a substantial part of the Avila Beach contamination. However, for human exposure to PAHs to be toxic, they need to be directly ingested, breathed into lungs, or absorbed through skin.

Testing in old homes is especially difficult, since they usually have lead paint somewhere in them. In some instances, lead paint degrades and flakes off, leaving some product to drift around the rooms. In any building, cigarette smoke and plastics that off-gas, auto exhaust coming in from the streets, and cleaning products used inside all have impact on the air samples, which meant that the list had to include products that can be identified, not all of which could be traced to their source.

Greenberg also had to map out the natural route of underground water as it travels toward the ocean, making the surf an important test site. He also had to test vegetation and trees, since heavy metals accumulate in plant tissues. The study complicated the lives of residents at Avila Beach and, worse, took dead aim at the businesses. With word out that the beach was covered with testers and equipment, tourists were a "no-show" at the busiest time of the year—again.

The pain in town was palpable, and as events moved toward a showdown, no one was spared the misery. The pace of activity was alarming to many, and without an end in sight, many residents expressed fear that it would never end. They expected to be ground down to nothing, either forced from their homes to escape the chemical dangers, or losing their businesses to the bad publicity that kept fearful would-be beach enthusiasts away.

When preliminary health study results revealed that there was no significant risk to human health as long as the petroleum was not airborne, there were still some people who didn't believe it, mainly because they felt the answer was too good to be true. Others were comfortable with the results, but in public meetings, comments still arose on both sides of the question. The idea of living on an enormous poisonous concoction was much too disquieting to end with the announcement that it wouldn't hurt anyone as long as it stayed where it was. Some people felt it was an invitation to let Unocal off the hook for cleanup, and that new fear rippled through the community.

At the health department, Curt Batson had to deal with both praise and condemnation regarding the results of the study. "It's the nature of my business," he said. "We are either moving too fast or requiring too much, or we are not moving fast enough or requiring enough. That is the nature of environmental health, because [the perception depends] on who is making the judgment."

Unocal tried to divide and conquer, but in Avila Beach that tactic no longer worked. While the residents lived every day and every hour with tension, fear, and apprehension, they remained resolute in their drive to get the corporate giant to take responsibility for the mess it had allowed to accumulate under the town.

At the Misakian house, Gladys could close her eyes and almost feel her house bobbing atop Unocal's underground petroleum lake.

TRUCE AND
CONSEQUENCES—
SETTLEMENT

O F all the partnership litigators, Rizzo had the least amount of experience in the field, but he had an inordinate amount of flair, dash, and daring. This, coupled with his uncommon sense of justice, made him a formidable negotiator. When he announced his intention to take the case to federal court in early 1997, he based his reasoning on the fact that federal judges are appointed for life and their caseloads differ in impact. Rizzo knew it was more commonplace for them to order a hundred-million- or two-hundred-million-dollar cleanup than it was for a local or state judge to do.

"We see federal judges get involved in school boards and discrimination cases trying to right these things, so it was worth at least giving it a shot there. If anything, the least we could expect was that it would give our case some leverage," he said. The strategy was firmly based, but the leverage actually came from Oakland when Deputy Attorney General Ken Alex joined the action.

Much of the time when government gets involved in a legal matter this way, attorneys expect for their own position in the matter to be compromised. Private legal counsels feel state attorneys do not understand the nuances of a local suit and what is important to the people involved. Putting together the legal partnership prevented the loss of local input, and the united front was pivotal in getting Unocal to agree to clean up the contamination. However, while that appeared to be the end of the legal wrangling for some of the team, reality dictated a different story.

The move toward reconciling differences was generally the responsibility of Unocal's lead corporate attorney, Mark Smith. It appeared to Rizzo that the company's board of directors finally came to the conclusion that excavation was the only way to get the matter settled. That was the one point on which there was no compromise for the partnership team. The crack in the wall of opposition Unocal had maintained for so long appeared when Smith took over the defense team.

Smith needed no time getting up to speed on negotiations, as he had been monitoring them for the corporate board. Rizzo credits him for convincing the decision makers at headquarters in southern California that cleanup was the best solution. "I don't know the inner machinations of Unocal," said Rizzo, "but I credit him. Mark spent time living here and dealing with Ken Alex. He could see the seriousness of the issues, especially with the agency boards and the explosiveness of public sentiment."

Letters to the editor in local newspapers made it clear that if Unocal had to get a jury in the region it was unlikely they would get a better solution to the problem than what they would get through negotiating for a settlement, which would include cleanup and some monetary compensation for the dislocation of residents. Word began to circulate wildly when a number of people in San Luis Obispo told the media they were called to participate in a poll concerning the controversy. The straw poll indicated that Unocal's popularity had shifted, putting the company somewhere between Adolph Hitler and Cambodia's Pol Pot. While it was never confirmed, Rizzo believed the poll was Unocal's way of testing public sentiment for a potential jury pool, since their acceptance of the cleanup demand came shortly afterward.

Negotiations for compensation were no easier than those for the cleanup dispute. County Supervisor Peg Pinard was suspicious of state involvement and attorneys in general. When Rizzo first worked with her, he got the feeling she didn't trust him either, because any time the prospect of getting money out of the disaster was mentioned, her general assessment was that greedy attorneys just wanted money for themselves. Rizzo knew she was still smarting over the loss of the PG&E settlement for Avila Beach, and she wanted passionately to ensure that the people who were affected were the ones who benefited. "I told her the money we expected to receive was going to a foundation we were creating for the townspeople," Rizzo said. "We were committed to fight to make sure that all the money stayed here in Avila."

Pinard was not the only official to make waves. State agency representatives on the MACC Coalition disagreed vociferously about the number of dollars that should be put on the table. Ken Alex was inclined to put out his best offer at the outset and remain firm. Steve Crandall and his associates at Milberg Weiss felt the preferred strategy was to come in high, pointing out that if they didn't do that, they would have no wiggle room in which to counter Unocal's anticipated low-ball offers. The differences in approach rocked the group to a point that moved Rizzo to anger.

At one momentous meeting, he gave what he laughingly calls his famous ten-hour speech. "I told all the government agencies basically to go to hell," he said. "We were sitting at the table and being attacked, with people who were saying how come these greedy attorneys are coming in, wanting to control everything." Rizzo felt they did not understand the mechanics of his lawsuit and had forgotten that it had been the genesis of their coming together. "I told the government agencies to go screw themselves, that we started this thing because they weren't doing their job." The tension had clearly taken a toll on his normally positive outlook.

He went on to rant about the fact that the people knew what was going on, and that Unocal had been there for eighty years, polluting the town, lying about it, and hiding the facts. "We know what's going on," he said firmly, "and the local government people are doing a great job, but you guys are not helping any by not supporting them. This has been dragging out for eight years, and the townspeople are now starting to get the facts when we have public meetings. Little or nothing has been done, and the state legislature says the law that we used is specifically meant to give the power to the people to take over and do the job. I filed it, I don't give a damn, we are going forward. We are not greedy environmentalists and attorneys. Furthermore, none of us would be here at the table if it weren't for our citizen lawsuit."

Rizzo was habitually positive in all his dealings, but in this case he was angry, upset, and brutally frank, adding that if it were not for the environmental court action, the agency attorneys would still be talking at board meetings, and Unocal would still be going over their heads to the state water board to appeal their decisions. In addition, the county would still be afraid of dealing with a polluting international corporation.

The meeting ended with a new focus for everything, but it did not remove the worry that the state would settle behind everybody's back. Ken Alex had been adamant about the cleanup and pushed for full excavation, having emphatically told Unocal that anything short of that would not be acceptable. Still carrying the taint of the unfair distribution of PG&E settlement funds, he was careful not to step into that quagmire again, even though, from a negotiation point of view, once the attorney general comes into a case, he can force a settlement, which would have been the cleanup. Alex could have gotten his settlement for both the state water board and Fish & Game without approval of the partner plaintiffs. Indeed, it appeared to Rizzo that Unocal was pushing to do just that, with a strategy to settle with the state and basically give the environmental group the finger. Suddenly the situation was "divide and conquer" again, with the environmentalists painted to look like they were in it solely for the money. If the tactic succeeded, the company could say that all public claims Rizzo's group represented had been handled as part of the settlement with the state. There was no way they would get any of the money, unless the settlement were kept "global," or inclusive of all parties.

All was not peaceful within Unocal's legal group either. Members of the group resented Mark Smith because he had direct contact with the corporate board of directors and had considerably more power to move negotiations than they had ever had. In addition, the team had been bruised and bloodied from years of confrontation, and legal outsiders wondered if they resented being left out of the final decision making.

In order to decide where to begin negotiations for the partnership, Milberg Weiss attorneys eased into the question of where to start the dollar demand amount for the partnership by determining the amount they hoped to eventually get. Rizzo was in the driver's seat again and found Milberg Weiss's veteran attorney Al Meyerhoff's rationale comical: "Okay we have water, everybody drinks water, ask more for the water than we do for salamanders and birds. How much do we have? Not enough, if we relate it to Prop 65." Then he turned directly to Rizzo and said, "Listen, kid, you have to ask for a lot more."

With sights on an eventual $20 million settlement, the partnership decided to begin by asking for twice that amount. They turned the case over to Rizzo, saying it was up to him to present the details of the settlement request. Not everyone thought they could get it, but at least they were back together again: "We ask for $40 million," Rizzo said.

The unity in the partnership was back in high gear. Following the meeting where Rizzo presented the demand to Unocal, both sides met at the company's local associate legal office of Andrew, Morris, and Buttery. Talks seemed to be going nowhere, and after the Unocal team withdrew to talk over the latest offer to settle, Steve Crandall started to get edgy. He had come two thousand miles and was missing his son's baseball game. Instead of spending an enjoyable weekend at home, he was sitting at a table waiting for Unocal attorneys to agree to an offer he knew would not stand. The more he talked about it, the thinner his patience got. Finally, he stood up and announced that the company had had more than enough time to assess the offer. "Let's go to lunch," he said. With a look at one another, the rest of the group agreed and walked out. They did not return after lunch. Crandall predicted that, not to be outdone, Unocal attorneys would return the favor at the next meeting. They did.

With negotiations in the final stages, San Luis Obispo County counsel finally became an official partner to the suit. There was some residual resentment because the county legal department was perceived as having contributed little except to get involved in the periphery of the case. Rizzo was unhappy that they took so long to come on board, but Crandall cautioned him, saying it was okay, because the county would have to be the overseer of the settlement and would be deeply involved with the permitting process required for the cleanup. With thousands of trucks, a potential for polluted air once the spill was exposed, and a myriad of regulations to deal with, Crandall said that Unocal might not realize it at the time, but it would be better for them to have the county involved as well. While Ken Alex could provide pressure in Oakland, a local presence was needed as well. The county would be the vehicle by which the company would be kept at the table.

Unocal attorneys were taken by surprise when County Counsel James Lindholm arrived with the partners at the next meeting. One of them said to Rizzo, "I thought you said everything was okay with the county." To which Lindholm replied simply, "We have responsibilities." However, even with the major stumbling block of agreeing to do the cleanup no longer in contention, the meetings did little toward reaching a consensus about the dollar amount. Rizzo said it appeared to him that Mark Smith was unable to get his team of attorneys to dump the emotional baggage they had accumulated over the years of stonewalling and controversy. In an audacious move, Smith sent Unocal's entire legal team to the mountains for a skiing weekend and then offered to meet with Rizzo and Alex privately.

There were seven Coalition attorneys at the meeting, with only Smith from Unocal. Negotiations went well, until they reached a $5–6 million difference, when Alex and Rizzo both sensed that Smith had reached his limit. No one was able to come up with a fresh perspective on how to resolve the impasse. At that point Rizzo, with his deep and abiding connection with Avila Beach, came up with alternatives. He asked if the company would consider funding the Front Street Enhancement Project.

Smith consulted with the board and came back saying that Unocal agreed to do the enhancement project, putting a $3-million-dollar value on it. Then Rizzo thought about land. The company had been buying out property owners for the last ten years and had become a major owner in Avila Beach. One particular triangle near the beach that was Unocal's appeared to be a perfect place for a park. The location would allow a grassed area so children could go from it directly to the beach without having to cross the street. The area could also be made accessible for handicapped people to enjoy. He posed the question to Smith, "You've got a lot of land down there, what about that corner piece of property? Can you give us that for a park?" Smith phoned corporate headquarters. They agreed to donate the land, build a park, and give it to the county.

As they drove toward completion of the settlement, Smith also offered a small building on another piece of land, saying it could be made into a historical center. Eight attorneys stood up, shook hands on the agreement, and settled the monumental case that had vexed the collective minds, security, and serenity of Avila Beach.

The historic settlement listed as plaintiffs: Avila Alliance, Communities for a Better Environment, and Environmental Law Foundation, plus: People of the State of California ex rel. Regional Water Quality Control Board Central Coast Region, Department of Fish & Game, and County of SLO (San Luis Obispo).

Unocal agreed to pay $18 million in cash, transfer title for three parcels in Avila Beach to the county for a park, and construct a "turnkey" community park, meaning it would be complete and ready for immediate use. Of the cash settlement, the Front Street Enhancement Project received $3.5 million; $6 million went to California Fish & Game for restoration projects in Avila Beach; $2.5 million was set aside for biological studies and restoration of the oil contamination; $3 million went to the Avila Beach Endowment Foundation established by the Avila Alliance; $1 million went to the Regional Water Board for projects in the Avila area; and $1.5 million covered attorneys fees for the Avila Alliance, Communities for a Better Environment, and the Environmental Law Foundation. Another $3.5 million was awarded to California Fish & Game for restoration projects related to recreation. With Unocal no longer a part of the town's economic base, this last part of the package was very important for the town's future. Rizzo felt the settlement represented a successful closure to his quest for a beach-cleaning machine.

Unocal accepted responsibility for the reconstruction of the seawall following the cleanup excavation, replacement of utilities, and repairs of any damage to the Avila pier and Yacht Club. The company declined to estimate the cost of the cleanup, but industry insiders were quick to put a quarter-billion-dollar tag on it. Coupled with buyouts and private party settlements for upheaval, the cost to Unocal is conservatively estimated to be a half billion dollars—quite a sum for a town less than a half mile long and having fewer than four hundred residents.

In accepting the judgment, plaintiffs agreed to resolve all parts of the suit under California Water Code, Fish & Game Code, Proposition 65, California Business and Professions Code, and California Hazardous Waste Control Act.

Every dime of the $18 million was to be either sent to Avila Beach directly or held in trust for the town to use for projects, by the State of California through the Department of Fish & Game and the water board. Avila Beach was finally recognized as having been damaged and deserving of redress.

16

THE WAY WE WERE

OVERNIGHT everything changed—again. It took a major shift in consciousness for Avila Beach residents to cope with the reality of cleanup because with it the town faced massive destruction. Until the agreement was made public, everyone knew what was necessary to clean up the contamination. People had read and reread reams of documents about what the spill contained, where it was located, and what it would take to get rid of it. The scientific data put emotional distance between the people and the problem, but now it was intensely felt. The elephant that had sat quietly in the parlor for so long had mutated into a raging leviathan hell-bent on trampling the town.

With one proclamation, Unocal morphed from a besieged behemoth into an active partner in meeting the enormous challenge of decimating a town and way of life, then setting the stage for the birth of a new one. To cope better with the dreadful future, residents imprinted the way it was on their memory and minds—every detail of a beloved funky oasis that would soon be gone. It was even more disturbing than living daily with the impending death of a loved one. It was the death of the Avila Beach family itself, and hardest to take was the fact that the decision for the town's ruin had been forced on them when they had to make the wrenching drive for a complete cleanup. There was no lady behind one of the doors of choice, as in the famous Frank Stockton tale. Tigers were behind both doors. The Avila Beach that had survived for a hundred years was about to join the San Luis Obispo lamplighter to exist only in the hearts and minds of the residents and in the history books.

The two opposing sides in the long struggle became united in a single purpose, as residents slowly shifted to new groupings: those in the area surrounding the downtown who would not lose their homes, and those whose lives would be disrupted for an unknown number of years as their homes and businesses were destroyed and rebuilt again. The rest were resigned to move out permanently.

Unocal assigned Jim Allen, a local insurance broker, to help residents deal with their relocation needs and make financial settlements with those who made a claim. Allen, who shared his name with one of the prominent town residents, was immediately dubbed "The Evil Jim Allen" by the townspeople. By dealing openly with everyone, it didn't take long before he won over the town, and, although everyone eventually agreed he was not evil, the name stuck.

Saro Rizzo and the Avila Alliance also shifted gears and started the legal steps to establish a foundation that could accept their share of the funds that were awarded in the settlement. At the county planning department, David Church moved in a new direction after years of confrontational dealings with Unocal. He began to put together the Avila Beach Specific Plan, incorporating what the people wanted to keep and what they would be willing to see changed. "There were a few people very sad about it," Church remembers, "but overall I think people who rallied for the cleanup project were resigned to that kind of emotional magnitude. They were amazed it was happening."

The first hurdle was to define *funky,* since that was the one quality most people said they wanted to see preserved in the business district. It had never been necessary to define the word before. "The character of this town is uppermost in the heart of everyone who lives here," Lucy Lepley said.

Avila Beach faced a scorched-earth, start-from-the-ground-up kind of planning, meaning changes to the level of the streets, the placement of utilities, and the flow of traffic, as well as a host of tourist-friendly amendments. However, when it came to defining funky, no one could do it specifically. Church brought hundreds of slides to community meetings to show what other beach communities looked like. Hour after hour they looked at building facades, layout plans, window arrangements, construction materials, and architectural details. The only thing everyone could agree on was what they didn't want: metal, too much glass, glitz, and what was derisively termed "Newport Beach," a synonym for upscale Yuppie sameness.

Some residents feared rampant growth of businesses that would turn the town into a pricey Malibu or Santa Cruz. They foresaw the loss of friendliness with a dramatic change in character and wanted to keep Avila Beach mellow and neighborly. They addressed the lack of space and the single road into and out of town. Although many worried about high-rises producing a kind of southern California congestion, others looked forward to some modernization.

It wasn't that the residents were unalterably opposed to change. The families had adapted several times, from fishing to include the oil business, and then to absorb tourism. They were able to embrace those changes because they were a family—in their homes, in their neighborhoods, and throughout the entire town. Many longtime residents recalled changes in the past, especially Betty Woody and Betty Terra. Woody remembered the onset of World War II most vividly, and she kept some of her memorabilia from her husband's years as a corpsman in a small metal first aid box. "There were a lot of soldiers down on the beach, and in the hills above from here to Shell Beach," she remembered. "Mama had one of these big old blue speckled coffee pots, and she would fill it with hot coffee and then go up and down the whole beach with that pot. My sisters and I would take turns coming behind with the cups for the service people." Coffee was rationed at that time, and people who didn't drink it would give their coupons to Betty's mother so she could continue to serve the military men.

Woody loves to tell about an incident some years later when her parents were in New Orleans for Mardi Gras. "They began talking with another couple while on a boat tour, and Mama said she was from San Luis Obispo. She said that because she figured no one would have heard of Avila. The young man said to my mother, 'You know, I'm not too familiar with San Luis Obispo because I wasn't at Camp Roberts, but I was stationed at Avila Beach.'" Betty's mother told him that was where she lived, and she was shocked to find that what he remembered most about being in the tiny town was a lady and her daughters serving the soldiers hot coffee on the beach. When she told him she was that woman, he immediately wrapped her in a huge bear hug. "When they came back from that trip, Mama was still walking on air!" Woody said.

Betty Terra associates Avila Beach with Union Oil and fishing. Her father worked for the company, and she remembers him working on many oil leaks there. "Mom used to take his clothes up to the refinery so they could put them in solvent to get the oil off," she said. "Then you had to air them out and be careful when you washed them so they didn't explode." She was sad about the destruction of the town and prefers to remember the good times. Her fondest memories of growing up in Avila Beach are connected with the freedom, hikes in the spring and hot dogs on the beach, as well as times when the albacore would run and everyone stayed up all night to clean and ice them. Most of all she remembers hikes with her dad when he had time off. "We would hike from Avila to a trail behind the old Marre Hotel and up to the lighthouse, because my dad knew the keeper there. We'd take a picnic lunch and spend the day up at the lighthouse."

Other times the family would hike up a road to swim nearby in natural warm springs. "My mother would save lard cans and we'd go picking wild blackberries up there, too. My dad had this old cowboy hat, and he would line it with leaves and we'd fill it with berries first. That was for my brother and I because we always fell in the nettles. Before we came home, him and I invariably fell into those darned horse nettles, and I tell you I'm talking about something that stings." Blackberry juice was used as a palliative to ease the pain, and by the time the children returned home with their pickings, Terra said, "[we] looked like we were in war paint from the berry juice he rubbed on our faces and hands. We'd also have six lard buckets of berries." Terra said her mother would stay up until late making wild blackberry pies, which, later, she'd serve warm topped with sweet cream from the family's cow. Years later when her father was dying from a brain tumor, the last thing Terra got to do with him was hike up to See Canyon, where they picked a bucket of wild blackberries. "He didn't fill his hat that time, and I didn't fall in the nettles."

Life in Avila Beach was closely connected with the fishing industry. Many old-timers remembered that young men rowed out to the boats at night to hang kerosene lanterns in the rigging, to meet the U.S. Coast Guard's requirement that every boat have a light on at night. The following day the lamps would be retrieved and refilled with kerosene for that night's lighting. It was similar to the Cattaneo family lighting the streetlamps in San Luis Obispo city.

In a town that has changed so little, it's not surprising to find that the people there have strong memories of World War II. That particular time defined Avila Beach like no other, perhaps because danger was not imagined, but real. Japanese ships came to the port on a regular basis to take on oil until as recently as September 1941, just before the tragedy at Pearl Harbor in December of the same year. It was not lost on residents that the location of strategic oil resources was well known by the Japanese, and Avila Beach prepared to be another Pearl Harbor.

The night of December 7, 1941, the town was guarded by citizens and Union Oil Company employees, one of whom was given a twenty-four-inch-long drift pole to defend himself and the landing area at the end of the company wharf. The man remained at his post from midnight to 8 A.M. It was a long, cold night, and by the next day he was glad to see military units come to take over. A short time after the conflict began, a Japanese submarine landed a large shell onto U.S. soil near the town of Cayucos, twenty-five miles north of Avila Beach. The tanker *Montebello* was scheduled to sail, but since three other oilers had reported brushes with enemy submarines, the captain was reluctant to leave port. He refused to take the ship out, but since the chief mate had the necessary papers to captain the ship, he volunteered to do so under pressure. On December 23, a torpedo sunk the ship a few hours after sailing from the Union Oil pier. The entire crew made it to shore safely. The *Montebello* still lies off Morro Bay in about nine hundred feet of water, her oil cargo still intact.

The military units stationed at Avila Beach were well trained for everything except the demands and sounds of life at the ocean's edge. The strict blackout was hard on Union Oil employees, who were assigned to the end of the wharf when ships arrived. It was nearly impossible to find bowlines in the dark, and if they used a flashlight, soldiers threatened to shoot it out. In addition, the newcomers were unaccustomed to hearing tides come in and recede, the changing action of waves on the pier pilings and buoys, or the clanging of rigging against hooks on the boats. All the unfamiliar sounds made them edgy, and it was not uncommon in the early days of the war for townspeople to have to dodge bullets in the dark.

Early in the war there was no military protection for the port, but resourceful residents and the military created the look of huge artillery armaments by arranging pier pilings poking out from fishnets. Later real guns were installed, but residents remembering those days laughed, saying that they felt they were living in a defense situation that was like *McHale's Navy* meets the *Minnow* of *Gilligan's Island*. The U.S. Navy presence at the time consisted of purse seiners and tuna boats, with one three-inch gun on the bow and a dozen depth charges on deck. Until the U.S. Army mobilized fully, Avila Beach formed a militia that patrolled the coast and the lighthouse. It certainly was a homegrown navy.

U.S. Navy landing boats were taken on shakedown cruises in Avila before they were shipped overseas, and local fishermen towed targets from their boats for naval gunnery practice. It was no job for the fainthearted, considering the state of military preparedness at the time. The sailors' skills improved quickly to the point that, while they did not hit the targets, in order to avoid destroying them, tired men would sometimes deliberately hit the towrope to end the exercise for the day.

At a time when the rest of the county had to deal with the probability of war, the West Coast in general, and the central coast in particular, was reeling from the reality of it. People felt they were living in a town with a huge target painted on it, because while there was little danger expected from the air, it was graphically demonstrated that they were vulnerable from the sea. Just one shell into the tank farm could set off another 1920s kind of explosion and fire. Fearful residents in southern California moved inland to canyons away from shore, but in Avila Beach they defiantly thumbed their collective noses at the enemy across the ocean.

The war dictated that the lights on buoys be turned out and the bells be bound, so enemy subs would have no navigation aids. On foggy days, resident Joe Scuri would ring a large bell at the end of the pier so the lumber schooner and other friendly ships could find their way through the gloom. Avila Beach lore was enriched when Scuri signed on to a tanker that was hauling gasoline to the military in the Pacific. The ship was torpedoed not far offshore in the Indian Ocean. On deck was a load of mules destined for Burma, and when the tanker went down, some of the men, Scuri among them, survived by riding the mules to shore.

Young boys delivered newspapers to boats in the harbor. One time during World War II, two of them hitched a ride on a U.S. Navy boat. Soon after leaving the marina, the boat's captain received an emergency call, and the boys were left on a buoy, where they waited half an hour for another boat to pick them up and take them back to the mainland. The daily tension did not ease until the war in the Pacific changed to the American offensive following the Battle of Midway.

Some memories were sweet, especially when rancher Tony Dutra would bring a load of corn on the cob to the beach. Kids cooked it in pots filled with seawater over beach fires. Later they took large pillowcases or small bed mattress covers, wet them in the ocean, then ran along the beach to fill them with air. Tied off quickly, the cases became huge balloons on which to surf. There were five seasons in Avila Beach. In addition to spring, summer, fall, and winter was salmon and albacore season, when the town was open and working 24/7.

Growing up secure in a secluded beach community may have offered limited opportunities, but it provided people a close relationship to everything and everyone who lived there. During the 1990s as information ballooned about the huge spill under the town, loyalties were conflicted by remembering a time when fishermen were sometimes unable to pay accounts, and Union Oil Company had carried them. Sometimes, if they were unable to catch up, the debt was even forgiven. In the years before health insurance, the company helped employees with large medical bills, supported Little League teams, and helped build backstops as well as the Scout House, which is still in use. Company people transported Girl Scouts and Camp Fire troops to camps. In 1920, the company promoted a baseball team and encouraged other groups to form teams so that they could play regularly. At one point in job recruitment, Union Oil suggested that candidates for employment should be able to play baseball.

After the settlement, Archie McLaren was part of the group who remained in Avila Beach. He saw very little disagreement in the community regarding the town's future and felt the process had been cathartic. Although they did not come to a 100-percent agreement, there was enough of a consensus that McLaren felt the town had found a common ground. "We went from a dilapidated town to one with a future," he said.

Jim Cummings was happy to see the plans for growth and positive change. In the *Telegram-Tribune*, he pointed out that many of the old buildings were terribly termite infested, and suggested that it wouldn't be a good idea to spray, because the bugs were probably the only things holding the buildings up.

It was still hard to let go. The Avila Grocery Store had been built in the early 1900s as a garage. Sometime between 1912 and 1920, it became a general store and a post office with quarters in back for the postmaster/owner. The post office moved out in the 1960s, and the store continued as the social center of the town where people came for their first morning cup of coffee. It was also the place they met to talk over what was happening with the crisis. The two benches outside were in constant use, as residents who were not facing total destruction grieved with those who were.

The Custom House, which was slated to be razed, had been built in 1927 as headquarters for U.S. Customs agents, who occupied it until the 1930s. Then it was used as a barbershop for some years and later as a home. In the 1960s it became a takeout food establishment, and in 1979, a restaurant with a unique patio.

David Church did not hurry any decisions, knowing that the worst was yet to come. Making choices about the future was easier than facing bulldozers and wrecking balls. However, there was little time to spend getting used to the idea of destruction. Once Unocal came on board and agreed to do the cleanup, it set out on an entirely new path. Aware that permitting would require time, company representatives worked hard to get the process moving quickly. Unocal hired Jacobs Engineering to do the operation, and one important requirement in the contract was to have an ombudsman in town full time. Wisely, Unocal withdrew as an obvious presence, leaving it to Jacobs to begin the enormous job. In retrospect, it was a turnaround time for all concerned, in that it signaled the company's intentions to get the job done, do it well, and disappear. Unocal was about to make history again; this time for its method of cleanup and for the time it took to complete the job.

DAWN ON THE
BATTLEFIELD

‑‑‑‑‑‑‑‑‑‑‑‑‑‑‑‑‑‑‑‑‑‑‑‑‑‑‑‑‑‑‑‑‑‑‑‑

THE joy of settling the cleanup problem was undercut by the reality of the destruction the town faced and the impending loss of identity, lifestyle, security, and sense of belonging associated with it. The plume was under every building in the commercial area downtown except for the motel, and, in addition to homes, apartments, and the trailer park, they would have to be moved or destroyed in order to clean up the spill.

It was akin to telling Americans they had to write a new national anthem, draw up an alternate pledge of allegiance, and design another flag to honor. And, oh, yes, you're still Americans. Avila Beach residents had to reinvent themselves without their sacred sense of place and, worse, to witness the destruction of their comfort zone.

The idea of excavation left many people depressed and wondering how they would cope with living in a town that was slated to become a huge, open-pit mining operation. Lucy Lepley said at the time the stress level was high, and she was surprised that things had not gotten violent. "Life was once free and easy," she observed. "Now it's a continuing nightmare." Angel Reloquio worked at Mr. Rick's, a business that was located directly above the plume, and lived in an eclectic one-bedroom apartment that was decorated on the outside with a brilliant fish-and-mermaid mural. He faced the loss of his job *and* his home.

The long good-bye began, and it was heartrending, out there for everyone to see. Every available wall, window, and door in the area to be destroyed was a canvas for sweet sentiment and sad farewells. Emotional limericks, poems, drawings, and graffiti covered everything downtown. The following is one such sentiment:

> *We sat here and drank our beer and hung out with our friends.*
> *Unocal's tearing down our beautiful town.*
> *But here the party never ends.*
> *We'll miss you Avila Beach.*

The place where everybody knew your name was about to become more anonymous. People dreaded the loss of a Norman Rockwell kind of place, where kids could get ice cream on the promise that their parents would come to pay for it later. Not many communities are so comfortable that families can let their children roam freely, knowing that more than a few people in town will know them well enough to remind them when it is time to go home. Nearly half of all residents would be displaced, many permanently. Evelyn Phelan's collection of stuffed bears went into plastic bags for safekeeping, and they would remain there for two years. Living on the very edge of the pending destruction, she had her first vacancies in twenty-five years, when tenants could not face the change and demolition.

At the April 1998 water board meeting, where the historical agreement was to be accepted, businessman Mike Rudd, whose test drilling discovery had set off the ultimate agony of the town, invited Unocal to call him about rebuilding his business. His voice broke with emotion. Lucy read what her mother-in-law wrote: "The pain never goes away. We live with it. A precious feeling of security was destroyed." Her nine-year-old granddaughter Julie, speaking for herself and her younger sister said, "Please don't let this pollution be a part of our future." The family had lived in a town that still had three-digit phone numbers, when many U.S. citizens had seven-digit numbers.

Saro Rizzo spoke in favor of the settlement. He praised the hard work and cooperation among the agency representatives, and Unocal attorney Mark Smith for his efforts in seeing it through. His voice trembled when he thanked the people of Avila Beach for their support and attendance at so many meetings, as well as their willingness to face the disruption to come.

Stephen Sawyer, senior attorney for the California Fish & Game, observed, "There has never been a cleanup project in California with the impact on a community this one will have on Avila Beach." Deputy Attorney General Ken Alex emphasized, "All parties to the suit wanted excavation and agreed to keep penalty money in Avila Beach. We are a united front." The water board agreed to the settlement unanimously.

The Unocal cleanup plan was expected to take a minimum of two years, involve 100,000 cubic yards of contaminated material to be excavated, and require forty permits from twenty different agencies. The timetable listed the mobilization of field necessities, removal of structures, including a section of the Avila Pier, relocation of utilities, demolition of structures, installation of interlocking sheet pile forty feet into the ground around the entire area of contamination, excavation of clean sand, removal of the contamination, backfill and compaction of sand, return of saved structures, reconstruction of the pier, removal of sheet pile, restoration of the site, and completion of the Front Street Enhancement Project. It was an epic project for any city, let alone for a small town.

A Unocal spokesman said the company would restore the most cherished areas as compensation for those impacted by the pollution and declared it was committed to maintaining clear communications regarding all issues affecting Avila Beach. Coming from an organization that had fought to exclude economic impacts in the EIR, the declaration rang a bit hollow. The buildings deemed historically significant were the Avila Pier, the Avila Grocery Store, the Yacht Club, the Old Custom House, Mr. Rick's, the Sea Barn, and the Avila Café. Only two of them, the grocery and the Yacht Club, were deemed safe to move.

There was some remaining conflict when the California Coastal Commission required the town to build tourist facilities instead of permanent resident apartments above the new businesses. Peg Pinard took issue with the commission, citing the consensus in town that the changes would make the business district a ghost town during the off-season with all the old houses, apartments, and trailers gone. Watching out for each other was a part of the old ethos that had sustained the town for so long. Residents wanted hometown people in the downtown area to be a presence to balance the inevitable influx of strangers. It was a small matter to the commission, but a very large one to the townspeople. Happily, the people won, leaving the commissioners to wonder what the big deal was.

Avila Beach Fire Chief Robert Gorman Jr. had double the stress of the others in town. He had to deal with issues all day with Unocal and the agencies, and when he went home, he had to deal with additional problems as a homeowner. At work he needed to remain neutral for the most part. "I didn't choose the oil spill, and I didn't choose the cleanup," he said, "but now that we are at that option, let's get it done the most effective way possible."

Gorman's role in the cleanup was ongoing, having attended nearly every meeting, reviewing and signing off on the EIR and permits, then overseeing everything during the "Big Dig," as the cleanup was termed, when compared with the "Little Dig." Gorman was the person responsible for public safety, and to dig up sand soaked with thousands of gallons of flammable liquid was no ordinary project. Removing sand, pumping water, or cutting old pipelines with simple torches was potentially hazardous because of the always-present danger of fire and explosion.

The fire chief put together a listing of safety requirements Jacobs Engineering had to comply with, in order to ensure the safety of the people. Pounding sheet pile into the ground to form a barrier, for example, possibly could release toxic vapors. That required a monitoring system developed by the air pollution control district to detect and measure levels of possibly dangerous air. Gorman planned a no-smoking zone around the cleanup site. He also forced the company to use a canopy instead of the huge tent they had planned to erect at the tank farm to transfer contaminated dirt. Unocal was worried about strong odors, but Gorman was worried about an explosion or fire, especially with trucks and tractors inside the tent.

The fire department purchased equipment to measure the ambient air, so that if toxic odors reached a critical level, Gorman's crew could spray foam on the entire project to trap the vapors. Even with a consultant hired to help him make decisions, the small-town fireman at times had to face down a cadre of lawyers in order to create a plan that would anticipate possibilities within a project, the likes of which had never been done before. He met with other fire chiefs in the San Luis Obispo region and consulted with still others from the Los Angeles area. Some of the things that needed to be done had never been faced in the state, such as protecting a populated town, dealing with a high water table, and dealing with the type of product that had been spilled. On occasion these difficulties had been met on military bases in isolated areas, but never with people ten feet from the sheet pile and oil.

As the number of historical structures able to be saved dwindled, the number of homes and businesses to be destroyed grew. Some were determined to be too fragile to make the move or to withstand the vibrations from work that would be done in close proximity to them. Some slated to move were questionable, including Gladys Misakian's house.

Robert Gorman and his wife, Elaine, knew Gladys did not want to leave and asked David Church to explain her options. Church didn't tell her what to do, but did explain all the choices open to her. Gladys wanted Unocal to move her home and place it back on her property. It was not a technically difficult job or even a very expensive one to do, but inexplicably Unocal representative Mike Biggi refused her request. That left her with few options—move, litigate, or make a deal. She chose to make a deal. "She was pushed into a corner," remembers Elaine. "Before the decision was made, she was one of the spiciest people I know, and it was terrible to see her later, so tired and dragging." Gladys moved to a small apartment, but didn't have the boat in her window as she had for the last forty years. A large model, the boat had rested in her picture window, and each Christmas, she and her husband, Jake, would decorate it.

Despite the expected upheaval, most residents were positive about the outcome. Unocal spokesman Denny Lamb was not as upbeat as others about the project. He said publicly that it was a complicated project, and since there was a history of confrontation in town, it could be seriously impeded by sidewalk superintendents with cell phones. He added that the track record in Avila Beach was not good, and he had little confidence that the situation would change.

For a couple of months while the project built up steam, Beachcomber's Bill Price could still come to work wearing an Aloha shirt and sandals to sell souvenirs and rent boogie boards. He'd still have time to fasten a steely eye on children, telling them if they brought the board back clean, he'd give them a Tootsie Pop. Then he would snap the clipboard fastener sharply and say if they brought it back dirty, "I put your finger in here."

Price and his wife, Linda, had two businesses downtown, and when the Beachcomber was slated to be the first building to be torn down, he stayed open as long as possible, then moved the inventory to the Sea Barn. By a curious coincidence, one of his stores was the first to be destroyed in the initial phase of deconstruction, and the other was the last to go down in the final phase. Price was also the first to rebuild in the new downtown.

Regular tourists, who had vacationed in Avila Beach each year until the news of the contamination made them no-shows, began to reappear. They were seen taking pictures from one end of town to the other—all the beach shops, walk-up fast food places, bars, and restaurants—as if to preserve what was about to be lost. The people were very welcome, but Price found the parade of media satellite trucks and mobile antennas very unsettling. However, later he might gladly have traded them for the incredible noise made by the installation of sheet piling.

The settlement agreement had a palliative effect on emotions, but did little to bridge the gulf between residents and Unocal. Public opinion in the rest of the region was muted, but the *Telegram-Tribune* sympathized in an editorial likening the oil contamination to a plague.

Unocal opened a claims office in Avila Beach, and not surprising to residents, it was initially unmarked and not consistently manned from 8 A.M. to 5 P.M., as the company said it would be. From the time of the draft EIR hearings, townspeople had pushed for an Avila Remediation Center in town to give them a one-stop location for dealing directly with Unocal. The company robustly fought the proposal and won. The final EIR made no mention of a remediation center, leaving the company to do as it saw fit in dealing with claims.

Residents of the trailer park were the first to be hit with eviction notices. Renters had thirty days to vacate. The owners' attorney sent letters of apology for the need to move and yielded to pressure when the renters demanded more time and some compensation for having to move. That protest netted each of them an extra month and $500. One renter said she felt like life was a Pac Man game, and she was the dot being eaten. Others said they felt like they were at the bottom of the food chain, even though more than half of Avila Beach residents were renters.

Denny Lamb of Unocal showed a remarkable lack of compassion, saying he didn't think the company owed the trailer park residents anything, and that it was up to the owners to deliver a tenant-free parcel, as per the purchase agreement. In all fairness, Unocal was forced to purchase the entire property, when all that had been required was to test a small part of the parcel next to the contamination. The owners had refused entry, and since the company *had* to get access, Unocal was forced to buy the entire property in order to comply with the water board's order to clean up the entire plume. The poor treatment of the tenants was unjustly attributed to Unocal.

The Lighthouse Bar and Grill was scheduled for demolition in the first phase. It had been a second home to fishermen, students, bikers, surfers, and tourists, and the last day of business, the bar opened with a potluck and offered a "happy hour" all day long. T-shirts were sold, showing a picture of the establishment and the caption, "Last Call at the Lighthouse." Patrons came in droves to write love notes all over the inside and outside walls, leaving thank-yous and good-byes to the bar and to the owner, Oakland Raider Dan Conners. A group of workers from the Diablo nuclear plant, who met regularly each Thursday after the shift ended at 1:30 A.M., made their final salute to the place.

The project began at a time when weather forecasters were on network television describing what was expected to be the worst El Niño ever to reach the West Coast. Before Unocal and Jacobs Construction could start digging, it was necessary to truck in tons of new sand to cover the contamination under the beach so it would not come to the surface as a result of weather. That same sand would have to be dug out again to get to the oil beneath, when the project got to that point. Residents had to face not only the destruction of the town, but also the possibility of the additional wrath of natural, but extraordinary, weather. The weather lived up to its billing, and at one point Gerhardt Hubner observed ocean waves pushing up pier planks.

A month after the announcement of the settlement in Avila Beach, Unocal also settled the problem at Guadalupe Dunes with the State of California for another $43 million. California Attorney General Dan Lungren was quoted in the *Los Angeles Times* as saying it was "possibly the largest environmental settlement in the history of California." However, it was not the costliest. Avila Beach was, because of the number of private agreements the company had made over the previous ten years with property owners and renters, over and above the cost of the cleanup itself.

DUST, DESTRUCTION
AND DISMEMBERMENT

EXCEPT for the feeling of vindication it gave, it mattered little to people on both sides that confidential papers had been leaked from Unocal files clearly demonstrating that not only did the company know about the contamination, but that it had opted to conceal that information from San Luis Obispo County agencies.

In one document dated July 21, 1977, the Unocal investigators into the explosion near Pete Kelley's restaurant admitted that it was the company's responsibility:

> *Preliminary low head pressure tests were imposed on our two gasoline lines. One was positively tight, the other showed a low rate decay of pressure, indicating either a small hole in the pipe or a small leak through a block valve. Further trenching and "well-pointing" in the area resulted in small accumulations of liquid hydrocarbon. Samples of accumulated hydrocarbon, saturated soil and of gasoline moved through our pipelines, were sent to Union's Research Department for analysis and identification. All tests are not yet complete, but preliminarily, there is close correlation between Union's Super Grade and the sample of the oil taken from the oil soaked soil.*

The gasoline lines were set in water and equipment brought in to impose a full head pressure test on the pipeline that was suspect. While imposing the pressure test, a rapid pressure decay developed. Continued injection of water into the line has caused water to surface at a point along the pipeline near the building where the explosion occurred.

The effect of public relations was not ignored in the report: *"To date, the publicity has been minimal. A small item about the explosion and the investigation appeared in the San Luis Obispo Telegram-Tribune. Union Oil was not mentioned in the article."*

In a September 1993 internal memo, years before the company insisted that their proposal for drilling wells to draw up the contamination vapor would work and work well in Avila Beach, Unocal experts said, *"They were also discussing what to do with the vapor extraction system since it is being less and less effective. Politically, it probably needs to say in place 'forever.'"*

The February 21, 1996, document from the Arizona State Attorney General's Office underscored Unocal's policy to do nothing until forced. The company employee witness said under oath, "Basically . . . he had documentation in his notes that we were to spend no dime before its time, which meant that an agency letter was in the file instructing us to proceed with some sort of investigation."

Asked if that meant he had notes instructing him to wait until the agency sent a letter before proceeding with investigations, the witness answered, "That's correct."

A surreal quiet descended on Avila Beach in the wake of celebrating the improbable win in the fight with Unocal Corporation. No one doubted it was the calm before the storm, but in the absence of angry rhetoric, it was a necessary time to recover enough equilibrium to meet the inevitable. Even before the destruction began, the community felt like a ghost town. Manager of the Custom House restaurant, Chris Chandless, said Front Street was "the boulevard of broken dreams."

Some people involved in the battle viewed the final settlement as a precedent for all communities contaminated by tank farms, refineries, and especially pipelines. The estimated cleanup costs for Avila Beach were surpassed in California only by those of Iron Mountain near Redding in northern California. That the case will impact future U.S. court cases is a certainty, even though some attorneys call it sui generis, or "of its own kind," in lay terms.

While residents might have felt they were sleepwalking after so much confrontation, debate, and turmoil, the quiet did not last. Once the decision was made to clean up the town, Unocal set to work as though it had planned to do it from the start, demonstrating a commitment to get the job done in the shortest time possible.

Work on the cleanup began quickly. The mural commissioned earlier by Unocal to make the town look less distressed was removed and returned to Bellevue–Santa Fe School where it had been painted by students. Water, sewage, telephone, television cable, and gas lines were rerouted around the afflicted area, and trenches dug for that part of the project immediately showed oil. It painted a black picture of the future *Big Dig*—Unocal's public relations term for what Lucy Lepley called "the coming desecration."

New estimates of destruction listed fifteen to twenty homes and businesses that would have to go. Saro Rizzo pointed out, "Everything will come to a stop. There won't be any tourism in a town that depends on tourism." On a larger but comparable scale, it was like General Motors shutting down for a year and a half, closing Broadway in New York, or fencing off the Loop in Chicago. The *Telegram-Tribune* pointed out that Unocal was on a buying spree in Avila Beach, having purchased seventeen properties in town since the contamination was discovered in 1988. That made the company the largest single owner in the downtown, with ownership of one-quarter of all properties there.

The project began as the West Coast braced for winter weather. Preparations in Avila Beach had to include extra precautions for the possibility of destructive hundred-year storms. One by one buildings were vacated, inventories transferred, and keepsake items taken for reuse and recycling. Specialized crews removed all toxic materials such as asbestos. Tourists continued to come, not looking to be entertained, but rather like they were coming to a wake.

Preparations for the sheet piling installation process were similar to those that would be done for an earthquake, and the comparison was apt. The pounding would last almost all day long, from 7 A.M. to 4 P.M., six days a week, for two months, with the only real respite from noon on Christmas and New Year's Eves, and resuming immediately after each holiday. Residents had to fasten shelves securely to walls; put heavy objects on lower shelves; assign breakables to low, closed cabinets; hang heavy items away from where people sit; brace overhead fixtures; repair old wiring and gas connections; secure water heaters to studs and bolt them to the floor; and store flammables on bottom shelves of closed cabinets that had latches.

The dance of destruction began when the Avila Grocery was raised and moved to the parking lot behind the community building. It escalated when the Yacht Club was also raised, dropped onto flatbeds, and rolled at a snail's pace to Wild Cherry Canyon, near the entrance of the Diablo Canyon nuclear power plant. It was ironic that for a year and a half the members would have to use a gate entry code that was a reminder of Unocal—76.

The sight of their utility mains lying atop the sand around the coming dig was disconcerting, like exposing lifelines to the whims of an army of giant machines. After the utilities were moved, the first demolitions happened just before Thanksgiving Day. No wrecking ball was necessary to take down the old buildings. Instead, a demolition claw took monster-sized bites out of each building after the windows were broken. Three apartments were the first to fall, followed by some of the trailer park structures that remained after all the homes had been removed.

As the jaws of the giant destroyer took the first bite out of the Lighthouse Bar and Grill, people who lined up along the protective fence gasped. Some wept. David Sneed wrote in the *Telegram-Tribune* that it looked like "a rambling dinosaur from *Jurassic Park*. The huge claw of the machine needed only an hour and a half to destroy five structures."

Beachcomber's Bill Price observed dryly, "It's their beach. We just live here . . . where the debris meets the sea." He watched as the remains of his store were fed into a grinder and turned into mulch. He put it into perspective with words from a Jimmy Buffett song about "changes in latitudes, changes in attitudes," meaning that nothing remains quite the same. As the front of his store was crushed, he said quietly, "There goes my front door. Thirteen years of therapy being swept away."

Matt Farmer was equally saddened. "I've seen buildings come and go in this town, but to see them *all* go under the bulldozer in one swoop is pretty sickening."

Longtime resident Connie Allen recalled the days when she and the fire chief constituted the entire emergency response team. Each time the siren rang out across the bay, she would yell to her neighbor to come down the hill to watch her kids, then run all the way to the fire station. She laughed about the time a gang of unruly motorcyclists threatened to take over the beach as their private turf. The squatters were chased off by a crowd of residents, backed up by Connie driving the fire engine ready to hose them down.

The owner of Café Avila, another business to be destroyed, was proud that it had an all-woman kitchen crew. People had said they came to eat there because of the great food and the girls who made them feel at home.

Resident Zeebe Benzler was scrutinized closely by camera crews, as first her home and then the Lighthouse Bar was demolished. Her misery and tears were caught on tape and broadcast around the world. She told David Sneed that it "wasn't just a bar—it was a gathering place, and without it we don't know what will happen to us." Incredibly, as people watched the destruction from behind the protective fence, water cannons used to keep dust down met the morning sun and created an immense rainbow. It was seen as a breathtaking promise of rebirth to come from the ruin.

The deconstruction was hard on the Jacobs crew, as they had spent weeks preparing to dig. During that time they had gotten used to seeing the buildings and had patronized the businesses along with the regulars. Now they, too, were saddened by the loss.

A steady stream of demolitions turned the life of the beach town into piles of splintered wood, metal, and glass. Most observers took a deep breath, cried, and then found a way to go on. Chris Chandless was heard to whisper as he watched his building fall, "Rest in peace."

19

THE LAST GOOD-BYE

I N the final analysis, it was connections that made the difference. It was partnerships, meetings of the minds reaching out
across an abyss of conflict to come to an understanding. The
ties were legal, financial, and emotional, none of which could have
succeeded without compromise, compassion, and conscience.

If ever a referee was needed for a construction project, it was in
Avila Beach. Arrie Bachrach brought twenty-five years of experience to the job, having worked on many environmental projects
for Jacobs Engineering. While his role as town ombudsman was
unusual, Bachrach had previously helped manage company projects by doing the upfront environmental studies and planning, as
well as working to help community and agency relations function
smoothly.

He said that, in retrospect, the Avila Beach job was the most
rewarding and pleasurable project of his entire career, partly because he found the setting on the central coast beach incredibly
beautiful, but mostly because the people were warm and welcom-
ing. By contrast, other jobs he had worked were in the middle of
nowhere, or within a gritty industrial city. Avila Beach was blissful
to him.

"I ended up meeting and making a lot of friends among the
community and the government agency personnel working on the
project. It ended up feeling like they were family," he said. "One

of the hardest things I ever did was to have to leave there when the project was completed."

Before it was over, more than a mile of sheet piling would be thundered into the sand, and between 150,000 and 200,000 cubic yards of polluted soil trucked out in 2.6 million road miles of travel. One of the things about which the construction crew was most proud was that those millions of miles of truck travel were completely accident-free. Out of the hundreds of thousands of person-hours the project took, the most serious accident was a cut finger.

A total of 300,000 cubic yards of earth were dug up, removed, and replaced. Five city blocks were razed. As the inevitability of the dig was accepted, the scope of the project escalated, and the number of buildings that would go down increased, as did the volume of earth to be moved.

The project took over the entire town, using the beach parking lot for construction storage and a "laydown" lot next to the spot where the Avila Grocery building had been moved. Bachrach was apprehensive that the previous acrimony would be a factor in meeting the extraordinary needs of the townspeople. One fundamental fact made the difference: Jacobs and Bachrach represented the solution.

Bachrach was sympathetic and would use the same analogy to describe the work itself that a Unocal representative had used in reference to Perry Martin's participation in the cleanup negotiations. "Everyone—the community, the construction crew, Unocal, the agencies—knew it would be disruptive and difficult. It was like going to the dentist for a root canal. I always thought that was the perfect metaphor. It hurts, you know you have to do it, but you know this is part of the cure, of the healing process. We had to do surgery on the town to make it well."

Bachrach regularly told the workers to remember that they were working in somebody's living room and front yard. By that, he meant that every Jacobs employee and every subcontractor had to treat people with a respect and consideration that went above and beyond that they would afford mere onlookers. "We insisted that it be that way," said Bachrach. "That decision came from the Unocal managers, the Jacobs Engineering managers, to all the crew and to the subcontractors. The order came from the top."

Reasoning that it was counterproductive to fight yesterday's battles, Bachrach didn't pressure people because some had an easier time letting go of the past than others. To counter the prevailing mood, he put a strong emphasis on communication, which was made easier for him by the fact that once Unocal decided to do the cleanup, it was clear that it was a firm commitment. Nearly everyone involved made an effort to get past the divisive issues and get the job done well. It also helped that Bachrach brought his guitar to the impromptu barbecue the community held when the Avila Grocery was moved.

Unocal Project Manager Rich Walloch assured Bachrach he would have the support he needed to do the job right. That was notable, because during negotiations, it appeared that Unocal's early testing had not been done well, which put their people in a difficult position, leaving them without much credibility. The result was that people were suspicious of Jacobs Engineering in the role of contractor hired by the beleaguered company, and Bachrach had to deal with those immediate past tensions and the emotional baggage. He was so successful in assuring residents that Jacobs was working hard and even ahead of schedule, he was able to begin some relief for the town even in the midst of the destruction.

For all his good intentions, Bachrach was unable to ease the intense pain of residents during the destruction. For Fire Chief Robert Gorman Jr. and his wife, Elaine, the hardest part was when Gladys Misakian's house went down. Gladys's move was hard on everyone, and it was compounded by the fact that the sweet old neighbor and friend had to be hospitalized shortly after she had left her house for the last time. To their utter dismay, the Gormans learned that Gladys had watched the destruction of her home on the television news from her hospital bed. It came as no surprise to anyone that she passed away not long after. Everyone who knew and loved her was certain she died of a broken heart.

Once the first stage of destruction was complete, the project moved to the actual digging. At the site, installation of sheet pile began in order to keep the underground fluids contained and later the soft sand from caving into the dig. Just unloading the huge pieces of metal was unbelievably loud. The metal clanged sharply, then boomed as each section was dropped onto the earth from low-bed trucks. Echoes of each landing rumbled underground, bounced into the salty air, and seemed to run reluctantly out into the ocean.

Each three-foot-wide section, weighing from four thousand to six thousand pounds and measuring forty-five to sixty-five feet, top to bottom, was driven into the ground. One section nested into an adjoining one all around to form a cofferdam. The ground around each section liquefied as it was pounded, much like often happens near aquifers and bays during an earthquake.

Not only was the noise like a constant succession of sonic booms, the vibrating concussion was felt no matter where one stood, sat, or reclined, nearly every day for weeks. With a sound meter measuring one hundred decibels as a crane hoisted each section and a vibrator hammered it into the sand thirty-five or more feet down, everyone working close to the equipment, and even those just watching from directly behind the fence, needed ear protection. Ninety-year-old Evelyn Phelan, living immediately next to the work zone, chose Day-Glo earplugs from those offered by Jacobs workers.

The ground trembled like an angry earth god. Compared to the installation of the sheet piling, the grinder that had previously made mulch of the buildings had been quiet. Work progressed slowly because of the danger of fire from the oil-soaked dirt. The action of driving the metal sheets into the ground caused a buildup of heat in the pit. No sparks could be tolerated, which required that many of the pipes be hand cut, making the job seem as though it were being completed in slow motion.

The pounding of sheet pile caused collateral damage to buildings nearby. Houses began to shift. Delores Lepley's home rotated several inches, and Betty Woody's old three-story boarding house split in a number of places. Every time Betty discovered a new crack, she would write the date on a sticky note and put it next to the damage. In time, the interior of her home was covered with dozens of yellow notes. In other homes, the pounding broke floor joists and gas lines, despite earlier preparations.

A steady parade of sightseers came from miles around to watch the deconstruction. People parked everywhere, including in residents' driveways. The strangers stood and stared in awe of the work and then wandered around looking at what remained of the town. One resident found some of them peering through a window into her home and said it felt like the town had been in an accident and people were coming to watch them bleed.

During the digging, freed petroleum products mixed with the water table and the floating oil was suctioned off and separated for transport out of town. Sand at the bottom of the lagoon that formed in the enormous hole was dredged up and cleaned in machines that shook and blew out the oil products, which could be recycled or transported to the state toxics repository for hydrocarbon wastes.

The excavation covered a total of about nine acres. Layers of clean soil, called overburden, had to be removed and reserved on the beach before the equipment reached the top of the pollution. The clean soil was set aside for later refill of the gaping hole. Typically a dig of this nature was treated like a layer cake, with complete removal of the overburden from the entire site, excavation of all the contaminated soil, and replacement of clean sand over the entire area. While thorough, it is a slow method.

Jacobs and Unocal improvised a train sequence, by dividing the excavation into six sequential cells. The sheet pile used in Cell 1 was pulled out when that part of the dig was complete, and reinstalled in the adjoining area. The train method was a sequence of digging and filling from one end to the other. As soon as crews reached a sufficient distance from the beginning of one cell from which the soil had been removed, they began to refill it with clean sand.

Contaminated dirt was dumped onto a paved area nearby to drain before it was loaded onto trucks. Before leaving, the exterior of each rig was washed down and the load covered. Traffic was a problem, since there were only two lanes through town, one of which had to be isolated for project traffic. The solution was for trucks to follow a one-way route through the downtown and return the back way for the next load.

After unloading in the interim exchange area at the tank farm on the bluff, each vehicle was washed down again before returning for another load. The $200,000 canopy used at the transfer location, rated to withstand eighty-mile-per-hour winds, covered huge piles placed on paved areas, where soiled sand was received, tested, and left for a while to ooze petroleum products into a drainage system.

Sent up in single dump trucks, the sand was later moved to long-haul double tandem trucks for transfer to an environmental dump. The system reduced the number of trucks in town by half, but they still lumbered up the hill every two minutes. The larger rigs came into and left the area by way of a back road and never had to come into town. The system required double handling of the dig material, but it was a better use of trucks and curtailed traffic. In the end it was apparent that the traffic solution also minimized the impact of contamination removal on residents.

Noise was only one part of the system that was unnerving. Each time a load labored up the hill it let loose a scattering of oily dirt that shook off the load or dislodged from wheels and the undercarriage of the chassis. After so many health warnings that the contamination was dangerous if exposed to the air, residents tried to get county officials to see that the system was flawed. In the face of noisy operations and concerns about what they would find as they dug deeper, no one paid any attention to complaints from Lucy Lepley and others about the scattered dirt. It was not until County Monitor Rod Farrell was hit on the head with one of the clods that fell from a truck that the dig was temporarily shut down until an alternative solution could be found.

Jacobs engineers installed an additional system of cleaners and a rumble strip over which trucks ran before heading for the road, which allowed trucks to shed excessive dirt before they drove past the remaining residences. To keep the dirt from blowing past the dig and to limit the occasional terrible stench that resembled a combination of tar and rotten eggs, Unocal erected fences and lined them with black plastic—a fitting color for the death of a town. Undeterred, sidewalk watchers moved up the hill, where they could continue to see the pit and watch the dig. Work resumed, and haulers beat a steady path through town toward Unocal's tank farm.

The day following the installation of the black-cloaked fences, a storm with high winds shredded the canopy at the tank farm as well as the safety barriers surrounding the dig. The winds caught the plastic covers like sails, flattening the fences and scattering heavy traffic control barrels like fallen leaves. As soon as the weather cleared, workers replaced the barriers and the canopy, and the digging began again.

Digging revealed the remains of the Pacific Coast Railroad, which had once connected the town to the rest of the world. The small rail line had been built with irregularly cut hand-hewn redwood ties. Holding spikes had been notched to resemble a dog's head and were specifically identified with the letters *PCRR*, a railroad fondly remembered by old-timers as a real-life *Petticoat Junction* line.

Thousands of huge abalone shells were unearthed, remnants and reminders of the thriving fishing industry of a half-century ago. Many of the people who worked on the dig took them to keep as a reminder of the part they had played in another segment of Avila Beach history.

Engineering was the easier part of Arrie Bachrach's job. His sensitivity to people's feelings was his strength, and he left a lasting legacy in town. Bachrach had become friends with many of the Avila Beach residents, including the Lepleys. Dolores moved to Grover Beach before the digging began, but her black and white cat, Cookie, was too old to move. Lucy asked Bachrach to feed Cookie, and he did so for months. Every day, including weekends, he went to the Lepley house to feed the cat. Learning that the Martin house was slated for demolition, Bachrach realized that the yard full of rosebushes would be destroyed as well. "This was an environmental project," he said, "and here was a beautiful part of the environment that was going to be destroyed. I had to do something about that." The bushes had been blooming in the Martin yard for nearly forty years, and digging them up proved to be a huge job. Bachrach spent several days after work digging them up and replanting them at the post office, at the Avila Beach Community Center, by the school and churches, and in anyone's yard in town who would accept them. Then he commissioned a small plaque to be installed at the community center, dedicating the roses to Evelyn Phelan for her ninetieth birthday. "It was an important continuity with the past," he said. "Longtime family roses. We found a way to preserve them, and it touched people." The symbolism was more than appropriate, reflecting the community's uprooting and its reconstruction. While Bachrach knew it was the right thing to do, he had no idea how strongly his act would affect residents.

He also helped make a celebration out of moving the Yacht Club, a building that was potentially eligible to be included on the National Register of Historic Places. Right before the Yacht Club was scheduled to be moved, Bachrach heard about Gerard Parsons, one of the men who had had a hand in the original construction of the club in the 1930s. Parsons was one of the first commodores of the club and still maintained active membership in it. Bachrach invited Parsons to help mark the occasion. He was given a hard hat and construction vest to wear, and he walked beside the low-bed truck that carried the building as it moved toward Wild Cherry Canyon. Bachrach made arrangements for Parsons to be interviewed by the media. A year and a half later, Parsons returned to lead the parade of engineers and construction workers as the building returned home. An accomplished woodworker, Parsons made a beautiful display board on which he mounted photographs of the building as it was moved. He presented it to Bachrach and Jacobs Engineering as a memento of the event.

Ceremony was important, and Bachrach knew that residents held to the secret hope that every building would be moved and returned exactly like it had been, even though they knew the chances for that were slim. He was dealing with a population with an incredibly strong sense of place, something that the late environmentalist Wallace Stegner articulated in lyrical fashion.

A distinguished writer and one-time poet laureate of the United

States, Stegner was possessed of extraordinary clarity when it came to a sense of place, calling those who were sensitive to it "placed people." Stegner claimed that in a country settled by restless Europeans, a sense of place happened only after people had been born, raised, and finally died in the same location, having lived in it long enough to have molded it. According to Stegner, placed people have a history that is remembered, revered, and repeated, where names are carved into trees and each rock and path is well known.

The United States holds a rich history of frontier people who looked to settle in a little utopian neck of the woods. Their treks remain fresh today in writings, song, story, and in still-visible initials that were carved into huge rocks along the Oregon Trail, giving mute testimony that a place was claimed only if it is felt. That sense of belonging was key to the fight in Avila Beach, where people keenly felt their sense of place each time the sun set in the Pacific and rose again in the east, over the inland mountains that sheltered them.

Some places are set in the mind with memorable writings, such as Bret Harte's "The Luck of Roaring Camp" and Damon Runyon's stories about New York City. In some unusual circumstances, the connection is made instantly, as it was for poet Stephen Vincent Benét, who wrote:

> *I have fallen in love with American names,*
> *The sharp names that never get fat,*
> *The snakeskin-titles of mining claims,*
> *The plumed war bonnet of Medicine Hat,*
> *Tucson and Deadwood and Lost Mule Flat.*
>
> *I shall not rest quiet in Montparnasse.*
> *. . . You may bury my body in Sussex grass,*
> *. . . I shall not be there. I shall rise and pass.*
> *Bury my heart at Wounded Knee.*

Other places have the aura of monumental history that will never change. Some will always hold a spiritual connection, like

Gettysburg, Valley Forge, and Washington, D.C., where, rather than residence, people feel connected to each other through the historical formation of the nation.

Cal Poly psychologist Dan Levi feels that social reality is more about people than places, suggesting that a strong connection to a location is the reason why people in Iowa and Big Sur both have the same attitude toward their individual homesteads. It is this connection that also draws people back to the place of their birth or upbringing. Levi observed that the connection could be related to time, meaning that the longer a person remains in a location, the more attached he becomes to it, something that happens in neighborhoods in larger cities as well. "Avila did not change much," according to Levi, "so people's sense of place was not disrupted by the environment changing in the region surrounding town."

According to Levi, the oil spill in Avila Beach compounded the sense of unity for the townspeople in the same way that the September 11 attacks in New York, Washington, D.C., and Pennsylvania did for the people of the United States. Coming together to fight an enemy is extremely unifying, especially when a communal sense of security has been threatened. The history of Avila Beach exemplified the American ethos of finding utopia, cultivating ownership of it over a long period of time, and fighting to preserve it. The difference as exhibited by residents of the little town was that they wanted more to stay there to fight for a righteous cause, rather than take the money and run. In the end, some did both.

In Avila Beach, prior to the contamination crisis, there was a constant sense of peaceful transition with the changing world around them. Residents lived not in ignorance of the cultural shifts in the rest of the country, but tolerant of choices that differed widely from their own. There was no conspicuous consumption, little competition, and a great deal of the strong community connection. The moment the settlement was announced was one of truth for the residents. It was a time to cheer, to laugh, and to weep. A time of reaching out to hug one another, while holding on to the impossible hope that the town could be moved out, cleaned up, and returned to what it had been for so long.

Arrie Bachrach saw this and respected it. He became one of the family, even though he was part of the solution that ultimately destroyed the town. By opening his heart to the people, he became connected to them as well.

HOLDING HANDS
WITH HERITAGE

T HE crisis at Avila Beach not only affected the present and the future of the town and its people, it impacted a vital part of history for Native Americans. Leilynn Olivas Odom is Chumash, a native group that anthropologists believe were the first inhabitants of North America. Leilynn often works with state and federal agencies to preserve as much as possible of nature because it is a major part of the Chumash heritage. She was a member of the cleanup team.

I am Leilynn Olivas Odom. My Chumash kinship is through my father, Timothy. His father was Francisco, and his mother was Rosario. Now we are speaking of Rosario Kuhn, who is my great-grandmother. Rosario was at the mission during her early childhood time, and her family is our genealogy. We started keeping a written language from this time. We have many villages in the area, including Pismu, which is now called Pismo Beach.

We try to trace our villages from our Chumash oral history and archeological surveys. We can date them that way. We say the village of Tsipxatu is located in Avila Beach under the inn. It is still there, but the inn is on top of it. It is here for five thousand years and has very high status. When the Spaniards came, they referred to the people here as very important—politicians, doctors, lawyers, astrologists—we just have different words for them. This village was likely the capital because of the presence of these respected people who lived there.

Leilynn points out that Chumash see their heritage through the family line and others identify them by the village, town, or city where they live. As soon as one heard the place of residence, that person's heritage would be known from the tradition of storytelling. The oral history saved much of what otherwise would have been lost during the Mission Era.

This [Avila Beach] is where El Buchon lived. He was known as the chieftain when the Spanish came and met him. The chieftain came out to meet them because it was the proper thing to do. The chieftain is written about as El Buchon, but we do not know his native name. He was the patriarch, and a village protected its people and fed them.

On the other side of Avila at the tank farm, we believe was a Chumash mint, where we made bead money. It was usually done on the Channel Islands, but we find other places where it was also done.

One of the most revered stories concerns how the Chumash came to be on the mainland. It is told that the Channel Islands were getting overpopulated, and the people were told by the goddess Hutash some should leave. Hutash created the Rainbow Bridge, which reached from the islands to the Huasna. As people walked over the bridge, some fell into the water and became dolphins. That is why Chumash believe they are related to dolphins as well as to whales.

The village of Tsipxatu, in what is now called Avila Beach, has the root word of whale, and they are very important to us. The first thing the Europeans did (not the Spanish ones, but the American ones) was to set up a whaling station in this area because the whales come into the harbor. They didn't have to go out to capture them. I often visualize the whales coming in while they are making their migration and since we are the people of the sea, we are related to the whales. We showed the Europeans the things we know of the sea, and they named one area Diablo [now Diablo Canyon]. We were told not to go there any more. They disrupted our cycle of friends and everything we gained knowledge of for thousands of years. Modern day archeology is a help that we can marry to our old stories and what the Spanish know plus the diaries of some of our people and others.

Leilynn, one of her family, or another Chumash representative was in attendance at the cleanup from the start of the Big Dig. Chief archeologist on the job, Robert Gibson, knows her well and has worked with the Chumash for twenty years. Although he did not expect the dig to uncover a significant village, the possibility existed, since the ocean shore had been at least a mile farther west ten thousand years ago. What is beach and wetland now was a landform at that time, and the Chumash were already living in the region.

Gibson also knew that soil had been brought in from other areas to fill the lagoon, meaning that some artifacts could have been transported to the Front Street area from their original resting places. A large volcanic stone bowl was found in a utility trench, and because there was no other indication of regular habitation in the area, the bowl was categorized as having been transferred from elsewhere and added to the other small items that were determined to have been reburied.

I can certainly understand the people in Avila Beach, especially after they have been here for several generations. Some of them understood our concerns, and not all of them were affected the same, by having to move and having their life taken away from them because of being occupied, in a sense. Maybe even invaded.

We felt that for the people here. All of us working on the dig were told not to talk with the people too much and not talk with reporters. It was because of security due to the high degree of emotion. Some people might think about doing things in another way. We might call it destructive, and people were certainly outspoken. Some of the people stayed the whole time and even slept in their cars.

When you dig up the earth, we feel that a lot. It is our job, but we are also Chumash, and that is difficult. All this ripping and tearing into the earth, sometimes the smell—the hydrocarbons, the H₂S—it affects us, and I know it did people in the town. It was tearing at us.

Leilynn sees her family history in the massive amount of soil taken away, and she knows the testing is not over. There are still pockets, including a part under the ocean at high tide.

We have seen the ocean go out [recede] two to three miles from where it is now. We also know some of our older villages would have been at the edge of the water at that time, so they are under water now. We are looking out there at our villages where they want to build oil platforms and drill new wells. That is a big impact for us, and they don't even want to hear about that. They will be finding human remains, and archeologists have documented that Chumash human remains are the oldest ones found on the North American continent.

Natives throughout the United States find it impossible to understand ownership of private property. Their understanding is that the earth cannot be owned. Rather it is cared for and tended to by people who live on it. Leilynn understands that taxes are a means of sharing resources; however, it is the same in her mind as sharing any resource, and the Chumash have been doing that for each other forever.

At the beach, you get fish and clams and share them. The deer came down to the shore, and the hunters share the meat. We gathered from things growing and share that. We certainly used parts of the whale, and what you refer to as bones are very significant to us. We did not go out whaling. We have a different relationship. If the whale came to us, we had an offering, because they would beach themselves for us. The vertebrae of a whale was the throne for El Buchon, and it was a sign of a very respected person. The ribs were used to make an arch door into homes or for separations inside.

It was noted by the observing people that what is referred to as the sweat lodge is an act of purification and meditation. To sing the old songs and recall the old stories is to get in touch with ancestors. What you call work, we call family time, gathering food to dry and preserve or cook. I work with CalTrans [California Department of Transportation] to locate and preserve different basket making materials that grow, as well as what you would call musical instruments we use. We try to protect that plant life today. It all comes down to family for us. We understand the emotions in protecting history and family. Not that we get to live in Avila Beach, but we do understand. It was heartbreaking to go through all the steps.

The Chumash are not strangers to crude oil. They gathered tar balls on the beach for their baskets and watercraft, and they thought of them as a gift for good use. Although the pipelines represent an assault to the earth, the Chumash came to observe if any artifacts were unearthed during the cleanup, especially human remains. It was a difficult balancing for them to take part in the cleanup.

We have always waterproofed our tomol [plank canoes] with tar balls melted by the fire. The earth gives it to us, and we also use it to waterproof our baskets so we can cook in them. Going back into what Europeans call prehistory, we have done this for a long time . . .

The Chumash have always come to Avila Beach to reconnect with their roots, greeting the dolphin with respect by throwing beads and tobacco into the ocean. They still do. Just as the residents of Avila Beach treasure their memories of growing up on the beach, Leilynn has fond memories of childhood.

I remember playing on the beach, but we didn't go out into the ocean. Although we were lost, assimilated into the population, we are still Chumash. We had to be called something else for our survival. Our villages were laid out in streets, and our people traded with many other groups from what is now California, Nevada, and Oregon. We have always done that.

We had large gatherings for trade and ceremonies, meeting at special times of the earth. Nowadays we call them the Winter Solstice, the Summer Solstice, harvest in the autumn—all connected

*with the earth. You could see it in the stars at night. All our knowl-
edge was passed down in the oral tradition, but we do have some
written symbols. People refer to them as rock paintings, but they
are written symbolism with stories that we have passed on for thousands of years. Another word that describes them is icon.*

*We had all that information until it was disrupted. We do work
with other anthropologists in developing guidelines for states and
the U.S. government. In working with pipelines, we have learned
that companies expect to lose 1 percent just getting it from here to
there. There are massive amounts of oil transported underground.
In the twenties, thirties, forties, and fifties, they did not believe
those products were very harmful to people and the earth. Nor did
they believe leaks would persist.*

Unocal and Jacobs insisted that the Native American concerns
take top priority, and that was evident every day. It was not uncommon for a dozer driver to pull up to the side of the pit and
shout to archeologist Robert Gibson that there might be something in that shovelful of soil. It was a lighthearted moment when
one of them stuck an unearthed bottle into the edge of the bucket
load, lumbered the dozer to the side of the dig, and gently depos-
ited the soil near the archeology team.

The pace was so fast that Gibson commissioned a small trophy
for each member of his working group. It featured a rodeo bull
rider in mid-ride and bore the caption, "A Great 8 Second Ride!"
It was a thinly veiled poke at the contrast between the usual slow-
paced archeological dig he was accustomed to. The cleanup was
done at top speed without any sacrifice of quality.

When all the artifacts had been gathered, more than sixty bank-
er's boxes full of them were given to the San Luis Obispo County
Archeological Society and the Avila Beach Foundation for public
display. The artifacts identified as Chumash materials were reburied near where they were found while a Tobacco Ceremony and
Blessing were performed.

"I think the Chumash were happy to be there in order to protect
the dolphins and Mother Earth," said Gibson. "It was important
enough for them to have to deal with the stress for about two
years—a good trade-off." Gibson recalled another remediation

project he had worked at Vandenberg Air Force Base, where a choice had to be made whether to relocate a fence closer to the water or inland toward the dig itself.

The Chumash representative at that site was a basket maker, Juanita Centeno, who said it would be better to put the fence in the site, because the wetlands and willows contained food and medicines. The site, she said, only held the crumbs of her people. Placing the fence at the site would be less of a loss than placing it in the wetlands, which would serve the needs of and ensure the survival of future generations. "Mother Earth is more important than archeology to the Chumash," said Gibson.

It was personally difficult for Leilynn to work at the dig. Not only was she conflicted about witnessing a desecration of the earth, she was surrounded with things foreign to her.

There were times back then . . . the sheet pile I called the Iron Wall. I called the other one the Black Wall. It was storm fencing [chain link or Cyclone] *covered with black plastic. It encompassed all areas, and you could only see a very little distance, but not the ocean. I would get into areas there at the dig, and I couldn't tell which direction I was in because I couldn't see the ocean. It was very confusing. I was standing back there many times thinking I don't know if I can make it through this job. Those storm link fences were supposed to hold up against eighty-mile-an-hour winds. The wind came through here and bent some of those fences over!*

Jacobs engineers were always watching out for the safety of people, and the men came and shredded the black covering so the winds could get through them. I was thinking that was too bad, but I was sure happy to see it happen. There was a lot of huge equipment and a lot of noise, pulling down foundations, old memories, and stuff. I gathered some of the broken glass to try to make a picture out of it later, so the memory would not be completely lost to Avila. It was almost like going to battle in a way every day. It saved my sanity to be able to walk down to the beach. We come as often as we can to honor the dolphin with tobacco and beads. Every day if we can make it.

The Chumash have no sanctioned *reservation*, only one village in the Santa Ynez region of Santa Barbara County. The reason they have one village is due to it having been continually occupied, predating written history. According to Leilynn and the Chumash Council, somewhere in the archives of the U.S. government in Washington, D.C., eighteen signed but unratified treaties for promises made to the Chumash lie lost to the world. If one particular treaty were to be honored, there would be no Avila Beach, no contamination problem, and no massive dig. There would be only the village of *Tsipxatu*.

21

RIZZO'S DOLPHIN
CALLING

I N the fall of 2000, in an eerie foreshadowing of the tragic loss of the World Trade Center in New York, Avila Beach looked at a gaping hole in the ground where the business district had been. A thriving commercial setting was now a yawning entrance into the earth. The work and livelihood of scores of people had been turned into mulch, carried away, and the very roots excavated. Those who could stomach the sight got an enormous dose of reality. Whereas Unocal had expected to find no more than eleven pipelines, sixteen were unearthed.

One set of questions solved seemed endlessly to open the door to new ones, and although quite small by comparison to the effect of metropolitan contamination problems on large pockets of population, the problem, solution, and ultimate completion of the cleanup at Avila Beach was quite complex.

The engineering of the project included a scientific assessment of what was underground and the risks involved in both its being there and in the process of removing it—to humans, to wildlife, and to the ocean in close proximity. How would it affect air and water quality, should it remain? What constitutes the geology under the town that might complicate the process of removing it?

What should be done with the contaminants that would be removed?

Another area of debate was legal responsibility. Since several petroleum enterprises had been functioning in the area, whose oil was it? The businesses had been regulated for decades, and until the mid-1980s there had been no clear mandate to keep track of leaking pipelines. Should the companies be held responsible for what had been tolerated for so long? What about the companies themselves? After providing jobs and economic stability for so long, should they not be given some leeway for what was only determined of late to be bad? How could long-term dangers have been determined when oil had been naturally oozing through to the earth's surface long before the American westward movement?

Ultimately, the key to getting Avila Beach cleaned up was economic. Even though any interruption to the supply of oil results in a widespread disaster to a nation utterly dependent on it, the Avila Beach case rested on the fact that no one in town could do anything with their property as long as the contamination remained underground. Rizzo and the MACC Coalition rode to victory on regulatory requirements that had been set in place by enlightened legislators and a populace determined to see justice for the town.

The case of Avila Beach involved science, engineering, legalities, the economic vitality and social fabric of a community, the perceived threat to the region's beach-loving public, and the application of case law, as well as the initiation of new ways to meet unprecedented challenges that muddied the entire situation. Any resolution was preordained to please almost no one and certain to anger, disappoint, and dishearten everyone involved, because for every gain, there was a corresponding loss. Some of those exchanges were monetary, others emotional. None were without corresponding cost. One factor rose above the rest. Most people involved worked for the common good because it was the right thing to do. However, they did it knowing they were overseeing the destruction of a distinctive community.

Awareness of the crisis had grown slowly for close to ten years, picking up momentum as new information became available. It peaked with the announcement of the settlement and proposed cleanup, replacing anger with grief. Unocal announced they would give the pipeline pier to a nonprofit group that could outline a plan to put it to good use.

The winner of the pier was Cal Poly University, San Luis Obispo, which planned to use it for a proposed Marine Science Education and Research Center. The value of the gift was $18 million for the pier alone, but the company added $4.5 million to endow two professorships in marine science and provide income to maintain the pier and operate the center.

Cal Poly alumnus and former Unocal employee Jack Spaulding had an intimate experience with the pier when he rode it down into the ocean during a strong El Niño storm in 1983. Spaulding and two other men were more than halfway out the length of the pier, assessing damage to the structure. While it was not raining at the time, ocean swells were strong. The men finished their inspection and were headed back, when one shouted that a big wave was headed for them. Spaulding said it felt like they were riding an express elevator as the pier went down.

The men floated on a sixteen-by-one-hundred-foot "raft" of the remains of the pier until help came nearly an hour later. By the time they were back on land, a mere sixteen-by-sixteen-foot section of the raft refuge was left.

Unocal rebuilt the old wooden pier in concrete. At the peak of oil transportation in Avila Beach, two million barrels of oil went through pipelines in the pier each month. Unocal employees considered duty at Avila Beach to be one of the most desirable company locations. However, Denny Lamb was heard to say that he had given thirty-five years of service to the company, of which thirty-four had been fun and one had been pure hell.

Bill Sharrer, Unocal's manager for environmental affairs, admitted to reporters that the company did not respond well to the crisis in the beginning, which left them with a tarnished image that did not change even when the company did. The reason the company's reputation didn't change was largely because the people were convinced that Unocal would walk away from the problem, which Sharrer said would have been impossible, because the company couldn't shirk its responsibility with the California Regional Water Quality Control Board.

Unocal's additional responsibility at the Guadalupe Dunes was described in *Oil and Gas Journal* at the time as "an incredible task and probably the most highly scrutinized environmental cleanup in the world." Among other technological methods of dealing with the cleanup at Guadalupe Dunes, the company used thermal desorption drums, baking the diluent out of the sand in huge drums of revolving kilns at 700°F. The machines were the largest in the United States at the time.

Unocal Vice President John Imle Jr. publicly announced that he personally owed an apology to the region for what happened there. He went on to say that the company accepted full responsibility for the crisis and vowed Unocal would spend whatever it took to clean up the spill.

No one involved was left unchanged, and with the exception of grudges held fast, that meant everyone looked back as well as forward. County planner David Church observed that Unocal had originally chosen to play the stiff-arm, and people had been livid at their stance. That made his job easier since the company was seen as the Evil Empire, while he and his agency collaborators were working to help the town.

Church felt the low point for him, after being involved longer than most of the others, was waiting for Unocal to agree to have the Environmental Impact Report done. He and Gerhardt Hubner of the water board had watched as many people were worn down to the point that they sold to the company just to get away from the tension and heartache. At one poignant meeting the two men observed that even people who had been so vocal in protesting were disappearing. It led to dark humor as they told each other, "They can't get rid of us all!"

They consoled each other with the assurance that they were government and would remain long after the perpetrators were gone. Their message was consistent: Do an EIR that meets the people's needs and then get the project done. In a strange irony, their insistence that the contamination be cleaned up dramatically increased the value of the property Unocal bought in Avila Beach once they did the project.

Church still misses the people in Avila Beach, especially Gladys Misakian, who touched him deeply. He thinks about Pizza Pantry owner Jim Cummings, with his unique angst, as well as Perry Martin and his public anger. In retrospect, Church felt Unocal never understood the people because they were always too busy defending their position to get to know them. He never wavered from his original stance that the spill had to be cleaned up, and he spent the most time of all the agency representatives working toward that end.

Gerhardt Hubner never lost his positive approach to the constantly changing problems, but he came close to it near the end. At the final meeting when all the agencies appeared to be finished with their internal processes for acceptance of the EIR, the U.S. Army Corps of Engineers suddenly wanted it in an Environmental Impact Statement (EIS) format. Representatives of that body had attended every meeting, but did not express any opinion about the report until the very end. It took another six months to get the thousands of pages into the format the Army Corps wanted. Hubner made it his personal responsibility to get the Corps of Engineers through the additional process, pushing and tugging everyone to get it done in the shortest time possible.

San Luis Obispo County agencies are uniform in their praise of Unocal for their efforts once the fight was settled. "They did a terrific job," said Hubner. "One of the comments they made on our EIR was that it was technically, logically infeasible, uneconomical, and couldn't be done. Even if it could be done, it would take five years. They did it in eighteen months." A. D. Little, the EIR preparer, said it would take three years, but Unocal was motivated to get the job done sooner, and they did.

At one point, the company told Hubner they could not meet the standards in areas where sand was on top of bedrock. Cracks in the stone held unknown quantities of petroleum products. He gave them some leeway, and Jacobs Engineering not only met the standards but far exceeded them. They used steam under pressure to extract the petroleum products. While the water board's cleanup demand specified 100 ppm, Unocal ended up accomplishing an incredible average of 23 ppm, and the cleanup was completed a record-setting eleven months ahead of schedule.

At the main plume, the remaining contamination was 66 ppm, and Gerhardt Hubner estimated that 99.7 percent of the total spill had been removed. The groundwater cleanup goal of 1 ppm TPH was achieved by the end of the year 2000.

In the weeks following the Big Dig and partial restoration, Hubner sat on a new bench by the beach talking with his girlfriend about the project and how hard it had been to see it through. She laughed about mounting a plaque to commemorate the project, but Hubner just shook his head, admitting he was proud of the accomplishment. He considers it his mark on the county and on his career, but always adds that others made a difference as well.

Hubner recalls that when he moved to San Luis Obispo from the Los Angeles area, people told him there was nothing much to do there except watch cows graze. "I think Unocal expected that, too," he said. "They came with the attitude that they were the power, and we were the yokels who didn't know what we were doing."

Hubner believed that Unocal representatives and their environmental consultants were continually surprised, and he remembers one time when they challenged the soil cleanup levels, asking them to be changed to standards permitted in Los Angeles County. It appeared to shock these same representatives and consultants to find that Hubner had worked in the Los Angeles Regional Water Quality Control Board at the time and had helped develop those standards. "It was almost fate," he said.

During the time he had worked at the Los Angeles Regional Water Quality Control Board office, Hubner had been involved in similar large coastal cleanup projects with a Chevron refinery in El Segundo as well as military bases at Point Mugu and Port Hueneme in Ventura County. Those were huge projects with contaminations that were on valuable properties such as shopping centers, which provided a greater incentive to get them cleaned up. Four hundred people in a small town did not have the same kind of clout.

"I think they didn't expect us to do our homework," said Hubner. "I called the Los Angeles and Riverside Water Board offices to find out exactly what was done down there, and repeated it at the next meeting. Since they cleaned it up with good result, I told Unocal they could certainly do it here. I think the company was not prepared for that kind of response."

Deputy Attorney General Ken Alex gives Unocal attorney Mark Smith high praise. "He made a compelling difference," he said. "I spoke with him many, many times and feel his presence and his view of the situation were key, because he helped the corporation make the decision that the best way to resolve the problem was to do more cleanup than they originally intended and spend the money to try to make the town whole again."

Alex said the Avila Beach case was one of the fastest he had seen, especially for a spill so large. "We never expected it to resolve so quickly. After the first meeting that Saro Rizzo had included attorneys from Milberg Weiss, I felt we were on the way to resolution. This was one for the books . . . an unusual case."

One of the MACC Coalition attorneys described Rizzo as the first to run out at the spear. "What I initially demanded was nothing, really—a beach-cleaning machine," Rizzo said. "I was willing to just sit there and ask for them to work with the agencies and to fund the Front Street Project for $2 million. I would have gone away, closed the case, and settled. When they told me to go away, I said, okay, and then I'd come back with my big brothers!"

That got to be a recurring joke in Avila Beach. Every time talks went nowhere, Rizzo would come to the next meeting with another group added to his suit. His Avila Alliance is responsible for raising awareness in town and encouraging people to work with the agencies involved. Rizzo said it is a testament to the people that national television reporters interviewed them as knowledgeable experts.

The case set precedents, but not legal ones, since it did not go to trial to be resolved by case law. However, it did make a difference in the delay and appeal process within the state system of agency responsibilities. Much past litigation has been embroiled in this kind of legal manipulation, often resulting in one party running out of money, time, and patience. Rizzo ran his case with his personal credit card, with much the same kind of dedication that Jan Schlichtmann exhibited in *A Civil Action*.

The practice of stonewalling is the target of tort reform in Washington, D.C., and with increasing public awareness of due process and consequent dilution of its effectiveness, the settlement will affect environmental conflict for decades to come. The reform will more likely be unnecessary now that the public has seen the results of ignoring a problem. It is not always a successful strategy in light of effective partnerships. Indeed, it is clear that integrity is the best cost-saving tactic. Corporate culture is best served by recognizing that the ultimate defense is integrity. In the long run, it is the most cost-effective approach as well. If Unocal had thoroughly investigated the first indication of a serious underground spill when it became known in 1977, the cost to clean it up would have been minor by comparison.

The lesson goes down hard in U.S. boardrooms, because business has a long history of clinging to budget forecasts and measurable results. Succumbing to fear of the unknown quantity has dictated more legal maneuverings than stalwartly facing whatever comes and dealing with it. Unocal's turnaround was roundly applauded by Avila Beach residents, who maintained their condemnation of attorney Ed Masry and his assistant, Erin Brockovich. Lucy Lepley felt that the Masry team behaved like a ringmaster at a circus taking advantage of and controlling vulnerable people. *New Times* reporter Steven P. Jones wrote that Masry blamed San Luis Obispo County for his failure to win a large settlement, because in his view, officials deliberately covered up the health risks. Jones went on to say that Erin Brockovich left clients feeling "used, neglected, conned and just downright angry."

Matthew Farmer mourns the loss of nearly half the town's residents. "I miss the people I talked with all the time at meetings. I've lost touch with so many people who were deeply involved and didn't want anybody to pull the wool over their eyes," he said. Farmer also feels sad that they were not allowed to talk with Unocal employees in the last ten years of the company's presence in town. The outcome was a far cry from the old days, when there was no division between the town and the company. Everyone had been neighbors for so long, and suddenly Avila Beach faced an identity crisis. The *San Diego Union* called the town "a blip of a place that overnight became California's *Love Canal.*" Cracked sidewalks are gone, and the downtown is slowly growing again. With 70 percent of downtown owned by Unocal, it is certain no one will ever call Avila Beach "funky" again— another loss to mourn.

Attorney Richard Racouillat said that it was a significant crisis for many people because their wealth was built around their home, and the loss of it created a psychological war zone for many of them. "I'm an observer," he said. "I know some where marriages were tested, some where people had near breakdowns, people who had medical treatment, and people who had to move out of their homes very early because they were suddenly unable to cope with the noise, the dust, the aggravation. Some were forced to move from homes inherited from fathers and grandfathers, forced literally to change their lives and their goals."

Racouillat feels strongly that Unocal is not wise in their pursuit of bioremediation as the answer for any new discoveries of underground contamination. The company is working with Cal Poly University to continue research on ways to improve the viability of petroleum-eating microbes. Racouillat said reliance on the procedure would marry the company to a site for years and years, without any foreseeable resolution. In addition, they would still be liable should the process fail within a reasonable length of time.

The law is clear, said Racouillat. "The catalyst for the suits was that Unocal knew about the pollution and took no steps to correct it. In this case, they were the ones who were committing the tort, and under American law, you have a duty to mitigate it, as well as to take steps to prevent further damage. Their viewpoint underneath your property is not 'further damage.' That was Unocal's failure, with the knowledge of what was happening to take steps to correct it."

Residents credited Supervisor Peg Pinard with taking on their cause. Some smile when they recall she "kicked butt" in every department to make things happen for the people. While she re-

214 ♦ David, Goliath, and the Beach-Cleaning Machine

spected the county workers, she sat in office after office asking questions about requirements and finding ways to help Avila Beach residents file the necessary forms and get through the hurdles necessary to move, return, and rebuild.

"The Avila Beach cleanup happened," said Saro Rizzo, "because of the unique character of the people in Avila. They are open-minded, and if there is one common thread among them, it was they were looking for what was good for Avila. No matter how many tourists come, the town remains the same. You can go down there any Tuesday in October at 5 P.M., and local people still walk the beach and visit."

♦ ♦ ♦

The old storm-battered sidewalk along Front Street is gone, and a smooth one runs all the way to the new marine artwork imbedded in the approach to the stairway to the sand. The Avila Grocery Store was returned to its original site with the graffiti still bravely declaring, "Party On! The spirit never ends!" A row of palm trees lines what is now a Mediterranean promenade, complete with nautical design street lamps, a water fountain disguised as a tide pool, and benches painted with sea creatures. Children play in the park Unocal built, taking turns commanding the pirate ship that dominates it. Lucy Lepley calls the new Avila Beach a "beautiful graveyard."

In September, following the completion of the Big Dig, Unocal offered to put on a celebration picnic, although they were a bit fearful that no one would come. But they did come, especially after Lucy Lepley asked the company if they could bring pictures of the old Avila Beach to put in the tent that would be erected for the event. Pictures were everywhere, and the history of the little-town-that-could was celebrated. Fire Chief Robert Gorman remembered that when he was growing up the town held work parties to enhance community building. After chores were done, families brought food for a potluck, and later they brought out home movies showing what their parents looked like doing the same things they were doing a generation ago. The Unocal picnic tied it all together.

Saro Rizzo: "Bye Bye Sweet Avila!" In a sweet, sad goodbye, Saro Rizzo takes one last long look. His part in the massive cleanup complete, Rizzo left his heart in Avila Beach with the dolphins. © *Los Angeles Times/Anne Cusack*

On a day not unlike the one when he decided to do something about the contamination under the beach, Rizzo stood near the same spot on the beach, facing the ocean, his back to the newly clean, but barren, downtown. The sun was sharp and the ocean calm, sending waves lapping gently to the sand. Sea birds again dotted the edge of the water, and offshore, two fishing boats bobbed with each passing wave. After a year and a half of constant legal challenge, often with acrimonious debate, miles of travel, and a steady succession of meetings, Rizzo was quiet, recalling a day that had changed his life forever.

Two years before he became involved in the crisis at Avila Beach, Rizzo had graduated from law school and passed the Bar examination. He was a full-fledged attorney working to find clients, wavering between sweet relief at having few demands on his time and feeling uneasy about his future in the profession. Living at the beach with brother Marco and helping at the family restaurant left Rizzo with a lot of free time on his hands, something he hadn't had much of throughout the years of his demanding education. The summer crowds were gone, leaving a few locals and tourist couples sitting along the strand or strolling into shops. The ocean water was still warm, drawing Rizzo to dive into the waves and swim out well beyond the breakers. A dolphin appeared alongside him, and he swam with the animal, matching its exuberant dips and rolls. Having company so far from shore engaged him to the point that Rizzo failed to notice the water had turned cold.

Slowly, the dolphin outdistanced him and disappeared. Rizzo realized he was moving in slow motion, taking water into his mouth. He didn't realize he was hypothermic, but he did know he was drowning. Struggling to get through to his numbed limbs and brain, he talked himself into relaxing, turning on his back to float in an effort to conserve energy.

Rizzo was far from land, but near the end of the Avila Beach public pier. He could see a fisherman well enough to recognize him as Southeast Asian, but each time he tried to speak, the words were lost in the water. His cries for help were a muted gargle that no one heard. If he were to live, Rizzo realized he would have to save himself.

He floated for a few minutes, then turned toward shore and swam a few strokes, letting the movement of the water carry him along. He tired again and reverted to a float, keeping his body moving toward the shore by riding the swells. Over and over again, he floated, swam, floated, swam, continuing until his feet could touch the ocean bed with his head above water. Half walking and mostly stumbling, Rizzo finally made it to shore, close enough to call for help. A friend walking her dog realized his plight. Fully clothed, she ran into the surf to lift him by one arm and struggled to get him out of the water. It was several moments before he could speak, and when he did, Rizzo pointed to Mr. Rick's Bar and rasped, *"Brandy!"* Another beach walker saw what was happening and offered to help. Hanging onto the shoulders of his two rescuers, Rizzo made it to the bar and took a long time to recover.

In the weeks following the incident, he wondered what the message of the experience could be. He felt strongly that the ocean had come close to taking his life and then had let him go. He thought about his father who had passed away and his own strong belief in karma, but try as he might, the near death experience yielded no clarity at the time.

In the fall of 2000 it finally came together for Rizzo. If there were a personal rationale for his involvement with the cleanup, he believes it was the ocean that sent him. "I'll always love the water, and what happened gave me a tremendous respect for it and its power," he said. "I got my life back, but the ocean wanted me to do something for it."

A PEBBLE IN THE
WATER—EVER-
WIDENING RINGS

O N its own merits, the story of Avila Beach deserves to be told, but the reality is that it is destined to happen again in hundreds of other locations in every state across the country. The worry California shares with the rest of the world is pipelines—160,000 miles of them in the United States alone—and not all of them are in remote and rural places.

Homes thirty years or older are more likely to individually face the same kind of economic disaster Avila Beach did, because until recent years, little attention was paid to what was built over or near old pipelines. Buildings have encroached on oil company rights of way, and in some cases sit above the pipelines themselves.

Within the city of San Luis Obispo and others in the county, there are private properties owned by oil companies because of petroleum products in the soil below them. Consider what happened to businessman Anthony Gomez and his real estate associates. For several years Gomez and his partners owned a house on Pismo Street, two blocks from downtown San Luis Obispo city. They kept it as a rental, and with enough room in back to build out, they decided to apply for a permit to build an additional unit. It came as quite a shock to find that several years previously, while working on a sewer project in the street adjacent to the house, city workers had discovered that oil had leaked from a pipeline, which was determined to be one of Unocal's lines connecting Avila Beach fifteen miles away to the central valley oil fields a hundred miles to the east.

The company had quietly cleaned up the majority of the spill and repaired the line. The water board installed monitor wells to see if the product broke down naturally, and until Gomez was refused a building permit, he said he knew nothing of the problem. Concerned they would be liable for any further cleanup, Gomez and his partners sold the property to Unocal, and the house continues to be a rental unit managed by the company.

Rightfully called America's lifelines, there are enough pipelines in the world to wrap around the United States eight to ten times. That they are important to living today is a given. To say that they leak is an understatement of immense proportion, and it is a mistaken belief that pipelines represent a problem only in remote areas as the result of oil wells or petroleum storage facilities.

Information about small contamination cases, meaning those that affect one or a few buildings and homes, is available for public scrutiny by checking county records of ownership. In California, local fire departments keep records of leaks as mandated by the state. In addition, regional water boards maintain information through a database called Geotracker. The records of both are also open to the public.

While most of the properties bought up by oil companies in these cases of contamination are single units, one particular site in Santa Barbara County is exemplary because of the scope of the buyback. In the late 1980s and early 1990s, a development of large homes on spacious lots was built on an oil field previously owned by Unocal. The company had a number of oil wells drilled on the property, and when they abandoned the project, they properly capped and sealed the wells. However, they did nothing for the sumps, which are large holes or depressions in the ground, one for each well drilled.

While natural crude oil holds limited risk to people, the sumps are a special case, because into each was dumped leftover drilling mud, gasoline spilled from pumps and equipment, heavy metals, diluent to thin the crude, motor oil from the myriad necessary vehicles, not to mention a variety of toxic chemicals used in the operations.

It is estimated that three thousand of these sumps were in use in the Santa Maria Valley alone, and few of them were properly decontaminated. Not all the blame rests with the oil companies; much responsibility attaches to rogue contractors who agreed to pump out the gunk and dispose of it legally. Some of these companies accepted the contract and pumped out the contents of the sumps. Instead of taking the toxic soup to legally designated environmental dumps, they chose to spread it on their own farm and ranch properties, pocketing the profit after bulldozing over the mess with clean earth.

However, that left the contamination in place in both areas to wait for unsuspecting homeowners of subsequent development. It was a disaster that waited for people who bought homes in the $400,000 range at the tiny town of Orcutt in northern Santa Barbara County. To his shock and dismay, property owner Henning J. Roug found crude bubbling up in his backyard. Concerned neighbors found they, too, had various kinds of erupting petroleum products in their homes, yards, and driveways.

In 1990 Unocal bought six of the homes in the tract. The next year, they bought an additional eleven, along with three more the following year. That was not the end of the buying, and by the time it finally concluded, Unocal had purchased thirty-eight homes in the tract. The contaminated houses are isolated from the rest of the tract with a permanent fence across the road. For a long time the houses remained empty, but well maintained. With timers installed to turn lights on at night, one could imagine people actually lived there. However, with uniformly mowed grass, no cars in the driveways, and no evidence of life—radios, deliveries, children, bicycles on the lawn—Palomino Estates is a unique ghost town. Even birds and small wild animals appear to avoid the place, and a horse trail that once ran through the properties has been rerouted to skirt the area.

A few of the houses are temporarily occupied by Unocal employees, all of whom must sign a document that they were apprised of the danger under the buildings. Women of childbearing age have to additionally promise not to have children while they stay there. In the event a woman does get pregnant, she must leave within two months of discovering it.

In July 2002, two new upscale homes in the city of Santa Maria near Orcutt were destroyed by Unocal after they purchased them—again because of erupting petroleum. The homes on St. Andrews Place were only a few years old and located not far from a major shopping mall, Santa Maria City Hall, and a country club.

In another curious twist in a story having many of them, private investigator Alan Bond was surprised to get a phone call from a Unocal representative after the Avila Beach project was concluded. The last thing he expected to hear was, "Would you consider working for us?" but that was the reason for the call. Bond laughed and said, "No." The caller persisted that this time the company was one of the good guys. Again Bond refused, but the caller would not be put off. He insisted they were not in the wrong. Bond asked the caller if they would still want him to work for them if he found that not to be the case, and the reply was, yes.

The case this time involved a part of the Orcutt property where a number of oil companies had drilled in the past, including Unocal. The other companies had pulled out, leaving Unocal solely responsible for contamination spread over private land by contractors who had emptied sumps illegally. Again Bond did a thorough job, and the case went to court. His testimony was pivotal in getting Unocal exonerated.

The entire history of oil and market demand has seesawed back and forth between good and evil. It is undeniable that no one product has made a greater contribution to American advancement in industry and lifestyle than oil. A vehicle fuel and home heating substance, oil also produces feedstock for many industries— plastics, rubber, chemicals, and lubricating products. Both Japan and Germany went to war to secure oil supplies, and Britain spent a fortune in human and financial resources to secure their source in the Near East. U.S. foreign policy leans heavily toward protecting its oil sources. The use of oil in developed countries is ubiquitous, and alternatives for it are limited. Few would disagree that oil is the most significant product in U.S. and foreign economies.

The idea of putting oil into pipelines was suggested a year before the Civil War began. Seventeen-year-old Samuel Duncan Karns attempted to run a six-inch wooden line from a well in Parkersburg, West Virginia, to a planned refinery on the Ohio River. The onset of the war put off the idea, but eventually a line made of cast iron pipe was laid in 1862, a mere twenty-six years after the epic battle of the Alamo in Texas.

Regional teamsters took exception to the construction as an assault on their business of hauling barrels of oil from the well to the refinery. They attacked the pipeline and dug up sections of it, some of which lay on the banks of a river for years afterward. Despite the controversy, pipelines became more and more efficient, although threaded pipes had to be tightened by hand. That led to an observation in the vernacular of the day that pipelines had a reputation of leaking "like a fifty-cent umbrella."

These small pipelines of a few inches in diameter proliferated slowly across the United States until World War II. With demand growing for the defense of Britain, increased shipments of oil were running from the fields in Texas and the Southwest, sailing to refineries on the East Coast. During the year before the United States entered World War II, German U-boats decimated the oil tanker fleet, and in an effort to minimize the amount of oil moving by tanker, it was proposed that a larger diameter pipeline than ever before used be laid from the Texas oil fields to the East Coast. The idea did not evoke much support until December 7, 1941, when the Japanese attacked Pearl Harbor, Hawaii. Then the pipeline was put on a fast track to completion.

Begun in August 1942, the Big Inch, as the pipeline was dubbed, required imaginative engineering, and within eighteen months was carrying 50 percent of all crude oil coming to the eastern part of the United States. A second pipeline, the Little Inch, even longer at 1,475 miles, was built in just over a year. It transported gasoline and other refined products from the southwestern part of the country to the East Coast. The amount of oil coming by pipeline to the eastern United States increased from 4 percent to 42 percent by the end of 1944.

The pipeline industry went into high gear and even proposed a system to link Britain with France by laying a line in the English Channel. The line was laid, but, fraught with technical problems, it never did produce the quantity of oil necessary for the European campaign. However, with advances in radar and a strengthened Allied effort, German U-boat damage was curtailed, and the tankers were able to keep the supply of petroleum safe for the D-day invasion that led to the end of the war. Joseph Stalin described the conflict as one of engines and octanes, and he saluted American ingenuity in getting the petroleum where it was needed.

Consumer demand and the growth of the American oil industry during the war created an increased awareness of the necessity of oil, which in turn led to laying more and more pipelines, spreading them across and around every state after the end of hostilities. There are countless numbers of oil wells in every state, all with an underground connection called a gathering pipeline. That line connects to a larger trunk or transmission line, which moves the product to a central point for collection or delivery to a refinery or export. Underground transport carries more than fifty refined petroleum products from varying grades of gasoline, diesel, jet fuels, and crude oil, to home heating oil and kerosene. Lines also transport the chemicals necessary to refine crude, such as liquefied propane, ethylene, and butane as well as some petrochemical feedstock. In some cases, petroleum products are mixed within a line and separated at the destination.

Until the mid-1980s, when the Santa Barbara oil spill gave rise to the environmental movement, little attention was paid to spills. Even though the safety record of pipelines is much better than that of surface transportation, the incidence of spills has taken center stage. The Association of Oil Pipe Lines said the annual *known* spill amount of oil has decreased by 40 percent in the thirty years preceding 2002.

However, it is not the known but the unknown that lurks underground, because record keeping is not fully available or even correct. These leaks are the skeleton in the closet that is waiting to be discovered. Ignoring the probability won't make it go away, because so much of the comforts of life today rely on underground installations. While a homeowner may choose not to worry about what is under his property, accidental discovery of an oil leak could bring that home or business to ruin, in the event the responsible party cannot be located.

In California, a seller of real estate must give any known information about underground contamination to the listing agent and potential buyers. However, testing to determine contamination is not required, so the buyer is at risk if testing is not requested as part of the negotiations. Accidental discovery can come from city or county work on sewers, power company maintenance of underground lines, septic tank failure/maintenance, construction of an addition to the building, installation of fiber optic cables, replacement of water mains, and any number of other scenarios that require digging.

Moreover, even if the contamination is under a street, properties in the vicinity are redlined by banks and lending institutions as possibly contaminated sites adjacent to the discovery. City and county agencies are vested with the power to require cleanup. It happened to Anthony Gomez with his Pismo Street property, but in that case the responsibility for cleanup was traceable. With ownership of pipelines having changed hands a number of times over the years, responsibility for heritage pipeline leaks can expect to be in the court system for a long time. Not many homeowners or small businesses can afford that kind of legal fight. Nor can they afford to clean up the contamination themselves. In a very real sense, this kind of legal action is akin to proving you are *not* guilty rather than the court hearing arguments that you are.

Accidental discovery is an elephant in the parlor, just as it was in Avila Beach. If the town had not managed to get enough water for increased development, if Michael Rudd had not applied for a building permit, and if that permit had not required a test boring, half a million gallons of toxics would still be marching toward the sea, with four hundred people bobbing on top of a cauldron of petroleum products.

In his book *The Prize, the Epic Quest for Oil, Money & Power,* Daniel Yergin points out that during World War I the United States produced 65 percent of the world's oil. The contribution oil made to that war effort turned the adversarial relationship between the

U.S. government and the oil industry from conflict to partnership. From trust busting the oil barons, the U.S. government moved to working with the industry, a change that would have worldwide impact during the decades to follow.

In the Cold War years, the United Soviet Socialist Republic chose to challenge the North Atlantic Treaty Organization by a power move, flooding the world market with oil sold at half the prevailing price. It was no small thumb-at-the-nose to the West, since the use of oil in the United States had tripled by 1972. Europe's demand for petroleum increased fifteen-fold, and Japan's an astounding one hundred thirty-seven times, in the same period.

By 1973, oil politics resulted in a stunning rise in crude coming from the Mideast, when OPEC initiated an embargo that was keenly felt in the United States. Six years later, in 1979, the hostage crisis in Iran again caused a world oil crisis. Both of these political events resulted in long lines at gas stations and a new frenzy of oil exploration by U.S. oil companies to meet both domestic and export demand.

With the advent of underground utilities and pipelines, much of the evidence of these underground installations has disappeared from sight, but they exist everywhere. The nation is bound together with millions of miles of these necessities, whether in the middle of a metropolitan area like Los Angeles, or in an agricultural county like San Luis Obispo. Every area has its share of both the benefits of progress and the costs involved.

Say the word *contaminated* and the prevailing picture that comes to mind for most people is one of a large metropolis choked with smog, a port with heavy equipment dripping crankcase fluid, or in the case of a traumatic spill, Santa Barbara in 1969. Few would picture the rural countryside or small towns, and certainly not an isolated beach community with sparkling sands and a breathtaking view of the Pacific.

Other pipelines are of major consequence in other states, for example in Ohio. Former Twinsburg City Manager Grace Kizak knows the state is crisscrossed by thousands of miles of petroleum and natural gas lines. Her file on them is two inches thick and bulging. Several lines, one of which has ruptured in the past, run not far from her own home in the woods.

So many agencies have jurisdiction—Summit County, the State of Ohio, and the federal government—that by the time Twinsburg enacted their own regulations for pipelines, the majority of the lines were grandfathered. The lack of information about them can be costly, as the city found out when it purchased one thousand acres of land on Liberty Road. "They found out the property is covered by oil well leases, some of which are dry," said Kizak. "The City paid $10.5 million for it, and one of the attorneys who worked on the sale told me they would be happy to get half of that in the event of a sale. The leaseholders have allowed the city to utilize eighty of the thousand acres for recreation facilities, and that story will continue to unfold as the years pass and the Mideast turns off their spigot."

Kizak walks every day in her country neighborhood, and in conversation with a friend she learned he lives with a twenty-inch high-pressure gas line under his house. "I thought he was joshing me," Kizak said, "until I noticed the warning tag directly across the street from his house." The gas line feeds all of northeastern Ohio and is patrolled by air. That gives little comfort to the homeowner, after news of a major fire in a gas line eruption in Maple Heights about sixteen miles away.

Eastern pipelines are often thin because it is easier to send the product through them. Some of the thirty-six-inch lines are only half an inch thick. The lines are coated inside and out, as well as often protected with a cathodic system to counter the electrical current produced by the movement of product inside. However, the lines still need to be monitored, and for many years that has been done by air. Pilots fly small planes over pipelines every day, looking for leaks and construction work around them. It is not uncommon to find heavy equipment moving earth in close proximity to large pipelines, despite the fact that contractors are required to find out if their project is in the vicinity of underground lines. Former pipeline pilot Lt. Col. Jeane Wolcott (USA Ret.) recalls seeing a home under construction directly above the line she was patrolling. The ride-along observer reported it as an emergency, and by the time they made their next flyover, the foundation had been abandoned and another one begun a safe distance away.

The condition of pipelines is now monitored from the inside with the use of robots called *pigs*. A self-propelled device, the pig is introduced into the line and, as it travels the length of it, sends back a clear picture of the condition of every inch, including the thickness of the line as it ages and any leaks or potential spots that could leak. Newer installations are made of stronger materials and have much longer life expectancy than older pipelines. The greatest threat is with the plethora of lines that are still in use after fifty years. Oil companies have known for a long time that product was escaping in transit, because, for example, when a million gallons is sent from one place to another and only nine hundred fifty thousand can be accounted for at the destination, the rest had to have gone somewhere else in the closed system. That means there is a leak.

For all the obvious differences between big towns and small ones, mega-cities and rural expanses, one common denominator connects the dots in the economic fabric of the nation. The connections of roads, huge water transport, corresponding disposal of waste, electric power, rail transport, telephones, and oil make the difference between life two hundred years ago and life today. Oil pipelines are probably the greatest part of that network.

The growth of the oil industry is matched only by the increased clamor for more regulation, a ban on oil drilling, and a general distaste for anything associated with the not-so-clean production of petroleum. What detractors forget or ignore is the fact that without oil, people would have a much harder existence and could enjoy none of the incredible advances that now are commonplace in the world.

The only people not dependent on oil are those who live in homes made of trees, native stone, or bricks made of mud, manure, straw, and wood ash. These shelters are constructed with handmade tools, and these petroleum-free people forage for food or farm it by hand, with the help of animals. Most of all, they walk to get anyplace, only occasionally riding on animals. They wear clothing that comes from the same animals they hunt for food, using skins that have been tanned with the brains of those animals.

Some wear wool cut from animals and woven on handmade looms. *Everyone else* is dependent on oil in some fashion.

Luxuries have a habit of becoming necessities. Clean water, reliable sanitary disposal, electricity, telephones, heat in winter, transportation, medical miracles, flowers in winter, and fresh fruit year round—none of these would be possible today without the use of petroleum. The vast majority of clothing worn, the array of office products used, the sports played, the homes lived in and maintained, the way people get from one place to another, the extraordinary medical miracles taken for granted, computers—all are possible because of petroleum products.

The Illinois Department of Natural Resources' Office of Mines and Minerals has calculated that each person uses 5,000 pounds of coal a year, and the same amount of natural gas. However, their calculation for petroleum is 7,800 pounds per person per year. That means each person uses well over half a million pounds of petroleum in his lifetime, by using various products made from it or those transported to stores for purchase.

Trying to lay blame is like determining what came first, the chicken or the egg: the product offered, or the resulting demand by the public. It is far more productive to agree there is an existing problem, and come together to fix it. Underground contamination is the *Silent Spring* for this millennium, and to lay the responsibility solely at the feet of oil companies is folly.

Playing the blame game is a wasteful exercise in time, money, and energy. Unocal learned that in Avila Beach and has taken the lesson to heart. The company appears to be taking an extraordinary new path in meeting the challenges of cleanup, recognizing there are problems and it is counterproductive to draw that line in the sand. Instead, they are working together with other responsible parties to take proactive steps instead of waiting for that elephant to lumber onto the field of operations again.

Pipelines carry more commercial products than all other industrial freight, and there are not enough roads and trucks in the world to replace the work they do every day. Petroleum pipelines are vital to national security as well as to every citizen's lifestyle and well-being. The benefits of oil became a necessity a long time ago, but the payment that was deferred is coming due.

Epilogue: People

RESIDENTS scattered as Avila Beach entered the new millennium changed to its core. After the noisy, confrontive years, the real community left softly like a breeze shaking a dandelion seed puff. For more than a year, the empty Avila Grocery Store and restored Yacht Club were the only structures along the new streets, as business owners looking to rebuild wended their way through the permit process. The new promenade, lined with palm trees, looked like a barren Charlie Brown Christmas tree with two ornaments.

Of all the residents who toiled endlessly to see the cleanup a reality, only a few remained. Saro Rizzo moved to San Luis Obispo city and now has a real office a block away from the courthouse where he made his stand. One room in an office condo created from an old house, his office has warmth and charm—old wood, lush greenery. A playful, larger-than-life raccoon brass sculpture is his only extravagance. He will drop everything to help Marco and the family at the restaurant in spite of the rapid growth of his legal practice.

Bill Price is back in business in Avila Beach and was the first to reopen. Mike Rudd's business is no longer at the ocean's edge, but some miles inland in a new shopping center. In his green and pink house on the hill, Archie McLaren can see in his mind all that happened, along with the well-ordered Front Street Enhancement replacement.

Gladys Misakian will always remain in the hearts of everyone who knew her, especially Evelyn Phelan. Now in her nineties, Phelan still lives at the motel and can be seen walking slowly along the new promenade, a bottle of oxygen on wheels her constant companion.

Betty Terra lives in San Luis Obispo city and remains the rosy optimist she always has been. Betty Woody's house on the edge of destruction did not meet the fate of its neighbors, but needs repair inside. She took some of her UNOCAL settlement and replaced the siding on her old boarding house home. It fits well with the new look of Avila Beach, and she has an unobstructed view of the water, at least until the empty lots are rebuilt with businesses.

David Church has moved on to another job with the San Luis Obispo County government and still feels wistful when he speaks of Gladys Misakian and her boat in the window. Gerhardt Hubner has been assigned to another oil cleanup in nearby Morro Bay. He still looks like a college student except for some gray hairs he earned in Avila Beach.

Dolores Lepley now lives in Grover Beach, a more affordable coastal town to the south, with Lucy and her husband. The fight took a serious toll on Lucy's health, as it did on Evelyn Delany's, but there is no regret in any of them. Made of sturdy stock, these women exemplify leadership in the face of fire. They never flinched and lived a life that few others enjoy or even realize existed.

Glossary

Aquifer. A permeable geological stratum or formation that can both store and transmit water in significant quantities.

Benz Anthracene. One of a group of chemicals formed during the incomplete burning of coal, oil, gas, wood, garbage, or other organic substances, such as tobacco and charbroiled meat.

Benzene. A flammable product found in gasoline.

Bioremediation. A process by which living organisms act to degrade or transform hazardous organic contaminants.

Biosparge. A remediation technology that uses microorganisms to degrade organic constituents in the saturated zone using oxygen and nutrient to increase the biological activity.

Carcinogen. A cancer-causing agent.

Chemical Fingerprint. A way of identifying the source of a material by comparing the presence of trace elements that are present along with the main ingredient. The method is frequently used to identify the archeological mine from which a particular ore was dug, evidence at a crime scene, identification of materials used by terrorists, sources of dust that cause lead poisoning, gases collected at arson fires, and to determine the origin of illicit drugs as well as other forensic materials.

Crude Oil. Fossil fuel generated from organic remains of very old water and land plants covered by accumulated sediments, and created by pressure over a long period of time.

Demur. A formal objection to an opponent's pleadings.

Diluent. Combustible liquid composed of Isoparaffinic hydrocarbons.

Discovery Process. Compulsory pretrial disclosure of documents relevant to a case, which enables one side in a litigation to elicit information from the other side concerning the facts in the case.

EIR. Environmental Impact Report, a formal review of a proposed project and its environmental effects along with feasible alternatives.

Entrainment. An event that occurs when aquatic organisms, eggs, and larvae are drawn into a cooling system through a heat exchanger and then pumped out again.

Ethylbenzene. A colorless, flammable liquid that smells like gasoline, found naturally in coal tar and petroleum. It is also in manufactured products such as inks, insecticides, and paints, as well as used as a solvent.

Grandfathered In. The continued allowed use of property as it was when restrictions or zoning ordinances were adopted.

H₂S. Hydrogen sulfide.

HAZMAT. Acronym for Hazardous Materials.

Hydrocarbon. Compounds containing only carbon and hydrogen. Petroleum consists mainly of hydrocarbons.

Mitigation. Abatement or diminution of anything painful, harsh, severe, afflictive, or calamitous, as in the mitigation of pain, grief, or the rigor and severity of punishment or penalty.

MTBE. Methyl tertiary butyl ether, a product made of methanol and isobutylene for use as a fuel additive to raise the oxygen content of gasoline; a volatile, flammable, and colorless liquid that easily dissolves in water.

Natural Attenuation. A natural process by which compounds are reduced in concentration over time through absorption, adsorption, degradation, dilution, and/or transformation.

PAH. Polynuclear aromatic hydrocarbons, of multi-ring compounds found in fuels, oils, and creosote; common to combustion products.

Plume. In this case, something shaped like a feather, spreading outward.

PPM. Parts per million.

Product. In business, the end result of manufacturing or in other cases a service.

Receptors. A variable ranking of children and adults.

Remediation. That which heals again; in law, a judicial means of enforcing a right or redressing a wrong.

Seventy-Six Ball. An advertisement campaign run for Unocal logo recognition by wide distribution of rubber balls for automobile antennas, given to those who bought the company's gasoline.

Slap Suit. A harassment suit brought to drag out litigation without a reasonable expectation of success, designed to make the opposing side reluctant to continue other legal action.

Thermal Desorption. The mechanical release of a petroleum product from soil by means of heat.

Toluene. A clear, colorless liquid with a distinctive odor, naturally occurring in crude oil. Produced in the process of making gasoline. Used in the production of paints, thinners, fingernail polish, lacquers, adhesives, and rubber.

TPH. Total petroleum hydrocarbons, a term used to describe a broad family of several hundred chemical compounds originating from crude oil.

Wildcatting. Drilling an oil well in an area not known to have produced oil previously, a risky venture.

Xylene. Colorless, sweet-smelling flammable liquid used in paints, gasoline, thinners, and other products, which causes dizziness and confusion in people; can be smelled in air at 0.08–3.7 ppm and tasted in water at 0.53–1.8 ppm; one of the top thirty chemicals produced in the United States in terms of volume.

Bibliography

Alex, Deputy Attorney General Ken, Department of Justice, State of California, interviews with author and accumulated public statements, 2000–2002.

American Petroleum Institute, Washington, D.C. Website, various dates, 2001.

Avila Community News, Avila Beach, California, 1977.

Bachrach, Arrie, Jacobs Engineering, Irvine, California, interviews with author, 2001–2002.

Barrow, Jack, *California Polytechnic State University Senior Project*, Kennedy Library, San Luis Obispo, California, 1977.

Batson, Curtis A., director of environmental health service, San Luis Obispo County Health Department, San Luis Obispo, California, interview with author, 2002.

Blodgett, Roger, private pilot, Ashland, Ohio, interview with author, 2002.

Bond, Alan, private investigator, San Luis Obispo, California, interviews with author, 2001–2002.

Carson, Rachel. *Silent Spring*. Boston: Houghton Mifflin/Cambridge, Mass.: Riverside Press, 1962.

Catanneo, Bill, historian, Lexington, Kentucky, interviews with author, 2001–2002.

Church, David, San Luis Obispo County Planning Department, San Luis Obispo, California, interviews with author and accumulated public statements, 2000–2002.

Clark, J. D., AICP, and Chris William, Crawford, Multari, and Clark Associates, San Luis Obispo, California, interviews with author, 2000–2002.

Crandall, Charles S., attorney at law, San Luis Obispo, California, interview with author, 2000.

Delany, Evelyn, supervisor, San Luis Obispo County government, interviews with author, accumulated public statements, and information from Delany's personal archives, 2000–2002.

Dickerson, Art, professor emeritus, California Polytechnic State University, interviews with author, 2000–2002.

Duenow, James, attorney at law, San Luis Obispo, California, interview with author, 2001.

Dunes Center, Guadalupe, California. Website, various dates, 2001.

Farmer, Matthew, Avila Beach, California, interviews with author, 2000–2002.

Gibson, Robert O., Gibson's Archaeological Consulting, Paso Robles, California, interview with author, 2002.

Gorman, Elaine, Avila Beach, California, interview with author, 2002.

Gorman, Robert, Jr., fire chief, Avila Beach, California, interview with author, 2002.

Hubner, Gerhardt, senior engineering geologist, Central Coast Regional Water Quality Control Board, San Luis Obispo, California, interviews with author, accumulated public statements, and information from the Central Coast Regional Water Quality Board's Public File, 2000–2002.

Jones, Steven T. *New Times*, San Luis Obispo, California, 8 May 1997.

Kelley, Pete, businessman, Avila Beach, California, interview with author, 2000.

Kizak, Grace, former city manager, Twinsburg, Ohio, interviews with author, 2002.

Kocher, Sara, environmental psychologist, San Luis Obispo, California, interviews with author, 2002.

Lepley, Dolores, Grover Beach, California, interviews with author and accumulated public statements, 2000–2002.

Lepley, Lucy, Grover Beach, California, interviews with author and accumulated public statements, 2000–2002.

Levi, Daniel, California Polytechnic State University, San Luis Obispo, California, interview with the author and public statements, 2002.

Los Angeles Express, 1900 (complete date not available).

Lloyd, Jo Ann. *Cal Poly Magazine*, Spring 2002, California Polytechnic State University, San Luis Obispo, California.

Lyons, Silas. *San Luis Obispo County Telegram-Tribune*, San Luis Obispo, California, 21 June 1997.

Martin, Glen. "Toxic Troubles." *San Francisco Chronicle,* San Francisco, California, 25 February 1996.

McLaren, Archie, Avila Beach, California, interview with author, 2000.

McMahon, Jeff. *New Times,* San Luis Obispo, California, 22 September 1996 and 20 February 1997.

Meyer, Norma. "Funky Hamlet Revives." *San Diego Union,* Copley News Service, 4 September 2000.

Mustang Daily, California Polytechnic State University, San Luis Obispo, California, 3 July 1997.

Odom, Leilynn Olivas, Chumash Council, interview with author, 2002.

Oil and Gas Journal. "Unocal Goes to Extremes to Remediate Two California Petroleum Spills." Houston, Texas, 1999.

Pederson, Barbara L. *A Century of Spirit.* Los Angeles, Cal.: Unocal Corporation, 1990.

Phelan, Evelyn, Avila Beach, California, interview with author, 2000.

Racouillet, Richard, attorney at law, San Luis Obispo, California, interviews with author, 2001–2002.

Radis, Steve, principal, Arthur D. Little Incorporated, Santa Barbara, California, interviews with author, 2000–2002.

Rizzo, Saro, attorney at law, San Luis Obispo, California, interviews with author and accumulated public statements, 1995–2002.

Smith, Kenneth A., manager Central Coast Group, Unocal Corporation, tank farm, San Luis Obispo, California, interview with author, 2000.

Sneed, David. "Environmentalists Want Avila Mess Cleaned up Now." *The Telegram-Tribune,* San Luis Obispo, California, 25 June 1997.

———. "Avila Mourns the First Block to Fall." *The Telegram-Tribune,* San Luis Obispo, California, 25 November 1988.

Terra, Betty, San Luis Obispo, California, interviews with author, 2001–2002.

Wheaton, James, attorney at law, The Environmental Law Foundation, Oakland, California, interview with author, 2000.

Williams, Steven, attorney at law, Cochett, Petrie and Associates, Burlingame, California, interview with author, 2000.

Wolcott, Lt. Col. Jeane M., USA Ret., Ravenna, Ohio, interview with author, 2002.

Woody, Betty, Avila Beach, California, interview with author, 2001.

Yergin, Daniel. *The Prize, the Epic Quest for Oil, Money, & Power.* New York: Simon & Schuster, 1991.

Index

Alex, Ken, 114–17, 137, 142, 153–58, 173, 211
Allen, Connie, 183
Allen, Jim, 162
Andreen, Kenneth, Judge, 50
Arthur D. Little (company), 37–39, 59–60, 105, 209
asphaltum, 32
Avila Alliance, 16, 30, 40, 43, 55, 70–72, 79–80, 82
Avila Beach
    1977 explosion, 18, 27, 40
    1996 a watershed year, 103
    Advisory Council, 86
    boomtown, 23
    business district, 61
    cleanup level, 53
    cleanup of, 85
    cleanup proposal, 173
    Community Center, 192
    completion of cleanup, 205
    concreting, 104
    construction moratorium, 28
    contamination at, 16, 21, 55, 194
    dance of destruction, 182
    destruction of, 171
    dismantling the tanks on, 135
    division between families, 70
    entering the new millennium, 231
    excavation of, 71, 189
    funky defined, 54, 162, 213
    historic settlement, 159
    pipeline break, 11
    plume, underground, 71
    samples conducted at, 121
    sense of unity, 194
    sheet piling installation, 182
    smell of, 20
    socioeconomic impact on, 61–63
    Specific Plan, 162
    stigma of, 64
    test results, 149–50
    tourism at, 64
    tourists reappearing, 176
    underground pollution, 14
    unity of, 115
    World War II, 163–67
Avila Beach Foundation, 202
Avila Business Association, 109
Avila Café, 173, 183
Avila Community News, 17
Avila Grocery, 28, 107, 168, 173, 182, 186–87, 214, 231
Avila Remediation Center, 177
Avila Valley Advisory Council, 106

Bachrach, Arrie, 185–87, 191–92
Barbera, Barry, 91
Batson, Curt, 145–48, 150
Beach, Roger C., 108
beach-cleaning machine, 10–12, 15, 72, 111

BeachFest '96, 52
Belnap, Ray, 89
Benzler, Zeebe, 183
Big Dig, 174, 181, 210, 214
Biggi, Mike, 175
Big Inch (pipeline), 223
biosparging, 26–28, 31, 39, 42, 49, 52, 58–59, 65, 77, 113
Black Gold rush, 94
blame game, 229
Boggs, Melissa, 140
Bond, Alan, 138–40, 222
Bray, Jim, 32, 35, 53, 70, 78, 85
Brockovich, Erin, 81–84, 90, 123–25, 145–47, 212

Café Roma, 10
Caffey, John, 84
California Environmental Quality Act (CEQA), 59
California Fish & Game, 22, 32, 35, 113–14, 160, 173
California State Bar, 10, 75, 91–92
Cano, Raul, 77
Carr, Bob, 108
Cattaneo, Charlie, 136
CEQA. See California Environmental Quality Act
Chandless, Chris, 180, 184
Chumash, 197–204
Church, David, 20, 27, 29, 30–32, 47–48, 52, 57–58, 85, 169, 175, 208, 232
Clark, Chris, 62, 65–66
cleanup, 49, 62
Cleanup and Abatement Order, 49
Clean Water Act, 73, 87, 113
Committee for a Better Environment, 73, 80, 113
Cookie (cat), 191
Corps of Engineers, U.S. Army, 47, 209
Cotchett and Petrie (law firm), 81, 137–39
Crandall, Steve, 117, 142–43, 155–58
Cummings, Jim, 68, 168, 209
Custom House, 168, 173

Dahlgren, Dr. James, 123, 126
daylighting, 30, 78
Dee, Marvin, 28
Delany, Evelyn, 11, 20, 22, 24–25, 29, 31, 33, 52–53, 82, 106, 232
DeMille, Cecil B., 38–39
Diablo Canyon, 23, 86, 182
Duenow, James, 137–39
Dunites, 38
Dutra, Tony, 167

EIR. See Environmental Impact Report
Environmental Impact Report, 12, 24, 32–34, 40, 52, 54–55, 58–66, 76, 84–85, 91, 105, 209
Environmental Law Foundation, 73, 80, 113
Exxon Valdez, 14, 39, 43

Family Fun Days, 108
Farmer, Matthew, 71, 79, 183, 212
Farrel, Rod, 190
Frantic Five, the, 106
free product, mobile, 41
Front Street, 12, 17–19
  artifacts, 199
  contamination at, 145
  Enhancement Project, 54, 73, 103, 125, 158, 173, 231
  level of, 42
  plume, underground, 32, 40, 59
  storm-battered sidewalk, 214
  thriving year-round, 23
Front Street Project, 211
Funke-Bilu, Ilan, 50

gasoline, 76 Premium, 19
Geotracker (database), 220
Gibson, Robert, 199, 202
Gomez, Anthony, 219–20, 225
Gorman, Robert, 174–75, 187, 214
Greenberg, Dr. Alvin, 146, 149–50
Greenberg, Thomas, 124
Guadalupe Dunes, 14, 21–22, 33, 37–39, 46, 57, 74, 84–85, 90, 178, 208
Guernsey, Tom, 68

Harbor District, 11, 53
Harrington, Tom, 117
Hartley, Fred, 101
Hayashi, Mike, 72
health study, preliminary, 30
Hinds, Alex, 34
Hubner, Gerhardt, 45–46, 49, 52, 57–
    58, 78, 82–83, 85, 125, 178, 209–
    10, 232
Huntley, Dr. David, 140

Imle, John Jr., 208
Iron Mountain, 181

Jacobs Engineering, 169, 178, 185–87,
    192, 209
Jesuit Santa Clara Law School, 10
Jones, Steven P., 212

Karns, Samuel Duncan, 223
Kelley, Pete, 17–18, 42, 179
Kitts, Chris, 75
Kizak, Grace, 226–27
Kocher, Dr. Sara, 63–66
Krentzer, Rick, 124

Lamb, Denny, 176–77, 207
Laurent, Bud, 86–88
Lepley, Dolores, 68–71, 137, 188,
    191, 232
Lepley, Lucy, 68, 136–37, 145, 162,
    171, 190–91, 212, 214
Levi, Daniel, 119, 194
Lighthouse Bar and Grill, 177, 182–83
Lindholm, James, 158
Little Dig, 33–35, 42, 45, 51, 70, 73,
    107, 112, 174
Los Angeles Express, 95
Los Angeles Mirror, 100
Los Angeles Times, 24, 125, 178
Lyons, Roger, 33
Lyons, Silas, 119

MACC. See Multi-Agency Coordinat-
    ing Committee
Madonna Inn, 136
Marcus, William, 123

Marre Hotel, 164
Martin, Perry, 48, 53, 68, 75, 120,
    186, 209
Masada, Mark, 57
Masry, Ed, 81–84, 90, 119–21, 123–
    25, 136, 139–40, 145–47, 212
McLaren, Archie, 53–54, 73–74,
    103–7, 117–18, 168, 231
McMahon, Jeff, 77, 89–90
Meyerhoff, Al, 157
Milberg Weiss (law firm), 117, 137,
    140, 143, 155–57, 211
Miossi, Harold, 121
Misakian, Gladys, 29, 105, 145, 148,
    151, 175, 187, 209, 232
Morrison, Sharon, 50–51, 55
Mr. Rick's, 171, 173, 216
Multi-Agency Coordinating Commit-
    tee (MACC), 46–49, 73–74, 155,
    206
Mustang Daily, 85

New Times, 11, 36, 77, 87–89, 120,
    124, 212

O'Connell, Jack (State Senator), 85
Odom, Leilynn Olivas, 197–204
Old Maud (oil well), 95

Pacific Coast Railroad, 191
Pacific Gas and Electric, 23, 81, 86–
    89, 114
Pal, Professor Niropam, 74–75
Palomino Estates, 221
Parsons, Gerard, 192
Pete's Seaside Café, 17
Phelan, Evelyn, 105–6, 172, 188, 192,
    232
pigs (monitoring device), 228
Pinard, Peg, 82, 88, 108, 154–55, 174,
    213
pipelines, history and future of,
    219–29
Pizza Pantry, 209
plume, underground, 12, 14, 21, 82–
    83, 171, 210
Point Buchon, 67

Price, Bill, 176, 182, 231
Proposition 65, California, 15, 55–56, 79, 160

Racouillat, Richard, 213
Radis, Steve, 37–42, 59
Rather, Dan, 108
Regional Water Board, 20–21, 37
Regional Water Quality Control Board, 12–14
Reloquio, Angel, 171
Rizzo, Marco, 13, 71
Rizzo, Saro
  beach-cleaning machine, 10, 15
  big league legal fight, 79–92
  California State Bar, 10
  date with destiny, 9–16
  filing suit, 15
  forming the partnership, 17–26
  Jesuit Santa Clara Law School, 10
  move to San Luis Obispo, 231
  near-death experience, 215
  overcoming monumental hurdles, 111
  presenting the details, 153–60
  public meetings and excavation, 71–78
  stirred to action, 9–16
Rosenberg, Norm, 119
Roug, Henning J., 221
Rudd, Michael, 12, 19–20, 23–24, 50, 77, 172, 225, 231
Ryan, Mike, 86

San Diego Union, 213
San Francisco Chronicle, 107
San Francisco Examiner, 35
Santa Maria Group, 22
Sawyer, Stephen, 173
Scuri, Joe, 167
Sea Barn, 173, 176
settlement negotiations, 142–44
Sharrer, Bill, 126, 207
Shell Beach, 163
Smith, Mark, 141, 153–55, 173, 211
Sneed, David, 182–83
solidification, 36, 52, 104

Spaulding, Jack, 207
Standard Oil, 93
State Water System, California, 23
Stegner, Wallace, 192–93
Stewart, Lyman, 93–94
sumps, 220–21
Surfrider Foundation, 57

tar balls, 147
Telegram-Tribune, 16, 35–36, 74–76, 85, 91, 117, 119–20, 149, 168, 176, 181–82
Terra, Betty, 163–64, 232
Thomas, Dr. Greg, 124
Tosco Oil Company, 30–31
total petroleum hydrocarbons (TPH), 40–41, 43
TPH. See total petroleum hydrocarbons
Tucker, Dan, 21–22

Unfair Business Act, 56
Union Oil, 94–102
Unocal
  1920s spill, 40
  1977 corporate memo, 42
  1992 pipeline spill, 13, 20
  1992 Pirate's Cove spill, 50
  accepting disputed EIR, 142
  accepting the cleanup demand, 141
  beach-cleaning machine, 11–12
  Beach Fest '96, 52
  Beach Plug, 61
  biosparging, 26–28, 31, 39, 42, 49, 52, 58–59, 65, 77
  brochure, 84–85
  buying out protestors, 75
  cleanup proposal, 12, 84, 173
  communication with, 21
  cooperation from, 146–47
  corporate attorneys, 29
  creating concrete dam, 61
  delay strategy, 48
  discussing a settlement, 141
  Family Fun Days, 108
  four cleanup options, 51
  Guadalupe Dunes, 14

hard-line stance, 26
having doubts, 29
information exchange meetings, 20
invisible shield solution, 18–19
joint solution, 148
lobbying efforts, 55
lost records, 50
lowball offer, 116
maps of, 34
offshore oil platform spill, 100
plan for the cleanup, 33
playing the waiting game, 22
public relations offensive, 28–30,
    53–54, 58, 76, 102, 108, 181
sale of, 31

settlement conferences, 72, 111
at the settlement table, 81
test results, 146–47
underestimating the people, 24

vapor extraction system, 12, 27

Wattenburg, Bill, 118
West, Paul, 76
Wheaton, James, 92
Wolcott, Lt. Col. Jeane, 227
Wolloch, Rich, 187
Woody, Betty, 163, 188, 232

Yacht Club, 173, 182, 192, 231
Yergin, Daniel, 225